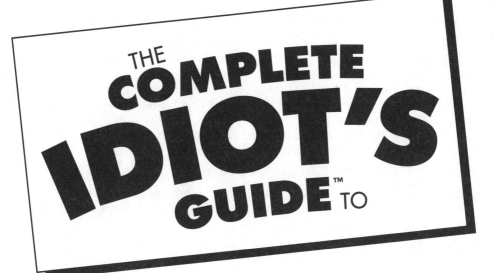

THE COMPLETE IDIOT'S GUIDE TO

Grandparenting

by Walter and Marilyn Hartt
with Will Cross

alpha
books

A Division of Macmillan General Reference
A Simon & Schuster Macmillan Company
1633 Broadway, New York, NY 10019

Alpha Development Team

Brand Manager
Kathy Nebenhaus

Executive Editor
Gary M. Krebs

Managing Editor
Bob Shuman

Senior Editor
Nancy Mikhail

Production Team

Development Editor
Carol Hupping

Production Editor
Robyn Burnett

Copy Editor
Susan Aufheimer

Editorial Assistant
Maureen Horn

Cover Designer
Michael Freeland

Cartoonist
Judd Winick

Designer
Glenn Larsen

Indexer
Tim Wright

Layout/Proofreading
Tricia Flodder, Aleata Howard, Megan Wade

Contents at a Glance

Contents

Foreword

Grandparents have a great opportunity. By sharing their wisdom, experience, and love they can help their grandchildren grow and thrive—while enjoying greater meaning and fulfillment in their own life journeys.

Studies show that children who have grandparents who are actively involved in their lives grow up with a more positive attitude toward life, service, aging, and the elderly, than those who don't. Active grandparents also benefit from a more satisfying and energetic life. Unfortunately, these studies also show that in the U.S., less than half of all grandparents qualify as active and involved. Many grandparents, instead, choose a loving but passive style. This stance deprives grandchildren of many of the benefits grandparents can bring.

Grandparents can take on many important roles that are often difficult for parents to assume. Grandparents can promote the family heritage; act as confidants for their grand-children; and provide a solid, comforting presence. Grandparents can expose their grandkids to new environments and experiences. They can also help their grandkids discover and develop their natural talents and gifts.

The Complete Idiot's Guide to Grandparenting provides beginning grandparents with many practical suggestions on enjoyable, effective grandparenting. It can help you build a strong foundation for a positive, trusting relationship with your grandchildren and their parents.

Experienced grandparents will find commonsense tips for a wide variety of family situations. The authors give sound guidance on sensitive, even stressful, subjects such as discipline, relations with other grandparents, and communicating with teenage grand-children.

In Creative Grandparenting™, a national non-profit organization that encourages active, involved grandparenting through a number of programs, we teach key points that are also discussed in this book:

➤ Be mindful of a higher purpose in your activities and transactions with your grand-children (for example, developing respect for yourself and for others).

➤ Be present in the moment. Give your grandchildren your undivided attention and listen receptively. This is essential to create a quality dialogue with them.

➤ Give unconditional love. Grandchildren need to know that someone cares for them, regardless of their behavior and performance. The key is to be non-judgmental, which isn't easy! It nurtures that precious but fragile childhood spirit, which often disappears in the schooling-socialization process.

I have five lovely granddaughters (ages 5 through 15) and a fine young grandson (16 months). I found this book full of good recommendations and new insights for getting the most from my interactions with the younger ones. For my older grandchildren, I found the later chapters very helpful. Chapter 19, "Keep the Faith," was especially meaningful, and Chapter 24, "Aging—So What's New!" seemed written especially for me.

I hope you too, find the book useful and enjoyable. May you be a living example of what your grandkids are to become!

Robert Kasey, Founder and President,

Creative Grandparenting Inc.™

Introduction

The tug of grandparenting is one of life's strongest forces. And that which pulls at us so powerfully also fills us with anxious wondering. During the process of writing this book, we were continually surprised at how much there was to think about—how much there is to the job of grandparenting. We are all, to some degree, "idiots" in this sometimes very challenging role.

Will we ever become expert at it? Perhaps not, but we can keep trying—and keep getting better as we go along. We hope that our own grandparenting experiences and our research will make *your* grandparenting easier.

Sure, you're a parent. You've raised your own kids. What can be so different about being a grandparent? Aren't the rules about the same? To be perfectly honest: *Everything* is different; and the rules are *not* the same!

Grandparenting is far removed from parenting, so the rules are completely different. You're not on the front line, as you are as a parent; you're a couple of steps back. So you can see things more objectively. It's easier to appreciate your grandchildren as people, instead of extensions of yourself, which, to some extent, is the way parents see their children.

In this book we explore how to make the most of grandparenting—how to be wise and loving grandparents, able to offer advice and guidance without infringing on the authority of the parents. We discuss potentially sensitive areas of grandparenting and advise on how to avoid grandparenting pitfalls.

We, Walter and Marilyn Hartt, are sustained and challenged by our spiritual faith. This faith has helped us struggle against the fear we felt when our grandchildren were born under the cloud of life-threatening pregnancies and births. And we now look apprehensively at the many challenges that face our adult children and our grandchildren in today's world.

But beyond fear there is hope and laughter, and the mystery of life and growth. A grandparent's journey may be hard, but as we have discovered, it is also blessed with happiness and delight.

We write often in this book about being "grandparents in good standing." By this, we mean grandparents who are on good terms with grandchildren, their parents, and other family members. Such grandparents are able to achieve and maintain this standing because they are considerate and thoughtful, putting the good of the entire family before their own desires.

Being grandparents in good standing often is not easy. It might mean postponing visits so that other relatives can have time with your grandkids. It might mean saying "No" when your grandchild asks you for the new team jacket that everybody in school is wearing, because you know his parents don't want him to have it. Sometimes things that are beyond your control may threaten your status as grandparents in good standing. But wise grandparents do all they can to resolve thorny issues, even those that they did not cause.

Think about grandparenting as an exciting, heartwarming, and sometimes rocky journey—and of this book as a traveler's guide to it all. We hope that it helps you to get over the rough spots, and that it enables you to make the most of all the wondrous sights along the way. It's a trip millions have taken before us, yet the joy and wonder come fresh to each new traveler.

How This Book Is Organized

The Complete Idiot's Guide to Grandparenting is divided into five sections, to make it easier for you to find the subject areas in which you're most interested:

Part 1, "Awaiting the Newest Member of Your Family," helps you get ready for the birth of your grandchild, whether it's your first or your fifth. It explores ways that you can help the parents through the pregnancy, and the best ways to welcome your new grandchild into the world.

Part 2, "Over the River and Through the Woods: To Grandparents' House We Go," covers the essentials that make grandchildren's visits safe and stress-free for all of you. It discusses childproofing your home and yard, avoiding natural and manmade catastrophes, maintaining discipline, and handling emergencies.

Part 3, "Memorable Pleasures with the Grandkids," explores the many ways that you and your grandchildren can enjoy time together: sharing the joys of sports and games, sightseeing, nature walks, holidays, and cooking together.

Part 4, "Growing Bonds with Your Grandkids," looks at the ways you can grow closer to your grandchildren. And there are many such ways. You can talk to them about your shared family heritage, and about matters of faith and values. We suggest ways to establish a meaningful and continuing dialog, show empathy and understanding of their problems and goals, and develop mutual respect for each other.

Part 5, "Uneven Roads of Grandparenting," suggests ways you can cope with common problems such as tight budgets; family breakups; abuse, alcohol, and drugs; sexual complications; and mental and physical disabilities. And it concludes on an upbeat note by explaining how grandparenting can make you feel young all over again, taking the spills with the thrills, and enjoying your grandkids.

Extras

To assist you even more on your grandparenting journey, you'll find helpful tips, warnings, and stories from real-life grandparents. You can identify these extras by the following icons:

> **Great Grandparenting**
> These boxes contain quick tips and advice to help you solve specific grandparenting problems.

> **Danger Zone**
> Look in these boxes for cautions about the physical or psychological hazards that can disrupt your activities or relationship with your grandchild.
>
> CAUTION

> **Hartt to Hartt**
> Look in these boxes for personal anecdotes and recollections about grandparenting from Walter and Marilyn Hartt.

Acknowledgments

The Hartts would like to acknowledge the many parishoners of Christ Church in Toms River, New Jersey, who gave us suggestions for ways to be the best grandparents possible to our older grandchildren. Our own daughters-in-law, Jennifer and Jeffrey, had much to offer us on grandchildren of younger years.

Trademarks

All terms mentioned in this book that are known to be or are suspected of being trademarks or service marks have been appropriately capitalized. Alpha Books and Macmillan General Reference cannot attest to the accuracy of this information. Use of a term in this book should not be regarded as affecting the validity of any trademark or service mark.

Part 1
Awaiting the Newest Member of Your Family

Whether this is your first grandchild or your fifth, the news of a baby on the way is always met with anticipation and questions. Will it be a boy or a girl? How about one of each? I wonder if the baby will be big or small. Have you thought about names? When exactly is my grandchild due? We're not anticipating any problems, are we?

As a grandparent, you have to use some restraint and abide by the wishes of the parents-to-be as they plan for the new addition. This first part of the book offers advice on what to do—and not to do—to start off as a grandparent in good standing.

So You're Going to Be a Grandparent!

Just when you thought your life was starting to calm down a bit....Your children's weddings are over and paid for, and all the kids seem to be doing rather well on their own. You've finally gotten those new drapes for the living room and replaced that worn-out carpet in the guest room. You've just settled in with a cup of cappuccino to browse through some travel brochures. Ireland? The Mediterranean? New Zealand? Alaska?

Whoa! Stash the brochures and break out the champagne! You've had a visit from your daughter and son-in-law and they've given you some WONDERFUL news. You're going to be grandparents! Think of it. A cute little baby to take for long, peaceful walks. All those adorable little outfits you'll be able to buy. Reading those fairy tales that your own kids liked so much. Having the baby sleep over at *your* house.

Don't your daughter and her husband look ecstatic? They're beaming, aren't they? Or, are they? Do you think she looks a little tired? Are those dark circles under her eyes? Does he look worried? They're so young! Maybe they should have waited, after all, they've been married only a year and a half. What will she do about her job? She just got that big promotion and she has to travel once a month! I hope she's not going to put the baby in day care! Yikes! They're not going to ask you to babysit every day; you've already raised your own kids!

Maybe this isn't such a good idea after all!

Getting the Good(?) News

Reactions to the news of impending grandparenthood will vary greatly, depending on circumstances. If your happily married daughter and son-in-law have been trying to conceive for three years and are absolutely overjoyed that it finally has happened, you probably will feel every bit as happy as they do. If, on the other hand, your daughter and her husband have been fighting and thinking about separating, the news of a baby might be more of a worry than a joy. In many, perhaps most cases, grandparents-to-be experience a range of emotions, including happiness, worry, doubt, and fear. These feelings jumble together to create what one expert calls "a feeling of ambivalence."

A good way to deal with the conflicting emotions you might experience upon hearing the big news is to buy yourself some time. Simply say something like, "Wow! That's really great news. I just have so many things going around in my head that I think I'm in shock."

Danger Zone

If you're fortunate enough to be reading this book *before* learning that you're about to become a grandparent, you'll be able to plan your response to the "news" and come out smelling like a rose. If you've already been given the news, however, and your response was *really* out of line, you need to apologize. If you were less than enthusiastic, simply be supportive, interested, and cheerful the next time you talk to the parents-to-be.

This will allow you to avoid causing any rifts while giving you a chance to sort out your feelings and plan your response.

Think about how you felt when you first found out you were going to be a parent. You were sure nobody else had ever felt quite like you did. You ate broccoli and drank milk because it was good for the baby. You worked overtime because the money would come in handy for the crib. The entire scope of your life was changed the moment you heard the good news. Trying to remember how you felt can go a long way toward understanding how your children are feeling. Excited, elated, nervous, scared—not sure at all what to expect.

Now, think about *your* parents' reactions to *your* pregnancy. Were they overjoyed or lukewarm? Did they give you the emotional support you hoped for, or did you feel that you were on your own? Consider their responses, and think about your own reaction to your children's news.

They're Not Ready!

You might be able to come up with all sorts of reasons why your kids aren't ready to become parents. First of all, they're kids! They live in a tiny house along a busy street; where would a child play—or sleep? They both work. They love to go away for long weekends. They don't have enough money. They don't have the slightest idea how to take care of a baby—she never even babysat, for heaven's sake! All he wants to do in his free time is play softball; he's not responsible enough to be a father.

The list goes on and on. Perhaps you have even greater reasons for trepidation. What if your unmarried daughter tells you she is pregnant and intends to have the baby? That's not too uncommon these days. Or, what if you haven't had successful relationships with your own kids and you worry about what kind of parents they'll be? Maybe there's drug abuse that worries you, or other situations that make you fear for the well-being of the unborn child. Tough, tough issues. Let's hear what experts advise:

If your reasons for doubt are based on things such as maturity, financial constraints, or a small home, remember that these obstacles can be overcome. A young couple will mature as they get older, their financial situation is likely to improve, and they'll be able to buy a bigger house. In other words, try not to worry about such matters.

But perhaps there is a more serious problem, such as drug abuse or another factor which makes you afraid the parents-to-be will not be able to care for a baby (maybe, for example, the expectant mom suffered abuse as a child and you fear the pattern will continue). In cases like these, you may need to intervene.

One expert advised sitting down with the prospective parent and talking about the problem, offering encouragement and support. Perhaps suggest that because now there is another life involved, the time is right for the mom-to-be to get some help to overcome her problem. Be ready with the names of some counselors or treatment centers if she sees this pregnancy as a chance for her to get herself better, while giving her baby the chance he or she needs. And, don't despair, even if you get no response or a negative response. No one knows what the future holds, and people do change. However, the expert warns, be careful not to let the pregnancy, and later the baby, become a tool for manipulating you.

If your single daughter announces she is pregnant and intends to have the baby, you are faced with a different kind of dilemma. Her decision may fly in the face of your own values, causing you to feel embarrassed and sorry for her and yourself. It's fair to point out the difference in values, but don't give up on her, a family relationship expert says. Ask her about her plans. How will she support the baby? Where does she intend to live? If her plans don't jive with yours (for example, she wants her childhood bedroom back with a crib installed), you have some serious talking to do. If she is an adult and able to support herself and her baby, consider whether you want to become alienated from her or to remain close. Your reaction could make the difference between the two.

If your relationship with your child has not been ideal, and the child is now expecting, use the opportunity as a chance to get closer. Express interest and support for the mom- and dad-to-be, and ask if there's anything you can do to help. It might take a while, but sometimes a baby has a way of bringing family members closer.

I'm Not Ready!

If you think of grandparents as gentle, white-haired oldsters who rock in chairs while dangling grandkids on arthritic knees, no wonder you're not ready to join the club! If you think of grandparents in a 1990s context, however, you'll want to head for the front of the line.

Grandparents today are young, compared to past standards. Thirty or forty years ago, to be fifty was to be heading into old age. Today, most fifty-year-olds are healthy, living their lives to the fullest. Some are heading back to college or retraining for new jobs. Some are finally learning to play golf, or putting in three mornings a week on the tennis courts. Others are in-line skating or mountain biking.

Of course, knowing you're going to be a grandparent can be a psychological jolt, no matter how you feel about your age. You are, in effect, preparing to pass the parenthood baton to your kids. While you'll always be a parent, you'll be moving into a new role of grandparent, with the primary parenting responsibilities turned over to your children.

Be glad about it, an expert advises. While moving up to what she calls the "next layer" may cause some anxieties, it also allows you to focus your energies on what is really important to you. By the time most people become grandparents, they have pretty much done what they wanted to in their careers. They're not so worried about making impressions or "finding themselves." They have more time to focus on family and other priorities, giving their lives greater meaning than ever before. They are likely to have more time and money with which to indulge their grandkids than they did while raising their own children. Grandparents are not old or trapped—they're liberated in many ways.

Get Over It!

Regardless of your initial reaction to this decidedly monumental news, it is important to do your best to support and encourage the parents-to-be. They are experiencing many of the same joys and misgivings that you did when you learned you were going to be a parent. Don't give them reasons to have to worry about your feelings of caution or disapproval. The fact is, you're going to be grandparents, and your child and his or her spouse are going to be parents. Whether or not this is what you would have chosen for them, they're going to want and need your support. They want you to be happy for them.

What to Do, Now That You Know

Once you have fully accepted the news that you'll soon be grandparents, you can start to get excited about it. You'll feel concern for the mother-to-be, and be anxious to hear how her first doctor visits went. You'll have dozens of questions you'll want to ask. What's the due date again? Where will the baby sleep? How much time will you be able to take off from work? What will you do about the vacation you had planned to take? Are you still feeling sick in the mornings? Have you been drinking enough milk? Getting enough sleep? Gaining any weight?

Uh-oh! Better stop right there! Concern is a good thing. Badgering is not.

Staying in Touch

You definitely want to stay in touch with the parents-to-be. This is a great time to really build on your relationship with your son or daughter and spouse. Regardless of how good or not-so-great your relationship has been in the past, this is a chance for you to show concern and willingness to help. Some supportive, sure-to-be-appreciated gestures you could make while keeping in touch include:

➤ Mail clippings of items related to baby care or parenting that you think might be of interest to the parents-to-be.

➤ If you have the time and skills, let it be known that you're willing to help remodel Baby's room (painting, stenciling, etc.).

➤ Offer to buy the crib or another large purchase. If you're not able to buy a major item, how about a helpful book, a lamp for the baby's room, or a pretty picture for the nursery?

➤ If the parents-to-be already have a child or children, offer to babysit while they go out to dinner or a movie.

➤ Send a check or gift certificate to be used for maternity clothes.

Visiting Hour

It is natural that you want to spend time with your daughter or daughter-in-law after you find out she is pregnant. It's an exciting time that you are eager to share. Figuring out when and for how long to visit, though, may not be easy. It's one thing if the mom- and dad-to-be live across town and you can ask them to come over for dinner and a good chat. It's quite another if they live across the state or country, and visits must be carefully planned around work and social schedules.

If you're really eager to visit and it hasn't been suggested, you could say something over the phone such as, "We hope we'll be able to see you soon, your news is so exciting." If your comment is met with silence or a mumbled, non-committal response, you'll know that a visit at this time is not a good idea.

Don't be hurt or put off, however, if you're not invited right over. It might be taking some time for the news to sink in that this couple is now a pregnant couple. Or, they may be working through the concerns and practical situations they're facing. Be patient. Keep in touch by phone, fax or mail (e-mail, anyone?), and wait for an invitation. Send a card, bunch of flowers, or a fruit basket to celebrate the news. If it gets too hard to bear, perhaps you could invite them to your house for an upcoming holiday. Let them know that you're thinking of them and anxious to see them, but don't be pushy.

Hartt to Hartt

Some friends of ours, who have four children and nine grandchildren, have developed a workable formula. After overreacting to the news of the very first grandchild (visiting without an invitation), they realized they had made a mistake. With the next eight arrivals, they took care to sound out the mothers-to-be and their spouses on their visitation preferences. The key questions to ask expectant parents, they suggest, are, "When, if at all, should we visit?" and "For how long?"

Advance Conditioning

It is nearly impossible for first-time parents to anticipate the realities of pregnancy and life with a newborn. No one really knows what it's like to have a baby until the baby arrives and becomes a member of the family. It's not something you can explain, either, because no two babies or families are alike.

You may be in a good position to help the expectant parents prepare for life with Baby. Suggest a comfortable rocking chair in the bedroom for middle-of-the-night feedings, and maybe buy some soft cushions to make it more comfortable. Mom-to-be has no way of knowing just how many hours she'll spend in that chair (and Dad, too, if they're bottle feeding), and will appreciate your thoughtfulness for months to come. But, render advice carefully. Many things (and attitudes) have changed since you brought your first baby home.

While you help the parents-to-be prepare for The Event, you, too, can be preparing. Get used to the idea that your daughter plans to go back to work six weeks after the baby is born, and accept the fact that your grandchild will go to a day care center. Trust the kids you raised to make good decisions concerning their baby, and enjoy the time you have together.

The Least You Need to Know

➤ Remember that your reaction to "the news" is important to the expectant parents. Enhance their joy and excitement by being joyful and excited for them. If you can't be those things, at least be supportive.

➤ No matter what you think about becoming a grandparent, it's going to happen. Be a good sport about it and think first of the mom- and dad-to-be.

➤ Learn and respect the wishes of the parents-to-be concerning visits and other matters.

➤ Let the parents-to-be make their own plans for the new arrival, without having to cater to *your* wishes and ideas.

➤ Maintain solid and continuing lines of communication with the parents-to-be, whether by phone, mail, or in person.

➤ Gently try to help expectant parents understand that having a baby is hard work, but it can be the most fulfilling experience of their lives.

Chapter 2

What to Expect When Your Kid is Expecting

In This Chapter

➤ Offering support for the mom-to-be

➤ How grandfathers can get involved

➤ How to handle troubled parents

➤ Understanding tests given during pregnancy

You've given the big news a chance to sink in, and even shared it with your closest friends. Everyone is thrilled for you and the parents-to-be.

Suddenly, though, you get feeling a little nervous. And then a little more nervous. Soon you've come up with all sorts of "what ifs" and you're waking up at night worrying. Relax! You've already been through at least one (pregnancy, that is) yourself, and the odds are pretty good that you'll make it through this one, too. These nine months will provide some wonderful opportunities for bonding with the parents-to-be. Just keep in mind that they might have ideas regarding their pregnancy that are far different from those you had. A little tongue biting, along with a lot of encouragement and understanding, will be necessary.

The bookstores and library shelves are full of volumes dealing with pregnancy and birth, but we never can be absolutely sure what we'll encounter along the way. It's best to try to remain calm no matter what happens, and remember you are far from being alone. Millions of other grandparents survived pregnancy and birth this year, and you will too. Establish and maintain good communication with the parents-to-be throughout the pregnancy, and you will look back fondly on these months.

Pregnant Ideas Grandmas Can Offer Early On

Let's face it. Being pregnant can be hard work. You know this. You've been through it. There are so many things you need to share with your daughter or daughter-in-law. Or...do you? You need to remember this is her pregnancy, not yours. She'll soon learn first-hand all the joys and tribulations, and she may ask you for advice or help.

When asked, feel free to share your knowledge, but do so sympathetically. A knowing "it will only get worse before it gets better," is hardly what a queasy mom-to-be, who is unable to squeeze into her favorite jeans, wants to hear. This would be a good time for you to do some reading on the latest procedures involved with pregnancy and birth so you can discuss them with your daughter or daughter-in-law when the subject arises.

Even after you've read up on 1990s procedures and are able to comfortably discuss glucose testing, amniocentesis, and underwater births, you still might be shocked when your daughter informs you she intends to fly out to the West Coast for a business trip at six months. Or those exercise classes your daughter-in-law refuses to give up may be a source of distress. Try to relax. Urge the mom-to-be to discuss these issues with her doctor, and trust that good sense will prevail.

Ideas about pregnancy have changed dramatically during the past several decades (that is, since you were wearing maternity clothes), and you'll need an open mind. Exercise actually is encouraged throughout pregnancy, and many expectant moms work right up until their due dates. These days, cigarettes and alcohol are completely taboo, whereas they once were tolerated.

Sprouts, skim milk, and lentils are "in," large quantities of beef, butter, and whole milk are "out." Breast feeding is definitely the preferred mode of feeding, and the baby may well come into this world in a birthing center instead of a hospital. If birth is in a hospital, Dad (and sometimes the entire family) will be present in the delivery room (maybe even with a video camera). Let the parents and their doctors decide what is right for them.

Danger Zone

Some things simply are better left unsaid. She doesn't need to hear how your morning sickness lasted the entire pregnancy, or how you didn't have one decent night's sleep during your last trimester. Nor does she need to hear the details of your three-day labor and forceps delivery. Keep your stories light and happy, and let her obstetrician or midwife deal with the other stuff.

Grandpa Has a Voice Here, Too

Pregnancy can't help but become sort of "a women thing," for obvious reasons. But that doesn't mean you're out of the picture, Grandpa. Men have their own perspectives on pregnancy, and you can be a huge help along the way to both expectant parents.

If you have a particular hobby or interest, you might want to do something special to mark the birth of your grandchild. A handmade cradle, toy box, or dollhouse would be a wonderful gift. Some grandfathers plant a tree to celebrate the birth of each grandchild. Of course, you also can be a great help in more practical matters, such as borrowing and setting up a crib in your guest room, or painting the old rocking horse that your kids loved so much.

With the new mom getting the lion's share of attention, the dad-to-be may be feeling a bit left out. He also might be a little anxious about the impending changes. Will he be able to adequately support this new member of the family? Will he and his wife ever be a couple again? Will he be a good dad? What about college—should he set up some sort of savings plan now?

An experienced father (that's you, Grandpa) might be the perfect person to discuss these and other issues with a nervous dad-to-be. Take this opportunity to become closer to your son or son-in-law, and try to get him to talk about his concerns. It is perfectly understandable for him to have doubts, and you probably can make him feel much better.

You also can cultivate a special relationship at this time with your daughter or daughter-in-law. You are an important person in her life, someone she looks to for advice and reassurance. Encouragement and support from you will mean a lot.

The Art of Listening

Did you ever notice all the classes and programs there are that can teach us to be better speakers? Isn't it ironic that there's hardly anything available to teach us to be better *listeners*? Pregnancy is a period of changes, which may be upsetting or overwhelming to the parents-to-be. They likely will need some willing ears to hear their concerns.

Smart grandparents already know it is often more important to listen than to talk. Often the answers will become clear as the person speaking tells the story. To facilitate good listening, keep the following guidelines in mind:

➤ Make phone calls only when there are no distractions at your end of the line. Trying to listen to a fretful mother-to-be while you're banging around pots getting dinner ready does not convey genuine concern and caring on your part. Make sure you're free to give your undivided attention, and try to gauge what is a good time for your children to take your calls.

➤ When discussing important matters over the phone, let the person speaking know you are listening carefully. Sounds such as "hmmm…" or "I see" let your son-in-law know you are as concerned as he is that the obstetrician recommended those tests. It lets him know you are with him in the conversation, and a good listener.

➤ Ask questions if you don't understand what's being said.

➤ Wait until the speaker is finished talking before you chime in with questions, advice, or news of your own. Nobody likes to be interrupted, especially an excited or concerned mother-to-be.

Mature Wisdom

Nobody is going to tell you that getting older is perfect. The creaky knees that complain after only two sets of tennis and the jaw line that just isn't as firm as it used to be are clear signs that aging has its drawbacks. You've got to admit, though, that there are advantages. Maturity tends to give us a more balanced perspective on the ups and downs of life. Many things don't seem as hard to handle as they once did, because we've handled them before. This allows us to convincingly reassure younger people who are experiencing difficult times that things will get better, and the storms will pass.

Tapping the Past to Enrich the Future

When a young couple has doubts and apprehensions (which tend to become more frequent during pregnancy), it helps to talk about similar situations that you've survived. While not making it into a contest ("Honey, those veins are nothing compared to the ones I got when I was pregnant!"), you can let the parents-to-be know that you understand and empathize with them. Share similar problems that you encountered, and let them know that you were as worried and unsure as they are. They'll see that everything worked out fine for you and be reassured.

Although it's great to be a source of wisdom and be able to comfort and give advice, it's really important to know when to back off. There are some issues relating to pregnancy, birth, and child rearing that simply must be resolved by the parents.

Show and Tell

As you and your spouse look forward to the birth of your grandchild, you probably will find yourselves recalling your own experiences of pregnancy, birth, and the early years of your children's lives. Share the stories with the mom- and dad-to-be. In addition to giving everyone some chuckles, they'll let your kids see that you were vulnerable in these situations, and felt much the same as they are feeling now. Remember when:

➤ It was full-go labor and time to leave for the hospital, but we couldn't find the car keys? We had the bag packed and everything we needed, except those darned keys. Fortunately, we found them—in the ignition!

➤ We invited the next-door neighbors over for dinner, but Baby was teething and when he wasn't screaming and crying, all he wanted to do was chew on the tablecloth?

➤ We used to immediately start singing "Old McDonald Had a Farm" (loudly, even in public) when we sensed an outburst in the making and needed to defuse the situation?

➤ Dad sat up with you practically all night because you watched that television show about sharks and were convinced that there were some under your bed?

➤ We almost named you Elvis, but your grandmom pitched such a fit we decided on William instead? We'll love whatever name you choose!

Great Grandparenting

A family scrapbook is a great project to start before the birth of the first grandchild, and to continue as other grandchildren come along. It is well worth the effort of researching the family tree (many libraries or historical or genealogical societies will help you at no, or little, cost). Everyone, regardless of age, will be fascinated with the picture of Great-Great-Uncle Will in his coonskin cap.

Solid Support—On Site and Otherwise

Nearly every parent-to-be can use some support of one nature or another. For some, moral support is enough; for others, financial or physical support might be necessary. If you are inclined to offer support of any sort, do so graciously and willingly.

➤ *Financial support.* If your child is financially strapped, and you are able to do so, you might want to offer some help. You could offer money outright, or take a more subtle approach by offering to pay some telephone or utility bills (or perhaps offering to do all the phoning from your end if your conversations are long distance). Perhaps you could pay for some groceries, offer to buy the baby's crib or treat the mom-to-be to some pretty maternity clothes.

➤ *Physical support.* Offer to run errands, help with housecleaning, make repairs around the house, or help with yard work. If pregnancy is keeping the mom-to-be from doing everything she is used to, she may be feeling frustrated and impatient. A little help might ease her concerns.

➤ *Other forms of support.* Order some gourmet treats from a catalogue and have them sent to the parents-to-be. Perhaps prepare a special dinner close to the due date, complete with candles and sparkling cider. Send over some "hospital gifts," such as pretty magazines, a book, or photo album. A fresh bouquet of flowers is always welcome.

➤ *Non-tangible support.* All the things we've talked about so far. Good listening, encouragement, and sharing the joy and anticipation of the mom and dad-to-be is the best gift.

15

Hartt to Hartt

We asked some of our friends who are grandparents how they help their kids and grandkids. Their answers told us that help is given in many forms, depending on need. Our friends provided everything from babysitting to help with paying mortgages.

One thing we learned, however, was that the young couples that they were helping all shared some common needs. They all desired the assurance of being loved, and the comfort of knowing that help is available when needed.

Testing, Testing

If your daughter or daughter-in-law starts speaking one day in what sounds to be a different language, she may be telling you about some of the tests she'll be having during her pregnancy. Tests early in the pregnancy can detect conditions that could lead to problems, such as rubella, infections, sickle-cell anemia, Tay-Sachs disease, or diabetes. Tests later in the pregnancy can detect abnormalities of the fetus. These tests are commonly done and are not a signal to worry that something is wrong. Some common prenatal tests are:

➤ *Ultrasound (also called sonogram)*—the use of sound waves that bounce off internal structures, allowing visualization of the fetus without the hazards of x-rays. Expecting parents can watch the process on a viewing screen, "see" their baby, and maybe even get a picture of him or her to hang on the fridge. Ultrasound's uses vary from determining how far along the pregnancy is to verifying breech presentation.

Danger Zone

CAUTION If there is a real problem, or even a possible problem, with the pregnancy, don't try to console the parents-to-be with cute stories or the "everything will be just fine" clichés. Understand that they are terribly worried, and be supportive, perhaps sharing some reassuring details from your own experience, or that of someone well known to the couple.

➤ *Amniocentesis*—the extraction of amniotic fluid to determine the possibility of genetic problems, present condition of the baby, or level of maturity.

➤ *Chorionic villus sampling*—a test to determine genetic defects in the fetus very early in pregnancy.

➤ *Triple-marker test*—a screening conducted at about the 16th week of pregnancy to determine the possibility of neural tube defects.

➤ *Non-stress test*—a test to determine the condition of the unborn baby. The mother is hooked up to a fetal monitor and the response of the fetal heart to fetal movements can be observed.

These and other tests during pregnancy can bring relief when they provide the news everyone wants to hear—that everything is fine. If something abnormal shows up, however, the test results can cause great anxiety. Some of the tests require a waiting period for the results, which also can be stressful. Try to remain calm and reassuring.

If the Pregnancy Gets Complicated

Nobody likes to think about it, but problems sometimes develop during pregnancy. Sometimes the problems are serious, and sometimes even life threatening. Some common complications of pregnancy are:

➤ *Pre-eclampsia*—pregnancy-induced hypertension

➤ *Hyperemesis gravidarum*—an exaggerated form of morning sickness

➤ *Placenta previa*—when the placenta is attached in the lower half of the uterus, possibly blocking or partially blocking the cervix and making vaginal delivery difficult or impossible

➤ *Abrupitio placenta*—when the placenta separates from the uterus prematurely

➤ *Ectopic pregnancy*—pregnancy implanted outside the uterus

Remember that most women go through pregnancy and childbirth without complications. If problems are detected, however, it is extremely important for grandparents to be encouraging, good listeners, and to let their children know they are there for them. Do some reading and learn as much as you can about the condition so you can better communicate with the worried parents-to-be. You also may need to help out with practical matters such as housecleaning, cooking, and yard work if the mom-to-be is confined to bed for a pregnancy-related problem.

Danger Zone
If something terribly wrong occurs during the pregnancy, it will be extremely upsetting to all involved. Your primary concern must be for the expectant parents. Don't panic! If it's too difficult to discuss the problem with them without becoming overly emotional, perhaps your spouse can speak in your place, or you can send a note until you are able to remain calm. The worried parents-to-be have enough to think about, without adding frantic grandparents.

The Least You Need to Know

➤ Pregnant daughters and daughters-in-law will welcome stories based on a grandmother's experience as a mother. Just keep them reasonably positive (no pregnancy or delivery horror stories, please) and remember to leave medical advice to the obstetrician or midwife.

➤ Pregnancy and childbirth are not for women only. Grandfathers offer special talents and perspectives and are welcome participants in these months of waiting.

➤ Learn the art of listening and pay close attention to what the mom- and dad-to-be are saying—or trying to say.

➤ Think about how you can best support your child, and do so willingly and happily.

➤ When the unexpected happens and a time of crisis looms, your wisdom and experience can be a great source of comfort to expecting parents.

Welcoming the Bundle of Joy

You've waited and waited for the news. The hours since you heard they went to the hospital seem like years. You've been up all night, hoping for the phone to ring. And now, finally, you know. You have a grandchild. It's a boy, it's a girl, it's big, it's small, he looks like his mom, she looks like her dad. It doesn't matter. You have a grandchild and you've just got to see him right away. Pack the bags, you're going!

Wait, slow down. New moms and dads react differently to the cavalry rushing in. Some enjoy all the fuss and attention, but others prefer to be left alone for a while. Some, hoping for a little time together with their brand-new child, might be downright annoyed to see you before they're out of the recovery room.

As grandparents, you obviously want the best for your children and their new baby. If you're not certain that visitors will be welcome the first hours after birth, proceed with caution.

Wait to Be Invited (or Dis-Invited!)

The good old days when a new mom got to lie around in a flower-filled hospital room for close to a week, waiting for her baby to arrive from the nursery and her dinner to arrive from the meal cart, are gone. Today's hospital stays typically are extremely short. Often, the new mom and baby are released within 24 hours of delivery. These very short stays might make a visit to the hospital logistically impossible. By the time Mom has nursed and bathed the baby, gotten a few hours of desperately needed sleep and gathered up her belongings, she and the newborn are on their way home.

Danger Zone

Even if you get a verbal go-ahead to visit, look for signs that the welcome mat might not really be out. Today's parents are advised that important bonding occurs with the baby during the first few days after birth. They may like to have that time to concentrate on their newborn but may be reluctant to say so. On the other hand, don't assume the new parents don't want company. They may mistake your concern for their privacy as lack of interest.

Ask the new dad how he feels about having you visit. Could you come to the hospital, or would it be better to wait and visit at home? Perhaps the new mom is not feeling up to having company (having a baby, after all, is hard, tiring work).

No matter how desperately you want to see your new grandchild, you must consider the wishes of the parents. Do go ahead and send a beautiful bouquet of flowers or a big basket of fruit. If the hospital stay is very short, it probably is a good idea to send the gift to the home. Include a card saying you love them all and can't wait to see the new family as soon as they're ready for company.

Hartt to Hartt

When Marilyn had her first child, she was scheduled to stay the customary five days in the hospital. On the morning of day four, the doctor told her she wouldn't be able to go home the next day, as planned. She had a low-grade fever, which he concluded had been caused by lack of adequate rest, brought on by playing hostess to so many visitors.

He gave her a choice: She could ban all visitors and rest, and perhaps be able to go home as planned. Or, she could continue entertaining and stay an extra day or two. Marilyn promptly put out the "Do Not Disturb" sign, went to sleep, and was home the following day.

Other Relatives Qualify, Too

Once you get a chance to hold the little bundle of joy, you might find it's addictive. The next time, you want to keep him in your arms a little bit longer—and then longer still. Before you know it, you've got to rock him to sleep, and can barely stand to leave once he's snuggled in his crib. He is just SO PRECIOUS! Grandparents have reported dreaming about new grandchildren and being unable to clear their minds of the images of their faces. If you've fallen hopelessly in love and feel that you've got to be with the baby as much as you possibly can, beware. It's very likely that another new grandma and grandpa are feeling the same way. And they happen to share the same grandchild. With you!

The point is, a baby is a very popular person. He attracts lots of attention—sometimes from people you don't even know. New parents tell of neighbors they've never met showing up to visit once the baby comes home. And there you are, trying to get as much time with your precious one as you possibly can. Throw in a couple of sets of grandparents (maybe more if there's been a second marriage), some aunts and uncles, cousins, a few neighbors, some of the parents' coworkers, and so on, and you've got a houseful.

You may need to be gracious and back off a bit. Remember, visits from everyone but the closest family members will quickly become fewer and farther apart. Don't let visiting the baby become a competition. Just enjoy the time you have together to the fullest.

To make the most of your visits, either at the baby's house or at yours, consider these pointers:

➤ *Schedule visits at times when you are least likely to be interrupted.* For instance, if you know the new mom's boss is going to drop by to see the baby, wait until that visit ends before starting yours.

➤ *Plan ahead!* Don't decide one morning that you'd like to spend the day with the baby, and be disappointed when you learn he has a doctor's appointment.

➤ *When the baby comes to your house, avoid the temptation to invite groups of friends in so you can show her off.* You already know she's the most beautiful baby ever born. Your friends will find out in good time. For now, be selfish and enjoy!

➤ *Start a photo album so you can "visit" any time you like.* Frame a couple of your favorite photos and put them where everyone will see them.

Sure You Want to Cope with Colic and Diapers?

Take One: You're sitting in a sunny room, gently rocking your new grandchild. Swaddled in soft, white blankets, he is looking peacefully into your face with what could pass as a smile on his lips. You've never known such calm and happiness.

Take Two: You've been rocking the baby for forty minutes, trying to get him to go to sleep. You're starting to get concerned because he seems agitated and nothing you do helps for more than a minute or two. Your daughter is trying to rest and you hate to disturb her, but you're beginning to wonder if something is wrong. This crying is really starting to get to you.

While the first scenario is certainly more pleasant, it may not be the more realistic of the two. Sometimes grandparents tend to look at child rearing through rose-colored glasses, forgetting some of the unpleasantness that comes with the job.

Colic

This unwelcome disorder, which doctors now believe may be caused by abdominal pain, can make life miserable, not only for the infant but for everyone nearby. Continuous crying, usually during a particular period of the early evening, can go on for hours. In severe cases, crying escalates into screaming, and becomes increasingly difficult to deal with. The baby may suck furiously for a few minutes when offered food, but loses interest quickly and resumes crying.

Colic is difficult to diagnose and even more difficult to cure. Less severe cases can be controlled for brief periods by cradling or rocking. Sometimes a ride in the car seems to calm the baby. Some mothers say they have found relief by putting the baby in her car seat or sleeping basket (always make sure she's secured) and placing her on top of an operating washer or dryer. (CAUTION: Never leave a baby unattended in this position. Vibrations from the machine could cause the seat to move to the edge and fall off.)

Some moms report that colic eases when the baby is switched from breast milk to formula. Others swear by a vibrating attachment that hooks up to the crib and mimics the action and noise of a moving car.

As terrible as colic seems, it does no lasting harm to the infant. Try to remember that it almost always ends by the time the baby is three months old.

Messy Bottoms

Changing diapers has become much, much easier in recent years, thanks to the advent of all sorts of disposable diapers. They come in all shapes and sizes; some of them feel so much like cloth that you may be tempted to wash them. And, all of them share a great feature (in addition to disposability)—they don't require safety pins.

Still, babies get diaper rash regardless of the diapers they wear. Most pediatricians recommend cleaning the baby's bottom well with plain water—no baby wipes at this tender age, please!—and treating diaper rash with zinc oxide ointment. Check the diaper frequently. Wetness is harder to detect in disposable diapers than in cloth, and a dirty diaper will aggravate a rash. Letting the baby go without a diaper also is recommended in the treatment of diaper rash. Just make sure there are several old towels underneath him!

And Then There Are Those Table "Manners"

You might look forward to dining with your grandchild as soon as he is old enough to sit in a high chair and be pulled up to the family table. After one or two tries, however, you may decisively change your mind. There is no sight quite so rollicking as that of an infant in a high chair, chortling with glee as the food leaves his spoon (or fingers) and spatters table, floor, and adjoining walls. If the table is an antique, the floor is expensive hardwood, or the walls are freshly papered, you may quickly lose your enthusiasm (not to mention your appetite) for dining with Baby. Think back to the days when your own children were babies. Remember all the spills, sticky floors, fingers, and dirty mouths?

The trick is to be patient and don't rush things. A baby only several months old has no interest in table manners, nor does she care whether you have a peaceful meal. It might be smarter to feed the baby first, then try to content him by putting him in a playpen or baby swing (within your sight) while you eat. Just don't expect that you'll dine uninterrupted.

I'm Too Old for This!

It's only natural that the excitement of being a grandparent will wear off a little over time. Don't feel bad when your daughter and grandchild drop by unexpectedly and you feel a flash of annoyance about being interrupted in the middle of the project you're working on. It's perfectly understandable.

You may also notice that a day of babysitting wears you out more than you expected. Your shoulders ache the morning after from carrying that cute, chubby baby around all afternoon. Or you get a headache late in the afternoon. Perhaps cleaning up the kitchen after his lunch of strained spinach and Cheerios has ruined your appetite for that dinner out you'd planned. And, it's not quite so cute anymore when he pulls all the magazines out of the rack and spreads them around the living room.

You might well think you're past your child-caring prime and it would best be left to someone else. You might even end up thinking, "I'm too old for this!"

Don't despair. You're not old, you're just tired. And with good reason. Caring for children is hard work. But—and this is the beauty of grandparenting—you can decline to watch the baby if you're not feeling up to it. You can beg off if you have something else to do. Don't feel bad about taking a day off.

As the child gets a little older and more mobile, you'll enjoy visiting places where you took your own children. Chances are you'll begin to look at life from a fresh perspective. You'll learn all about toys you never heard of (a play cell phone with realistic-sounding push buttons?), television shows you never imagined (a big, purple dinosaur? "Bananas in Pajamas"?) and the many wonders of Zany Brainy or a Disney Store ("You have *how* many different Snow White figurines?").

Fantasize about future visits to zoos and museums and walks in the park. New wonders, marvels, and magic will dazzle you and your grandchild. You may some days think of yourself as getting older, but don't dwell on it. There's too much to do.

I'm Not Fit for This!

If you have a physical problem or disability, you might have some serious qualms about your ability to be a *safe* grandparent. Arthritis could make it very difficult to hold a baby, or you might not trust yourself to hold him if you are prone to seizures or dizzy spells. Perhaps you just aren't sure of the safest ways to care for a baby anymore. Everything seems so different. Or, you doubt whether you could be effective if an emergency were to occur. If you are uncomfortable with your ability to care for your grandchild, *don't take any chances*.

Discuss your feelings with the parents and explain you would never do anything to jeopardize the safety of their child. They will understand that not being able to care for the baby by yourself does not mean you love him any less. In fact, they probably will be relieved that you recognized the problem without them having to say anything. Perhaps you could make arrangements to assist your spouse or another caregiver with babysitting. Maybe you can sit and rock the baby in a chair, but not have to carry him from room to room. You may also want to discuss the situation with your doctor.

Handy Tips if You Expect to Be on Hand

If you're the kind of person who always volunteered to chair the employee Christmas party at work, serve as president of the PTA, or teach Sunday School every single year, be on your guard. You're a likely candidate for overcommitment. Fueled by enthusiasm over your change from parent to grandparent status and anxious to help the new parents, you might agree to do a fair amount of babysitting. You may even agree to do a *whole lot* of babysitting. If this is what you want to do—great. Many grandparents have been very happy to see the babies grow into children and then teenagers under their watch.

If you do not intend to make babysitting your grandchildren a full-time job, however, make sure your children know this. Don't let them assume that a lot of babysitting early on means that you'll continue the service indefinitely. If you both are working grandparents, of course, watching the baby while your children work is out of the question. If you're retirees who are busy pursuing hobbies or volunteer work, you will find that many evenings and weekends are already filled. Your children, however, might not realize that. Just make sure you all are on the same wavelength!

Don't Get Locked In

As much as you've enjoyed having your daughter, son-in-law, and the baby for dinner the past few Sundays, look out. Habits are quickly established, and your lifestyle might not be able to accommodate a same-day, same-time, and same-place-next-week dinner date. Go slowly and let traditions form naturally, not be created artificially and regretted later.

The Question of Gifts

It's fun to take little gifts for a baby or young child. There are *so* many adorable things out there! That little snowsuit with the bunny ears… The mobile that winds up and plays "Rock Around the Clock" while it turns… Beware! No matter how well intended you are, you can overdo it, particularly if you live close enough to visit often. When the baby gets older, he will quickly learn to associate your visit with a gift, and you may establish a pattern of him expecting something each time he sees you. Breaking the gift habit will be difficult, but you don't want to create unrealistic expectations.

In addition, constant gifts early on can be overwhelming to parents who already are trying to find room in their home for a crib, sleeping basket, baby swing, and assorted other gear. In a particular case, new parents were so overwhelmed by the number of stuffed animals their son received, they packed up all but a few and delivered them to a Salvation Army shelter.

Never fear, you can avoid the bearing-too-many-baby-gifts syndrome and still indulge your desire to give. Occasionally take something for the whole family to enjoy. A home-made apple pie or a basket of apples or grapefruit would be appreciated by everyone.

Hartt to Hartt

Marilyn's family had an older friend who they affectionately called "Aunt Nina." Aunt Nina loved Marilyn, and began to pamper her practically from the moment of birth. The moment of truth came when Marilyn was eight. Aunt Nina, who by this time had showered Marilyn with gifts of every kind, asked the young girl if she loved her for all the presents she had been given, or just because she was Aunt Nina. Marilyn felt obliged to be honest and replied, "both." In spite of, or perhaps because of her honesty, the friendship between Nina and Marilyn continued to flourish.

Great Grandparenting

If there are other children in the household, keep tuned for any evidence of jealousy or resentment. Tell siblings about the roles they'll play in caring for the new baby ("You can hand Daddy the powder and help him dry Baby off after his bath."). Everybody knows how important big brothers and sisters are! This will make them feel important and excited about the impending arrival.

Grandchild Rivalry

Let's face it. The announcement that your daughter or daughter-in-law is pregnant is pretty hard to top. It definitely is BIG NEWS, which tends to overshadow other events for a while. Grandparents, along with the rest of the family, want to be kept up to date on all the developments as the weeks and months pass.

Don't let yourself get so involved with the pregnancy and birth, however, that you neglect to give adequate attention to other grandchildren. Children don't understand the intricacies of pregnancy, and normally aren't as enthralled with newborns as adults are (when is she ever going to stop howling?). They can quickly become resentful of all the attention given to the newest member of the family if they think they're being neglected.

Doing the Right Thing

It's a big deal for small people, there's no doubt about it. But, if you can somehow help your other grandchildren to understand how their family has been blessed with the birth of the new baby, you will have given them a wonderful gift. Don't think for a minute you'll rid them of the jealousy they'll feel when Mom says she can't get their apple juice because she's nursing Baby. And don't think you can take away the resentment they'll feel when Baby grabs a favorite book and shreds it to pieces.

If you can give them a sense, however, of the importance of the family, and an idea of how the members of a family must care for one another and operate as a unit, you will have given them a piece of the foundation that will support their lives. This may be a good time for you to try to spend extra time with the other grandchildren, despite the allure of baby coos and gurgles. Bring out scrapbooks and photo albums, and show youngsters what you looked like as babies and children growing up. Tell them stories about their parents as children and newborns. Let them see how a family evolves and grows from generation to generation. Show them how precious your family is to you, and hope they gain a bit of understanding.

The Dilemma of the Only Child

We all like the idea of a big family gathered around the table, sharing the events of the day, laughing and planning and making memories. Not every family, however, has as many members as the Waltons. In fact, some families have only one child. And, some grandparents have only one grandchild. If this is the case, do not think about what you might be missing (some grandparents would tell you that what you're missing is a lot of noise, mess, and carrying on). Focus on the grandchild you have and the opportunities to create a very special relationship with him or her. Think of some ways you could "multiply" your grandparenting of an only child:

➤ Get to know your grandchild's friends and classmates and include them in family gatherings and festivities.

➤ Have your grandchild meet and play with other children the same age when he or she comes to visit you.

➤ Communicate regularly by mail and phone (maybe even by e-mail) as your grandchild grows up.

➤ Give your grandchild incentives to communicate with you, such as including self-addressed envelopes with your letters. Tell your grandchild to call you for a surprise invitation, or ask questions you know he or she'd like to answer.

Hartt to Hartt

When we were raising our own children, we found that some of the most difficult people to deal with were parents with only one child. These parents sometimes failed to realize that all children are different, and what works with one child (their own) does not necessarily work with another. So, too, with grandparents—they need to be careful about jumping in with advice before they know their grandchild well. As grandparents, we have had more life experiences than our children and their peers, but that still does not mean we qualify as experts on any particular child.

Consternation or Collaboration?

It looks like the period of grace has ended. Your daughter, who was so grateful to you for all your help the first few weeks after the baby was born, now considers herself a seasoned mother. A bit more confident about what she's doing, she no longer calls three or four times a day to check something with you, the voice of experience. She has no qualms now about taking the baby with her when she goes on an errand, so you're not on call to dash over when she needs to leave the house. She's even gotten one of those soft little packs that allows her to snuggle the baby securely against her chest while she does chores or takes a walk. In some ways you're happy that things are easing up, but in other ways....

For starters, you don't think she should take the baby out of the house so much. It's getting cool outside and you're quite sure she doesn't always remember to put the earflaps down on his hat. Who knows—she might not even use the hat. Plus, she's started washing some of his clothes with theirs. Everyone knows you use Ivory Snow for a year!

She doesn't keep his room warm enough. And the other night they had friends over until all hours, and you're sure it was hard for the poor little thing to get to sleep. You're fit to be tied, but don't know what to do about it.

Start by putting yourself in the shoes of the new parents. Most likely they're doing the very best they can. They've had to make dozens of decisions during the past few weeks, most of them with the handicap of too little sleep. They've been overwhelmed, overtired, and overly emotional. Cut them some slack. Try to understand why your daughter put Baby's sleeper in with the family wash.

Could it be that modern detergents are different, and it's not as critical to wash Baby's clothes separately? (Indeed, this is so.) Is she perhaps taking the baby with her on errands because she doesn't want to bother you all the time, or because she's more confident in caring for the child? And, can you really blame them for wanting to have a few friends over that night? It's been ages since they've seen anyone! And besides, some kids can sleep through anything.

Of course, if something the new parents are doing poses a danger to the baby, you must speak up. If you simply don't like it because you would do it differently, you'd best look the other way. Feel free to offer some friendly suggestions if you honestly think you have a better method of doing something, but don't be offended if they continue to do it their way.

The Least You Need to Know

➤ Let the new parents call the signals and suggest the best time to visit—if they want you to.

➤ Don't view other grandparents and relatives as competitors. Be happy that there are others to share in the life of your grandchild, and make the best of the time you have with the baby.

➤ Don't worry about being too old for babysitting unless there's a safety concern. Revel in the magic of seeing the world again through the eyes of a child.

➤ Plan in advance what you should do, could do, and won't do. Tell your kids what to expect—or *not* to expect—and stick to your decisions.

➤ Treat the idea of the new baby as something positive and meaningful in your family, but don't let the new arrival become so all-important that other matters (and grandchildren) fall in the shadows.

➤ Practice collaboration and cooperation wherever possible, and refrain from fostering differences of opinion that can lead to dissension.

Ground Rules for Grandparents

Now that you are firmly established as a grandparent, you'll be facing some tricky territory ahead. If you think of your family as a generational sandwich, you'd be on the top (or close to the top if there are great-grandparents). Your grandkids would be on the bottom, and the parents (your kids) stuck right in the middle. A family is made up of layers, and if some are missing or they can't complement one another, you'll have a really bad sandwich.

Parents and grandparents don't always see eye to eye. That's no secret. You think they're too lenient. They think you're too strict—except when you "spoil" the grandkids with Twizzlers and Pixie Sticks. You think they let the kids watch too many videos. They say you don't understand that videos are an important learning tools. You think Mom should quit her job and stop shuffling the kids around all the time (watch it, you're on thin ice!). They say Mom has to work because everything costs so much, and besides, she *likes* having a career.

There's no denying that times have changed. Nor can we think they will stop changing. Look at your little grandchildren and think of the future. What will it be like for them? Will they race through childhood too quickly, as we all seem to be racing through life? Will they have time to dream, to explore, to experiment? Will they fear failure, or understand that sometimes life's belly flops eventually lead to successes? Grandparents have a special ability to provide perspective and insight to children.

Let's face it. Even if you're only 50, they think you're O-L-D. You've been around for a while. You might even remember World War II. When you were a kid, you not only didn't have a VCR, you might not have even had a TV! These things set you apart and give you special status in your grandchildren's eyes. Because you have that status, you sometimes can get through to grandkids when their parents can't. You're a step removed, therefore less threatening.

Now comes the tricky part. You want to—and should—take advantage of the special role you have in your family. But, it sometimes gets difficult to do that without causing conflicts with the parents. Let's see how we can avoid conflict.

Wanting to Get Involved

Did you ever know somebody who always knows more about what you're saying than you do? You can't tell this guy (or woman) *anything* that he doesn't already know. His way of doing something—regardless of what—is right, and that's that. Advice? This guy doesn't want advice about anything!

A guy like that can be *really* difficult to get along with. In fact, nobody wants to be around him at all. He's obnoxious!

If you're really honest, though, you probably have to admit that every now and then a little bit of that guy shows up inside you. It happens to everyone. Even the meekest and most mild-mannered people feel a need to really assert themselves sometimes. It happens to new parents, too. All of a sudden they're struck by the need to appear knowledgeable and in control. They've got a new baby and, by darned, they can take care of her all by themselves. Don't bother telling them the diaper is on backwards; they won't believe it. And they don't want to know that those little bumps all over their newborn's skin are perfectly normal. Hold your breath because they're already on their way to have them checked out by the pediatrician.

If new parents get a case of the "we-know-it-all syndrome," don't despair. It's normal. No matter how desperately you want to get involved, you just have to wait it out. Once they experience the never-ending work that parenting entails, they most likely will be happy for your help and more receptive to your advice. They might even recognize that you've succeeded in doing what they are attempting to do, and admire you for it.

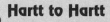

Hartt to Hartt

When Marilyn had her first child, her mother came to help her daughter for five days. She cooked and cleaned, and did everything else that was needed, but she was always careful to let Marilyn decide what she wanted to take care of herself. It was a good arrangement, but one person felt left out.

Walter, the new father, was feeling a bit unneeded, due to the competence of the two women. When the second baby arrived, however, Walter had his big chance to be the VIP, because Marilyn's mother couldn't be there.

What Is Your Role?

Once the "we-know-it-all syndrome" has passed, you should determine just how it is that you'll fit into this family mosaic of yours. Will you be very involved or more on the sidelines? You can determine this to an extent, but the parents also will affect your involvement. Grandparents in good standing are followers, not leaders. They take their cues from the parents, and gauge their involvement accordingly.

This can be very difficult, experts say, because you're used to being in charge. You have, or have had, responsibility at work. You've raised a family, you care for your elderly parents. And now you've got to sit back and wait for your daughter to indicate what your role will be? Well, an expert advises, you certainly maintain a say in family matters, but it's very important for grandparents to know when to defer to the parents.

One thing a grandparent always can do is offer practical, needed assistance. Taking care of a new baby is a full-time job. Even if the mother has the luxury of making it her full-time job, she'll probably be tired. If she has to work outside the home or continue a career from home, she is likely to be exhausted. The new dad will be tired, too, especially if he's taking bottle duty during the night. Listen for clues from the parents about problems they might be having. Then, come up with some specific suggestions as to how you can help. For example:

➤ *Give the new parents a gift certificate to their favorite restaurant and offer to babysit while they go.* If the restaurant is far away, choose one that's closer. Most new parents are more comfortable close to home the first few times they leave the baby.

➤ *Let the parents know if you hear about a good babysitter,* especially if he or she lives in their area. It's always nice to know of trustworthy, reliable help.

➤ *Offer to hire a cleaning service or person to help the new parents until things get back to normal.* Make sure the parents know you are offering this gift to ease them of a burden, not to criticize their housekeeping skills. Make sure all parties understand this would be a temporary situation.

You are likely to be well received if you make a specific offer, such as one of like these, rather than just asking how you can help or offering help in a vague manner. If there's any of the "know-it-all-syndrome" lingering, you might get turned down completely if you don't come up with a specific offer.

Avoiding Parent/Grandparent Clashes

Remembering to be a follower and not a leader (even if it makes you cringe) in the grandparenting game will minimize friction between you and the new parents. And, think of it this way: You've been the leader for a long time, and it's not always easy. Take a break and let somebody else do it for a while. With that in mind, when your grandchild is about to be left in your care, ask the parents for instructions:

➤ What are the usual nap and bed times?

➤ What is the feeding schedule? Are any foods off-limits?

➤ What toilet training procedures, if any, should be followed?

➤ With older children, find out what the favorite foods are if you don't already know, and ask if any foods are on the "no-no" list?

➤ Again, with older children, you might ask whether there are any sensitive subjects that should be avoided—some subjects *always* seem to start arguments between siblings.

You need also to be aware of, and sensitive to, the parents' attitudes concerning child raising. If the mom and dad differ on a child-raising issue, don't get involved. If they agree on a policy, defer to their judgment. If, for example, the parents are determined not to make a big fuss over a child who has fallen, you should refrain from rushing in and scooping him up after the first tumble. If they aren't going to insist that their little one clean up her plate at every meal—and this is what the experts now recommend—don't try to insist on doing things the way you did them back in the 50s, when your kids had to sit at the table until they ate everything. Try to adhere to their policies.

Danger Zone
Mom rushes to Baby's side whenever he makes a whimper. Dad feels that when Baby whimpers, he should be left alone for a bit to try to work it out. The three of you hear Baby crying. Mom wants to go to Baby, but doesn't want to get Dad upset. You know she'd be happy if *you* would go. What do you do? Nothing. Simply pretend you don't hear a thing. You'd be in a no-win situation, so don't get in it at all.

Remember these rules:

➤ **Rule #1:** Don't do anything to put yourself between the father and mother.

➤ **Rule #2:** Accept the fact that, when there are properly functioning mothers and fathers, grandparents serve to *augment* rather than substitute.

Hartt to Hartt

We recently babysat for our 4- and 5-year-old grandkids. With the parents in a hurry to get out, we neglected to ask them about the latest bedtime and bath routines. When we asked our grandsons if they were ready to take their baths, the younger one simply said no. Then his brother patiently explained that only moms and dads talked about baths—grandmas and grandpas did not. Obviously, baths were a hot topic at the moment. We took the coward's way out and decided that one night without a bath wouldn't make any difference. Next time, we'll get some definitive information on baths—from Mom and Dad.

You may have to retreat a bit from time to time, but there's no need to abandon your own tactics and child-raising style. What you offer as grandparents is a slightly different approach to daily life. While the parents may insist on fruit at every meal, for example, you can be a bit more lenient when the grandchildren are at your house. A "good try" will make everyone happy and won't compromise your authority.

Leave It to the Parents: When Not to Get Involved

Just when you think you know how to play the game, they go and change the rules on you! Apart from bedtimes and eating routines, child raising involves issues that are more serious and far-reaching. A late night or two won't make a big difference in the long run. Other matters can.

You know this, and you managed nicely with your own kids. The thing is, your child-rearing techniques may be completely out of sync with some of today's philosophies. Set aside time for a little reading in the field of child development and parent-child relationships. You may be surprised—even shocked—at how attitudes toward child rearing have changed. A few suggestions for up-to-date books are:

➤ *Complete Baby and Child Care Guide*, by Dr. Miriam Stoppard. Covers physical, emotional, and developmental issues.

➤ *Normal Children Have Problems, Too*, by Stanley Turecki, M.D., with Sara Wernick, Ph.D. Deals with issues facing today's children and how parents how can help them cope.

➤ *Common Sense Parenting*, by Ray Burke, Ph.D., and Ron Herron. A guide to raising responsible kids.

Among the issues on which opinion has changed dramatically during the past 20 to 30 years are behavioral problems (we didn't know those naughty kids in school were really suffering from attention deficit disorder), discipline (let somebody hear you talk about not sparing the rod and spoiling the child today and you may get a call from the child welfare department!), self-esteem (you can't promote it too much), gender (do girls *really* want to play high school football?), and nutrition (whole milk after the first two years? Think again, please!).

If these or other child-rearing issues are causing conflicts between you and your son or daughter and his or her spouse, you'd better back off. Your concern and resulting opinions and advice come from love, but your ideas might be outdated.

Experts recommend that parents take a firm stand against interfering grandparents. Before that happens, bow out graciously and stay away from these potentially dangerous areas. You don't have to agree with the child-rearing philosophies of the parents, but you need to respect them. One family counselor who is the mother of five children and grandmother of two has a firm policy of never offering advice unless she is asked. Sometimes it's difficult, she says, but it's too easy for a piece of advice to be misinterpreted as an insult to the mom and dad.

Hartt to Hartt

When one of our grandsons had eye surgery, we needed to keep his two-year-old brother, Max, at our house. He'd never been away overnight before, and we decided that rigid bedtime rules were unsuitable for this occasion. We felt that the guest room would be too lonely, so Marilyn cuddled little Max on the couch and read him stories. When he remained awake, she cuddled him some more and tried a soothing video about baby animals. The two of them stayed there all night, with pillows and a blanket. Grandma was a bit stiff in the morning, but felt privileged to have offered her grandson this special time of comfort.

Don't Leave It to the Parents: When Experience Pays Off

Conscientious new parents are often hard on themselves. "What are we doing wrong?" they ask when child raising hits one of its inevitable bumps. As a grandparent, you are a good source of reassuring stories about the bumps you encountered and how (hopefully) everything was successfully resolved.

Grandparents can offer a more relaxed perspective about everything from teething to telling lies than parents are able to do for themselves. You've been through it all before and know that in most cases this, too, shall pass. One expert says grandparents can see their grandchildren more objectively than they did their own children because their egos are not involved. They see, and can appreciate, the child as a separate person, not as an extension of themselves, as parents tend to.

If parents are receptive to advice, and you have some that will be valuable, feel free to offer it. Do so especially if the parents are upset about something and your advice will reassure them.

An expert in family relationships said grandparents who have limited involvement with their grandchildren must be particularly careful about offering advice. Grandparents who see their grandchildren only two or three times a year, due to distance between their homes or other reasons, have not "earned" the right to give advice. Grandparents who are closely and actively involved with their grandchildren may have more leeway.

Ideally, grandparents and parents should act as partners in raising grandchildren. Grandparents, however, must be ready to play the role of junior partner unless parents request otherwise.

Sharing with the Other Grandparents

While you're working things out with the baby's parents, you may be facing another potential source of conflict. Many a feud has been launched between two sets of grandparents that feel jealous or even threatened by the amount of time the other set gets to spend with a common grandchild. Conflicting child-rearing styles and philosophies can also cause some turmoil.

A good way to keep peace and avoid conflict is to get to know the other grandparents if you don't already. You'll probably like them! Once you become acquaintances (maybe even friends), it will be easier for you to "share" the grandchild. Who knows, you might end up in some sort of joint activity and have a great time!

Consideration should be given to the grandparents who are further away from the grandchild—or who, for whatever reason, find it more difficult to plan visits. Here are some situations that might need to be considered:

➤ One set of grandparents is many hours away by plane, while the other set is within convenient driving distance

➤ One set of grandparents is financially pressed, while the other can not only extend invitations to their children and grandchildren, but offer to pay travel expenses

Great Grandparenting
The baby was almost two and a joy to be around. She normally was pleasant and happy, but suddenly, it seemed, she became a cranky baby. She woke up crying and had trouble contenting herself during the day. Her parents were frantic. Grandma noticed the little girl sticking her fingers far back into her mouth. Suddenly, she realized what was causing the baby's irritation. A look into the baby's mouth confirmed it: Molars! Everyone was immensely relieved, and the problem soon abated.

Danger Zone
We advise that grandparents should be followers and let parents be leaders, and that it is unwise for grandparents to be too free with advice. But be alert for situations in which the child might be in real danger. Never hesitate to speak up when you know your failure to do so might put a child at risk.

➤ Physical disabilities limit the travel capabilities or participation of one set of grand-parents, while the other has no such limitations

➤ One set of grandparents more nearly matches the religion, culture, education, or politics of the parents, while the other is uncomfortable with one or more of these differences

The goal, here, is to make grandparenting a pleasant and rewarding experience for everyone involved. Be glad your grandchildren have so many people who care about them, and in no circumstances should you criticize the other grandparents in front of your grandchildren and children.

What If the Grandchildren Aren't Allowed to Visit?

This situation crops up more often than you like, and it's extremely unfortunate. Many grandparents will tell of being denied visits with their grandchildren because their child is upset with them about one thing or another. It is an effective "punishment" for grand-parents and grandkids, but an ineffective way of dealing with a problem.

Experts advise that the way to deal with this terrible problem is to meet it head on and talk about it with your son or daughter. Often, there are issues that have been festering for a long time and must be resolved before the situation can be settled. An adult child might say she is angry with you because you said she takes the baby out too often, but the real reason she's angry probably lies elsewhere. If you and your child are unable to resolve the problem, you might suggest you go together for counseling.

If, despite your very best efforts, the rift remains, you can petition the court for visitation rights with your grandchild. Be aware, though, that this puts the child directly in the middle of an adult problem. If your grandchild is old enough and mature enough, you could write a letter or talk to him on the phone, explaining that you would love to be able to spend time with him, but it is not possible just now. Do not go into specifics, and do not blame the child's parents. Simply say that some adult problems are preventing you from spending time with him, but that you love him very much and hope the matter will be resolved.

If worse comes to worst, you may just have to wait until the child is an adult, and hope you can resolve the issue with him then. But don't give up easily if this situation occurs. Grandparenting is one of life's most precious experiences, and to lose out on it would be devastating, not only to you, but to your grandchild who would be robbed of a wonderful dimension of his life.

Or, Is a Visit Forced on the Kids?

On the flip side, some parents "punish" their children by sending them to grandma and grandpa's house instead of letting them remain at home with them or taking them along on a trip ("If you're not good, I'll ship you off to grandmom's for the week!"). Needless to say, this could seriously undermine your relationship with your grandchild. The last thing you want is a visit to your house to be thought of as a punishment.

If this occurs, assure the child that he is welcomed at your home and loved very much. Be aware that the child might perceive a visit to his grandparents as a punishment, when it was not intended to be that at all. If in doubt, talk to the parents to find out what is going on at home. Once your grandchild is at your house, make the visit as pleasant as possible and try to set up a date for another visit before he leaves. That makes visits voluntary in his mind and not forced upon him.

Grandchildren sometimes are used as wedges or pawns in difficult parent-child situations, just as they sometimes are in divorce situations. Because a grandchild/grandparent relationship can be one of the most rewarding life has to offer, it is imperative to try to correct whatever situation has caused the rift.

If for any reason your grandchild is reluctant to visit you, try to find out what is causing her hesitation. Could it be she's frightened of your big dog, but doesn't want to hurt your feelings by saying so? If you understand her reluctance you'll have a better chance at remedying the situation. Make her visits as pleasant and fun as you can.

Special Visits

Terrible situations of withholding or forcing visits between grandchildren and grandparents do indeed occur sometimes, but no book is going to fix them. Such situations will be resolved only when the people involved are ready to do so. Let's focus now instead on those happy occasions when the kids—or one of the kids—come to visit, and everybody has a ball! Of course, in this business of grandparenting, it is imperative to treat all grandkids equally. Be aware of how your relationship with one grandchild affects your relationships with the others.

One Grandchild at a Time

While it's fun to have all the grandkids together, it's a good idea to arrange an occasional visit with just one. What a special treat for a grandchild to have one-on-one time with grandma and grandpa without those pesky brothers and sisters competing for their attention! This works out especially well if the grandchildren are different ages and have different interests. To avoid inciting a third world war, however, make it clear that each grandchild will have a turn for a special visit. You might even want to set up some dates ahead of time, so the other children will know when their turn is coming.

Another nice thing would be to have another grandchild from one of your other children's families visit at the same time. This is particularly good if the cousins don't live close to each other and don't see each other often. It gives you a chance to watch how the cousins relate to one another, and them a chance to get better acquainted. Having just one or two grandchildren in your company at a time gives you the opportunity to really get to know them. Children (especially when they get a little older) often find it easier to talk to a grandparent than to a parent. They look at you as a friend, and often a confidant. Take advantage of this unique opportunity and encourage them to open up to you.

Reward for Achievement

Recognize your grandchildren's special achievements with a special visit. Older children might enjoy going out to dinner and then back to your house to watch a movie. A shopping trip can be a reward for a child, while giving you a chance to visit. Make sure your other grandchildren understand that even though one of their siblings is the star this time, their time will come.

Birthdays

Visits can be planned to coincide with birthdays or other special anniversaries, as long as you plan to give special (and equal) attention to the other grandchildren on their special days. One grandmother and grandfather take each of their grandchildren (they're fortunate enough to have them all living close by) to a toy store on their birthday. The child gets to pick out one toy, and can take as much time as he or she wants to decide what to get. After the choice is made and the purchase complete, it's off to the ice cream shop for a treat. All the grandchildren look forward to these outings that have become a firmly established tradition.

A visit alone with grandmom and granddad can provide a child with a welcome "time-out" from his parent/child and sibling relationship. He gets some special attention and a change of pace. The rules are a little different. Bedtime is an hour later and he gets to go fishing with Grandpa at their special spot. Mom and Dad aren't around for a whole week so nobody will be bugging him about the "D" in algebra last report card period. His sister won't be teasing him about his haircut and his brother won't be taking his baseball glove without asking. Grandparents offer many gifts every time they babysit.

> **Great Grandparenting**
> Even children as young as four or five can understand the reasons for individual visits with grandma and grandpa. Waiting and looking forward to their own visit make the event even more special. These visits will be the fodder for some happy memories down the road. Make sure you think seriously about what you will do and where you will go that can make a one-on-one visit successful (see Part 3 for ideas about memorable adventures).

The Least You Need to Know

➤ Carefully consider your relationships with your children and their spouses, and discuss what they expect of you as new grandparents.

➤ Leave decisions about nap time, bath time, and other daily routines in the hands of the new parents.

➤ Do offer advice when requested to do so, and be obligated to intervene if your grandchild's safety is threatened.

➤ Respect the rights of the other grandparents and close relatives, and make it a cause for joy that your grandchildren have so many adults who care about them.

➤ Resolve any problems that may be causing your children to withhold visits between you and your grandchildren, and help create wonderful memories for your grandchildren with one-on-one visits.

Chapter 5

Tools of the Trade: What Every Grandparent Needs

The grandkids are coming and you need to be ready. But, what exactly do you need? In our society of "specialized gear" (walking shoes, running shoes, soccer shoes, tennis shoes—what ever happened to plain old sneakers!?), gathering the proper equipment can be a challenge, to say the least. Never fear, we'll sort out everything from car seats to playpens, baby bottles to baby wipes. You'll be prepared for anything—almost!

Two pieces of advice. Don't panic about what you might have or not have, and don't try to gather supplies for every situation that could occur over the next five years. Consider what you and your grandchildren will be doing during your visit, and take it from there.

To simplify things, we have described seven key categories in this chapter. Consider them one at a time and don't get overwhelmed. All this complicated "gear" isn't so complicated once you get the hang of it.

Rules of the Road: Car Seats and Belts

Car seats can be real pains in the seat, there's no question about it. Hoisting a squirming baby or child through the back door of a car and into the waiting car seat is a challenge, even for those whose backs don't twinge at the thought of such endeavors. But those bulky, cumbersome devices also are one of your best defenses for keeping your precious cargo safe. Never, never put your grandchild in the car without one, not even "just to run down to the corner store." The temptation to skip the seats and just use seat belts might be powerful, but it's dangerous and even illegal in many states.

Parents usually will give you the proper car seats to use during visits with your grandchildren. If for some reason they don't, you probably can borrow them from other grandparents or from parents whose kids have outgrown them. Car seats are hot items at yard sales and flea markets. You may be able to pick up what you need at very reasonable prices. Or, you can rent them at most rental centers. Just make sure you get the right seat for the size of the child who will be using it, and that it will work in your particular vehicle (some seats work fine in a Jeep, but not so fine in a Honda Civic). It's a good idea to try out the seat in your car before you buy, borrow, or rent.

Children who are too big for baby car seats—those in booster seats and on their own—should always be made to buckle up. Make sure the belts are adjusted snugly and worn properly. And, don't forget to set a good example by using your seat belt every time you get in the car.

Hartt to Hartt

It was a rush, as usual, to get the grandkids off to our house so their mom could get to an appointment on time. We ran into trouble while trying to transfer two car seats from mom's car to ours. As hard as we looked, we simply couldn't find one end of one of the seat belts! We knew it was there somewhere, but darned if we knew where. For a moment we thought about putting one car seat in the back and the other in the front. Thoughts of all the warnings against this filtered through, however, and we knew it was too big a risk. We solved the problem simply by switching cars.

Air Bags, Scare Bags

We've all heard the horror stories about kids and air bags. Designed to protect drivers and front-seat passengers during front-end collisions, they discharge with force powerful enough to badly injure, or even kill, children riding in the front seat.

Never, for any reason, let infants or small children ride in the front seat of your car—whether or not your car has air bags. Car seats properly installed in the back are the only safe way to go.

Free Wheeling: Strollers and Trikes

Strollers have come a long way, baby, but trying to figure out the best one to get for your visiting grandkids could require a degree in baby gear technology. They run the gamut from simple umbrella strollers to high-tech, three-wheeled joggers. Some models even fold up small enough to be tucked away conveniently for air, train, or bus travel. Consult with the parents before purchasing a stroller. They may have a preference as to what you buy, or be willing to haul their model along for visits. In these days of multiple baby showers—thrown at the workplace, by neighbors, family, college friends, and on and on—it is quite possible the parents have an extra stroller you'll be able to use.

Tricycles can be a lot of fun, but selecting the right one can be tricky. It is nearly impossible to do so effectively without having the rider along to test it before purchase. Many a trike has sat practically unused in the garage because: "it's not like the cool bike Johnny has," "it's too big (small, and so on)," "I wanted purple, not yellow," or "the seat hurts." Many children like Big Wheels, low-to-the-ground, plastic vehicles that let them zoom around like crazy while making tremendous amounts of noise. The advantage is that they're easy to ride and hard to tip over. The disadvantage, aside from the noise, is that they're hard for car drivers to see because they are so low.

Small bikes are another tricky proposition. You might think it's time for your grandchild to graduate from a trike to a bike long before he or she has any intention of doing so. Or, the child might beg to trade in the three-wheeler before he's fully capable of riding a two-wheeler. Training wheels can be invaluable when making the transition, but very adventuresome kids might shun them. As with trikes, it's probably best to have your grandchild with you to help choose a bike if you are going to buy one.

Danger Zone

Your grandkids may clamor for in-line skates and skateboards, but be wary: Many a child has been taken to the emergency room after an accident involving these modern modes of transportation. It probably is best to nix them for very young children. Older children who bring theirs to use should wear helmets and protective pads.

Let's Eat!

Dinner time can be danger time for unprepared grandparents. Picky eaters are hard to deal with, especially near the end of a long and tiring day. We can't get your grandkids to like your flounder Florentine, but we can give you some tips on how to make them comfortable and happy at mealtimes.

The Highchair

As you undoubtedly recall from your own parenting days, a highchair is not a necessity, but it's as close to one as you can come. The best thing about highchairs is that most kids will stay in them, allowing you to get dinner on the table without them underfoot. A spoon to bang on the chair's tray, or a first course of Cheerios will help keep a child occupied until dinner is served. Remember, however, that the most persistent children sometimes find a way to wriggle out the straps, stand up in the chair and topple over if not quickly restrained. If a highchair is unavailable, some (old) pillows or large books can be stacked on a chair with sides, but watch that they (and the child) don't slide off.

Assuming that you'll be using a highchair, we come to the question of what kind to buy, rent, or borrow. One with a plastic tray wipes clean, but certain foods (like spaghetti sauce) will stain it. Wooden trays with a durable finish are more practical, and perhaps a bit quieter, than plastic when being pounded with cups and spoons.

Seats that clamp tightly onto the edge of a table and allow a child to sit right up at the table with the rest of the family also are available. They're nice because they're easily transported and they fold up quite small for storing. Just make sure they're securely fastened to the table before the child is seated. Seats that strap onto chairs are another option. Always make sure to fasten the seat belts, regardless of the type of chair you're using.

Baby Bottles

Let's all drink to the advent of the modern baby bottle. If you haven't seen it, you're in for a pleasant surprise. Disposable plastic liners fit into a plastic bottle, eliminating the need for sterilizing anything but the nipples. They come in four- and eight-ounce sizes, are shatterproof and lightweight enough not to inflict serious injury if thrown at unsuspecting grandparents.

Bibs and Baby Wipes

Remember trying to scrub those baby food stains from your own children's clothes? If so, you surely can appreciate the importance of bibs. If you get stuck at feeding time without one, or you can't bear to use one of those plastic models that get so messy after the first few spills, simply place a hand towel across the child's shoulders to absorb splatter. Thick, terry cloth bibs work equally well, but be sure you have one large enough to cover that cute little outfit.

Baby wipes, moist disposal cloths that come in various sizes, are another lifesaver. They're especially handy to have at mealtimes, and are a must when traveling.

Floor Mats

No grandparent would think to put Baby's highchair on the new, barely beige carpeting, but the linoleum may be equally at risk. Remember how strained spinach and spaghetti rings can do a number on any floor covering. Protect your floor with a mat to save yourself some grief. Sure, you can buy adorable, plastic coverings with cute designs made just for this purpose, but a washable rug or old beach towel works just as well.

Dinnerware

Aside from "be sure it's unbreakable," there are no set rules concerning dinnerware. If your grandchild is training to be a major league pitcher and insists on practicing during dinnertime, you might want to invest in one of those plates with suction cups on the bottom that adhere to the tray of the highchair. Plastic cups with tightly fitting lids equipped for sipping are invaluable. But don't be overwhelmed by the vast sea of children's dinnerware on the market. It might be that your grandchild has a favorite cup at home and absolutely refuses to drink from anything else. In that case, make sure parents bring the cup along—and make sure it returns home with the child!

Hartt to Hartt

We have our share of plastic plates and spoons, but we encourage our toddler grandchildren to try "grown-up" dinnerware. We feel this encourages them to use their best table manners and really makes them feel that they're part of the group. And when there are several small children, it's best to separate them among adults. They're much less likely that way to engage in table-top games such as shoot the peas.

The Land of Nod and Three Men in a Tub

Ah, naptime! Ah, bedtime! As much as we love our grandchildren, there are few grandparents who do not welcome these times. To help them proceed smoothly, it's important to make sleeping (and nearby bathroom) conditions as close to ideal as possible. Quiet places that can be darkened and are out of main traffic areas are recommended. If your quarters are small and you can't get the child away from noise, just do the best you can and remember that they all sleep—eventually.

Cribs and Sleeping Arrangements

Babysitting young grandchildren in their own home is one thing—but putting them to bed in your home (especially the first couple of times) is quite another. Plan ahead of

Great Grandparenting

What a world! Now available are cassette tapes with the sounds of ocean waves, whales singing, bubbling brooks, and other soothing sounds to lull a restless child to sleep or block out distracting sounds.

time where they will sleep, and show them "their rooms" before nap- or bedtime. Let them put their stuffed animals in their cribs or beds, and perhaps leave a small, soft and welcoming toy the first time they bunk in. Ask the parents for advice when shopping for a crib or child bed. They've probably done significant research on the topic. Because these things are expensive, don't rule out the possibility of borrowing.

If you can make the bed or crib similar to the child's bed at home, so much the better. If investing in crib bumper pads or quilts, consider buying the same prints as those at the child's home. Urge parents to pack favorite dolls or blankets to give your grandchild a feeling of security. Find out about special bedtime rituals: Does the child have a drink before bed? Say prayers? And, of course, a bedtime story and lullaby can work wonders.

Above all, make sure you know the child's nap and bedtime schedules, and follow them as closely as possible. A little person's inner time clock is easily disrupted.

Disposable Diapers

If you long ago lost count of how many cloth diapers you pinned, rinsed, washed, bleached, and hung out to dry, you will be thrilled with today's disposables. Just put them on and fasten the tapes, take them off, shake them off, and toss them in the trash. Opponents of disposables sound warnings that they slow potty training because wetness is kept away from Baby, who does not feel the discomfort that would result when wearing a cloth diaper. Some environmentalists criticize disposables as adding to the landfill glut. Consider the amount of water and energy spent washing cloth diapers, factor in the convenience of disposables, and make your own decision. Just make sure to buy the right size and see if the parent has a preferred brand.

No matter what kind of diapers you use, you'll need some baby wipes (look for those with no alcohol) and perhaps some ointment in case of diaper rash. Check with the parent before using any sort of diaper-rash remedy. Pediatricians recommend different things, and parents might have a preference.

Bathroom Belongings

A basket kept in the bathroom and stocked with baby bath and health needs can save a lot of scrambling at bath time or in the middle of the night. Some things to include are baby soap, shampoo, and lotion; a small, soft washcloth; some bath toys (don't forget Rubber Ducky); some non-aspirin baby fever reducer (be careful here—always check with the parents before buying or giving any medicine); a little comb; and any other necessities. If the baby is very small, you'll need a small bathtub or a bath ring that attaches to the tub and supports the child while you lather and rinse.

Intercom Systems

If a child is sick, has any sort of breathing problem, or is likely to wake up frightened to be in an unfamiliar place, you might want to buy or borrow a baby intercom. The transmitter plugs into an electrical outlet near the sleeping baby, while the receiver (operated by either battery or electricity) remains with you. Intercoms provide peace of mind, but they also let you hear every burp, gurgle, and coo a baby makes during the night. If you're a light sleeper, be prepared for frequent awakenings when the intercom is on.

Fun Stuff: Playpens and Jingle Bells

A playpen stocked with stuffed animals, soft books, and age-appropriate toys (ask the parents what sorts of toys are favorites) is just the thing for keeping creeping crawlers safe while you throw in a load of laundry or answer the doorbell. Some kids will happily entertain themselves in the playpen (probably by throwing everything out of it onto the floor), while others will squawk like everything at being "banished." Regardless, it is a safe place that can offer some relief to harried grandparents. Just make sure the playpen meets current safety standards, and is located away from anything harmful that the child could reach out and grab. When stocking the playpen, be careful that there are no small pieces for the child to swallow and no harmful substances such as peeling paint.

Some nifty additions to playpens are:

➤ Hanging bells or chimes (remember how small children love anything that makes noise)

➤ An unbreakable mirror for playing peek-a-boo

➤ An overhead mobile that turns in the breeze or can be wound

Great Grandparenting
Sometimes even very young babies will snuggle up with you to listen to stories or look at picture books. It might not happen often, but it's worth a try. Babies seem to particularly like books with pictures of other babies, and some of these books are produced with big, soft pages for easy turning and safe chewing.

Security Stuff: Brought from Home

You've seen them. Those shredded, unbelievably worn and treasured blankets, diapers, bears, and dolls that kids cling to for dear life when they're unsure of themselves or their situations. Security blankets. Smart parents will always send along security blankets, in whatever form they take, and smart grandparents will make sure the cherished item remains with the child during the visit, and returns home with the child. Many a parent has had to turn around and drive back to grandma and grandpa's house because blankey was left behind. Nearly every child has something special.

Bedding

The security blanket indeed may be a blanket. However, security comes in many forms, so don't be surprised if your grandchild shows up with a favorite pillow or even her own favorite sheets.

Stuffed Animal

Be it a panda, pig, or porcupine, you can bet it will be threadbare and beaten from being hauled about and hugged. Regardless of its appearance, it is your grandchild's friend, and should be treated with respect.

Battered Old Toy

These are the things you would love to throw out, but know it would mean disaster. The wheel-less trucks, the headless dolls, the wingless planes. Still, they give comfort to small children who rely on their familiar presence.

The need for security doesn't end when a child becomes potty trained or starts school. Older children may carry family photos or other items from home to make them feel secure. Even adults (grandparents included) have been known to hang onto trinkets or "good-luck charms." After all, it can be a big and scary world out there.

The Least You Need to Know

➤ Before you even open the car door, make sure you know the car seat and seatbelt rules that apply in your state.

➤ Never, never, let a baby or small child ride in the front seat of your car.

➤ Mealtime calls for some special gear: highchair and dinnerware should be chosen carefully.

➤ Look for a quiet sleeping area where a child will not be disturbed.

➤ Be selective about choosing toys for the playpen or crib. You want to entertain, not overwhelm, the child.

➤ Don't underestimate the value of your grandchild's security blanket, no matter what it looks like.

Part 2
Over the River and Through the Woods: To Grandparents' House We Go

Safety is always a top priority when you're caring for your grandkids. After all, not only are you charged with delivering the young ones back to their parents in their original condition, you also want some peace of mind during their visit. You want to bond with your grandchildren and have fun—and, at the same time, you want to know that everyone is safe. How much freedom should you allow? How do you avoid being overprotective, especially with older grandchildren? What do you do to avoid panic in an emergency?

Although you may be inclined to skip over some of the advice in this section and declare that "it just won't happen to me," program yourself to enjoy the pleasures of good foresight rather than lament unfortunate events in hindsight.

Chapter 6

All Around the House: Childproofing Your Home

In This Chapter

➤ Danger zones in your home

➤ Safeguards you can count on

➤ Safety rules your grandchildren will respect

➤ What to do when disaster strikes

It's completely unthinkable that your carefully arranged and planned visit with your grandchild would end with a trip to the hospital emergency room. It just couldn't happen, could it?

As much as we don't like to think about these things, accidents do happen, and kids get hurt. They fall off bikes, out of trees or down the steps. Their great curiosity and enthusiasm, combined with lack of experience, makes them do things you can hardly imagine. A 4-year-old boy who has always wondered (unbeknownst to you) about that thing on the car, grabs onto the hot exhaust pipe. The same boy takes off his shoes and tromps around in the poison ivy at the creek ("I didn't want to get my shoes wet!"), while his older sister pokes a stick into that funny, papery looking nest hanging from the garage. Let's face it. Kids are walking invitations for disaster.

OK, you bring them into the house. Surely, they'll be fine in here. What could they get into?

Think again! Stairs, fireplaces, workshops with all sorts of interesting tools, cleaning supplies, and medicine cabinets are all tempting targets for curious kids. Vigilance and preparedness are your best defenses for preventing them from getting into something they shouldn't, and for remedying the situation when they do.

Upstairs, Downstairs

The older we get, the more respect we have for things like steps. Kids, however, see steps as something first to be mastered (did you ever watch a toddler climb the steps, descend in his own, peculiar way, and begin the process all over again?), and then as a fun diversion (railings to slide down), or a nuisance to be gotten up or down as quickly as possible (did you ever see a hurried child jump down a complete set of steps?).

For tiny tots, stairs can be a great diversion. As long as you stay on the scene to prevent a slip, you can count on a few steps to entertain a toddler for extended periods of time. Be sure to check with parents first; if stairs are outlawed in their home, you don't want to be encouraging them in yours.

If steps are not allowed, or you can't be close at hand to supervise, you may want to block them with gates to stop the explorer. It is recommended that you use gates at both the top and bottom of the stairs to eliminate access altogether. Also, gates that latch are preferred to pressure gates that could give way if a child crashes into them. Make sure the bars on the gate are vertical, not horizontal or crisscrossed, so that toddlers can't climb on them. Odds are, that old baby gate you've still got stored up in your attic from when your own kids were small won't meet today's safety standards. Toss it out and get a modern version.

It's a good policy to keep stairs to the cellar or garage off limits to toddlers. Even if they successfully navigate the stairs, no doubt there will be other dangers lurking when they reach their destinations. All stairways should be protected on both sides by walls or banisters. And, speaking of banisters....

Kids and banisters are an irresistible combination. Kids think of them as indoor sliding boards. If you have slideable railings, set some ground rules. Either outlaw them completely, or insist that they go one at a time, without pushing. Remember, if younger children see older ones sliding, they're sure to want to try it. Nixing the activity probably is preferable.

Caution: This Area May Be Hazardous to Your Health

Every house is fraught with potential perils. Thinking of all the terrible things that could happen to a child is enough to make you a complete nervous wreck. But don't let all the "what ifs" keep you from enjoying your visit. Do the best you can in making your home safe and keep a close watch while the child is in your care. Here are some common items that could cause trouble if you're not careful:

➤ *Head-high open cupboard doors.* Who hasn't taken a bang on the noggin from the corner of one of these things?

➤ *Open cupboard doors of any height, depending on what's in them.* Remember, what looks like a harmless selection of canned food to you might cause injury to a small child who reaches up and pulls some of them down on his head or feet. Shelves with precariously perched objects (especially your favorite vase) also should be rearranged and closed up.

➤ *Tables with sharp edges.* These corners are like magnets to kids' foreheads when they fall. It's wise to cover the tables with small blankets, which also serve to make hideaways underneath. Rubber, bubble packing material that comes in wide strips, or soft plastic bumpers also will help prevent accidents.

➤ *Low, open bureau drawers that snag shins.* Ouch! Keep them closed, and get kids in the habit of doing the same.

➤ *Furniture that is fragile or tips easily.* Put any rickety tables or chairs in the "keep out" zone. Make a no-climbing-on-furniture policy.

➤ *Plastic bags.* Most homes seem to be overrun with them, because everything you bring home, from groceries to dry cleaning, is in them. Children love to play with these bags, which might inevitably end up over their heads. The plastic can be sucked in over the mouth and suffocate the child. Pillows, cords, drawstrings and curtain pulls are also risks for strangulation, so beware.

➤ *Doors leading to the garage, basement or workshop.* Keep them locked when you're not in immediate proximity. Even outside doors should be kept locked for small (fast) children who could wander out without you noticing.

➤ *Low windows.* How many times have you read about a kid who leaned against the window screen and took an unexpected ride? Keep accessible windows closed, or protect them with window guards.

➤ *Plate glass windows and doors.* Paste colored stickers on them so they can be seen and avoided by running children and roughhousing youngsters.

Great Grandparenting
We all hear the warnings every year about the dangers of poinsettias, but there are a whole raft of other plants that are dangerous to little ones, including the common philodendron. Nibbling on that plant can make a little one's mouth raw and blistered. Daffodil bulbs are quite toxic, and the water in a vase of lily-of-the-valley can be deadly. Keep all plants out of the reach of small children, and know which ones are harmful.

➤ *Knickknacks and other small objects.* Remove any within the reach of young children. They're choking hazards.

➤ *Glass-topped tables*—especially those that can tip over easily. Remove them temporarily or cover them with suitable cloths.

➤ *Small, slippery rugs.* These probably aren't a good idea for anyone, but kids are particularly adept at locating them. Remove them, or secure them firmly in place with double-stick tape.

Hartt to Hartt

We thought our house was pretty well childproofed when our two small grandchildren came for a five-day visit, sans parents. Midway through the visit, however, we were cleaning and gathering trash, and we discovered some potentially disastrous oversights.

The bathroom wastebasket contained three half-full bottles of outdated prescription medicines and some jagged glass from a broken bottle. The kitchen container included three razor-sharp metal lids, another broken bottle and a torn plastic bag with remnants of powdered lye. Both baskets were located near where the children had been playing, and neither was covered. Blessedly, nothing happened. But, it made us realize how easy it is to overlook potential hazards.

Minimizing Ever-Present Dangers

Children are naturally drawn to water and fire. Electrical appliances can also be fascinating to little ones. All can be safety hazards and must be managed carefully.

Avoiding a Shocking Experience

Electrical outlets and plugs are a source of wonder to many small children, maybe because they're usually located at crawling-kid level. Kids must be taught early on that plugs are not something to play with (they seem to like to pull them out and stick them back in, especially if they can make a light go on and off by their actions). Use plastic safety plugs to cover all accessible outlets.

While the most obvious, outlets are not the only electrical hazards in your home. Older children should never use hair dryers, radios, or any other appliances near water. Never let a child play with a hair dryer or other electric bathroom appliance while someone is in the tub; it can cause electrocution if it's dropped in the water. Wet floors and counters create other hazards when using bathroom appliances. Make sure that all small appliances are unplugged when not in use, and warn children to never try to fix or clean an appliance that is plugged in. Be certain that all cords to these appliances are in good condition, and avoid using extension cords. Never leave an electric fan or heater running where a young child can get to it.

When there are very young grandchildren around, it is best to remove as many electrical cords as possible. Besides the obvious electrical danger, they also pose a choking hazard. At least, hide them under a rug or tape them down.

Be sure children know to avoid wires when playing outside, too. Teach them to NEVER touch any kind of wire, either one they might see while climbing in trees, or one that may have fallen.

Gun Laws

If you keep guns in your home for any reason, it is imperative that they be kept away from your grandchildren. Guns should always be unloaded and stored in a locked cabinet or closet. The key and extra ammunition must be stored separately in an inaccessible place.

Home Cooking: A Hot Topic

If your stove or oven is in use, children should not be nearby. We've found success in keeping grandchildren at bay by using colored masking tape or an erasable crayon to mark off a "no-no" zone around the stove. They can clearly see the boundary, and know not to venture past. If they're curious about the contents of those pots, you can meet them at the line to show them, or lift them up for a quick peek.

Just to be extra safe, we use the back burners instead of the front, and turn the pot handles inward so they're next to impossible for kids to reach. And, don't assume that because the stove or oven is turned off, it's not hot. Some burners stay hot for a long time, and so do some cooking pots and pans.

You tell them and tell them, but sometimes the temptation is too hard to resist. If you've found your grandchildren messing with the dials on the stove or oven, consider installing devices that make it impossible to move them. You also may need covers for your stove burners. These items are available at hardware stores, or you can improvise if necessary.

Repeated warnings about hot objects (irons, hair dryers, toasters, pots and pans) are necessary, as is watchful vigilance when kids are around any of these things.

Speaking of hot objects, how about matches? Make sure your grandchildren understand that matches are completely off limits. No exceptions. If you have them in your home, get them to a place where kids can't reach them. Same with cigarette lighters. DO NOT leave them lying around. And remember that lighted cigarettes, cigars, and pipes can cause serious burns. Keep them out of children's reach.

Danger Zone
Don't forget to safety-proof the medicine cabinet! Many pills look like candy, and nobody has to tell you how much kids love candy. Even a child's own vitamins can be deadly if they contain extra iron and your grandchild drinks the whole bottle. Keep all drugs out of their reach. Always.

Whether or not there are children around, you should have smoke detectors on every floor or wing of your home. You can buy approved models that are inexpensive, easily placed in key locations, and operated with batteries that last a long time and let you know by beeping when they're getting low. You also should have fire extinguishers in the kitchen, near fireplaces, or in any of the locations where fires could break out. Hardware stores carry small, effective models that are easy to mount and use.

Radiators sometimes get hot enough to cause burns, and might be at just the right level for small children to touch. Cover hot radiators with screened covers. Fireplaces, while cheerful and homey, also can be hazardous. Never use them without screens. Doors with glass panels that are spark-proof and can't be removed by little hands are recommended.

Water Worries

Water, that substance that we can't live without, is worth a worry or two of its own. Take hot tap water, for instance. Or how about boiling water? We've already mentioned the importance of keeping handles turned to the back of the stove, making it less likely that a pot of boiling water or other liquid will be pulled off and spilled. But water in the shower, bathtub, or sink can be hot enough to scald and cause serious burns. Always check the water temperature before bathing a baby or child in the sink or bathtub. Always add hot water to cold when preparing the bath, never the other way around. You can adjust the temperature control on your hot water heater so that water never reaches beyond 130°F. or 54°C. At that temperature, it will take about 30 seconds for serious scalding to occur. Keep all kettles and pots containing hot water out of reach.

After the water comes out of the kettle and into your cup, it still can be a hot hazard. Never leave a cup of tea or coffee, or any other hot food or beverage, where a child can reach it. Beware of what you pull out of your toaster or microwave, too. The steam from microwave popcorn has caused a nasty burn.

To give our grandchildren a real understanding and respect for what hot water can do, we poured some over the stub of a candle. They were surprised to see how quickly the water destroyed the candle, and hopefully, more careful about hot water afterwards.

Actually, any water can be hazardous. Bathtubs can be a fun place to play and splash, but they also are potentially deadly. Never, never leave a small child alone or with another child in the tub. Not to run and get a towel, not to answer the phone, not for any reason. It takes only a few seconds for the child to slip under water. Small children can drown in small containers of water, so take caution with the toilet (keep the lid down), with any large pots or buckets of water, and the like. Of course, children must be extremely well supervised in swimming pools, hot tubs, and ponds, all of which should be fenced in and locked.

Some of our older grandchildren insist on privacy in the tub, but we maintain our vigil by taking turns stationing ourselves outside the closed bathroom door. This allows us to communicate with the bather and listen for any sounds of trouble. We also use non-skid mats in all our showers and bathtubs to prevent slipping. Beware of slippery films from soaps or some cleaning supplies.

Danger Zone
Some of the most common household hazards are cleaning products and laundry supplies. Typically stored under the sink or in low cabinets, they are too often accessible to toddlers. Kids have strong impulses to taste substances, and even a tiny sip of some can cause disaster. Move them to an unreachable spot or put child latches on all cabinets containing them.

Light the Good Light

A tiny night-light can dispel fears of goblins, spooks, and sharks underneath the bed. It also can light not-so-familiar territory on the way to the bathroom, take the mystery from "a dark place," and allow a child to keep an eye on his stuffed friends all night long. It is solace and comfort, and worth its weight in gold. The light it casts also helps you to get to your grandchild quickly during the night if you need to. We like the kind that automatically turns on and off, responding to light conditions. If you have the kind that uses bulbs, be sure you have a few spares on hand.

Great Grandparenting
Good lighting is essential for the safety of everyone in your home. Be especially sure that stairs and other potentially hazardous areas are bright enough to see exactly what you're doing.

Childproofing Checklist

We've covered a lot of territory so far. So we've created a "Prevent-a-Calamity Checklist" to help you make sure you've covered all your bases before the grandchildren arrive. Use our checklist as it appears here or make up one for yourself.

Prevent-a-Calamity Checklist

Kitchen

Turn off stove when not in use.

Keep all cleaning supplies out of reach.

Close and latch cabinets after use.

Bathroom

Adjust temperature control on hot water heater.

Use non-skid mats in bathtub and shower stall.

Drain water from bathtub as soon as bath is over.

Keep all medicines (including vitamins) and cosmetics out of children's reach (don't forget the ones in your purse or on the night stand).

Close and latch cabinets after use.

Make sure grandchildren do not use electrical appliances near water.

Use a night light to prevent nocturnal bumps and falls.

Bedroom and Living Room

Remove or cover all furniture with sharp corners or edges.

Remove or stabilize any items on high shelves.

Remove or fix any rickety furniture.

Use a night light in child's bedroom to dispel anxiety and light the way.

All Around the House

Treat plastic bags as hazardous and keep out of children's reach.

Turn off and unplug all appliances not in use.

Use latching gates at top and bottom of all stairs.

Lock outside doors and those leading to garage, basement and workshop.

Remove or cover any wastebaskets that may hold potentially hazardous items.

Use safety plugs on all electrical outlets.

Keep all matches and lighters where children can't get them.

Install fire detectors on every floor.

Never, never, never keep a gun of any kind where a child could find it. Loaded or unloaded, it should be completely inaccessible.

Fun and Games

You know how you can remember that little ditty you learned in junior high school, or the cheers you used to shout at your college football games? A rhyme helps you remember every time. And safety is no exception. Here are a few rhymin' rules we've used with our children and grandkids over the years:

➤ "No balls in the halls."

➤ "Shouldn't you oughter test the hot water?"

➤ "If you don't mind going up in flame, lighting matches is a real hot game."

Puzzles, games, and books that teach safety also can be fun and useful. Your can find (in school and public libraries) numerous kids' books dealing with safety. For preschoolers, the Berenstain Bears series, by Stan and Jan Berenstain, covers a variety of safety topics and is fun to read. Kids love the books.

Get Them Where You Want Them

If your grandkids are where you want them to be (in an area that you know is safe and secure), it will be healthy for them and less stressful for you. Lure them into the "safety zones" with some of these ideas:

➤ *Customize the safety zones.* Arrange furniture, pillows and rugs in a comfortable place the kids can call their own.

➤ *Stock the safety zones with plenty of fun or creative supplies.* Crayons, construction paper, sparkles and glitter, glue, felt-tip markers, along with some games, puzzles, books, and maybe some dress-up clothing will keep them busy and happy. Arrange with some of your friends, who also are grandparents, to swap some games and books every now and then. Kids love variety. Just be sure not to give away their favorites!

➤ *Give the safety zones appealing names* such as "Carol's Corner," "David's Den," or "Natalie's Nook." Get the kids to make signs for their areas.

➤ *For older grandchildren, set up an entertainment center* (television, VCR, tape, or compact disc player) in the area where you want them to congregate. Don't forget the popcorn!

> **Great Grandparenting**
>
> If you have a sturdy and comforting old rocking chair, its time has come. Get some pretty pillows for it and put it in a safe space where kids can rock without banging into the walls. There's something about a big rocking chair that kids just love. And having them on the chair, either alone or in pairs, will assure that they're not getting into mischief elsewhere.

Regardless of where your grandkids are in your home, you want them to be safe. Just use your best common sense and follow the guidelines discussed.

Toy Story

If you're just starting out in the grandparenting business, you might be in for a real shock. Toys. Not the fact that kids have toys, or that the kids want toys. But rather the sheer number of toys they have, and the even greater number of toys available to buy. There are toys that talk back to you, beep like computers or phones, play music, light up, spin around, and seem to be pretty complicated (unless you're a kid). Two things about toys haven't changed, though. Kids still leave them wherever it is they happen to finish playing with them. That means you still run the risk of stepping or slipping on them or tripping over them. The other thing about toys that hasn't changed is that you still must be careful to check them before the kids start playing to make sure the toys are in good repair and present no safety hazards.

Limiting the number of toys or games allowed out at one time makes it easier to keep track of what the kids are playing with. Some things to watch for when checking their toys are:

➤ Any sharp or jagged edges

➤ Potentially hazardous materials like glass or brittle plastic

➤ Metal or other heavy materials that can cause bruises if dropped

➤ Any sort of potentially toxic or irritating materials, such as the contents in a chemistry set or glue in a modeling kit

➤ Paint that can be chewed or sucked off

➤ Pieces that are two inches or less in diameter and can be a choking hazard

It's a good idea for grandparents to have toys at their house for grandkids to play with when they visit. The toys will seem special because they're different from the ones at home, and you'll be able to pick out ones that you feel are safe. Make sure you have one or two that are popular at the moment—fads come and go quickly. But, don't overlook traditional toys such as blocks and dolls, and if you have any of your own children's toys around, get them out for the grandchildren. They'll love to see toys their parents played with. Encourage them to use their imaginations to create their own toys and games.

Be sure to tell your grandkids that all toys must be put away at the end of the day or visit. This will not only preserve some sense of tidiness in your house, it will also help eliminate accidents that occur when somebody trips or slides on a toy (especially ones left on steps).

> **Hartt to Hartt**
>
> Grandkids are kind of like cars. They run fine for a while, but when they start to run out of gas, they sputter and falter. Tired time for kids is a dangerous time. We've discovered that if we make the idea of a rest appealing, they'll be quite cooperative. We hand out pillows, blankets, and cuddly toys, and tell each grandchild to find a special spot. Quite often they take a nap, but even if they don't, they rest quietly. When quiet time ends, we have a snack, and they're ready to go again.

Furred and Feathered Friends

Kids and puppies. Kids and kittens. Oh, the Kodak moments you get when you put them together. Be careful, though. Kodak moments of kids and pets can turn into big trouble without some close adult supervision.

If you have a dog or cat, or both, and can't wait for your grandkids to get acquainted with them, you could be in for a disappointment. It's not at all uncommon for kids to be allergic to certain animals. Pet allergies can cause the sufferer to be absolutely miserable with sneezing, itchy eyes and congestion. Having an allergic grandchild together with your pets simply won't work. If the grandchild will be coming to your home, the only thing to do is ship out the animal and clean up all its fur from the carpets and furniture. A better alternative would be to find someone to care for your pet and go visit your grandchild at his house.

If your grandchildren are not allergic, but don't have pets of their own, they will need some pointers on how to get along with Rover or Tabby. Here are a few suggestions to keep the visit friendly:

➤ *Introduce the grandkids and pets and give them some time to get to know each other a bit.* Tell them to be gentle—that pets don't appreciate having their tails pulled or being roughed up. Stay close.

➤ *Be sensitive to the size thing.* Remember that your grandkids are small, and your dog might be big. Real big. A Saint Bernard to a toddler must seem like King Kong to Fay Wray. A large dog that jumps (such as an over-enthusiastic and friendly Labrador) can easily knock over and badly frighten a small child.

➤ *Never leave an infant or toddler alone with a dog or cat, no matter how companionable they seem.* Play can turn mean if a child yanks one time too many on a dog's tail or drops a full bottle of milk on its head. A cat awakened suddenly from a good nap might react by scratching the toddler who so rudely interrupted it. And some dogs, especially ones that have been around for a long time, show extreme jealousy of children who command center stage and too much of their grandparents' attention.

➤ *Teach grandkids that pets should not be hit, pulled, or pushed.* Show them how and where to pat a dog or cat and tell them to approach an animal slowly, not charge at it.

➤ *Teach children not to approach an animal that is eating or sleeping.* They should avoid getting a pet overexcited or trying to play with it when it is tired.

➤ *Teach children how to properly lift and hold animals.* It might look funny to see a young child trying to lift a large puppy, but don't let the game continue too long, the dog might become irritated and snappy. Many cats are leery of being handled at all.

➤ *Make it clear that animals are not be placed in wagon or strollers, or forced to sit on bikes or in bicycle baskets.*

➤ *Tell your grandchildren if a strange dog approaches them while they're playing, they should maintain some distance and be wary.* If a particular dog in your neighborhood is always roaming around and is a threat in any way, talk to the owner or notify the police if the owner is unknown.

➤ *Keep your pets free from fleas and worms with preventive treatments.* Children can contract ringworm and other conditions from dogs that have not been treated. Don't let small children kiss an animal on its mouth or nose, and encourage them to wash their hands after playing with pets.

➤ *Don't allow toddlers to feed your pets.* Older children should be shown the proper way to do so before they're allowed. Make it clear the pets are not to get any unauthorized snacks or handouts.

➤ *If a small child is really frightened of your large dog, it's probably best to kennel the dog while the child visits.* They'll have time to get acquainted when the child is a little older.

➤ *Teach grandkids about feeding, washing, and grooming.* Kids typically love animals, so you probably can count on some help with your pets from older grandchildren. It will be good experience for them, and a nice break for you.

Having pets can be a very rewarding experience, but is not without its problems. Keep a close watch on dogs and cats when young children are around. Realize it will take some time for them to get used to one another. And, make sure you have some extra film on hand!

Finny Folk

Many kids are fascinated by fish in an aquarium. Just make sure they know they are not allowed to throw in any small bits of food or to put their hands in the water. Fish are prone to various fungus diseases that could be spread to a child.

Also, a child running at full tilt and unable to stop before crashing into a fish tank can cause not only a mess, but a real safety problem. Teach children that the area where the aquarium sits is off limits for running and horseplay.

Winged Wonders

Birds also are fun to watch, or to talk and listen to, in some cases. As with fish, kids should be taught to never feed a bird except under adult supervision, and to keep fingers out of the cage. Birdcages can be quite unhygienic, and little fingers can get nipped. Birdcages should be kept away from very noisy areas.

Offbeat Pets

Animals such as ferrets, non-venomous snakes, and certain kinds of large lizards are enjoying increased popularity as house pets. If you or your grandchildren have such a pet, just be sure that you're aware of any safety issues relative to the animal. Some, like reptiles, can carry serious diseases such as salmonella.

Also, resist the temptation to buy things like chicks, goldfish, tiny turtles, or chameleons for your grandchildren. Often found at circuses or fairs, these animals could be sick when you buy them and infect other animals or even your grandchildren. Always buy pets from reputable dealers or stores.

Danger Zone
If you have animals, keep their food, medication, flea powder, grooming sprays and lotions, and other supplies out of children's reach. Medicines and grooming supplies for animals pose the same safety hazards as those belonging to humans. Make sure children know they should never eat any kind of pet food.

When Disaster Strikes

No matter how careful you are or how extensively you try to childproof your home, you can't anticipate every possible hazard. Accidents happen, despite all our best intentions. If accidents do occur, you need to be prepared.

Have a first-aid kit and manual on hand to treat emergency ouches. Make sure you know what's in the kit and that the expiration dates on antiseptics haven't expired. Also, it doesn't hurt to know something about emergency procedures covered in the manual, because you may not be calm enough to read carefully if an accident actually occurs.

In most parts of the country, 911 is recognized as the phone number to call in the event of an emergency. There are still some areas, however, that do not have 911 access. If you are in an area without 911 access, contact your phone company and/or elected officials about having it instituted.

Most important, keep a list of emergency phone numbers (doctor, poison control center, ambulance) next to each phone in your house. Some communities even provide such lists. Don't forget to include the names and phone numbers of neighbors, friends, or relatives who might be needed in the event of an emergency. Keep a list at every phone, because someone who doesn't know the numbers might be making the emergency calls, or you might forget the numbers in all the excitement. Check out our example "Important Phone Numbers" list we've put together. You can use it as-is or as a model to create your own.

Important Phone Numbers

Your names: _____

Your home address and phone number: _____

Your work addresses and phone numbers: _____

Your children's home address and phone number: _____

Your grandchildren's names: _____

Your grandchildren's ages and weights: _____

Any special medical conditions or allergies your grandchildren might have: _____

_____

Your doctor's name, address, and phone number: _____

The address and phone number of the nearest hospital: _____

_____

Police phone number: _____

Fire department phone number: _____

Ambulance phone number: _____

Local or national poison control center phone number: _____

_____

Names, addresses, and phone numbers of nearby friends or relatives: _____

_____

The Least You Need to Know

➤ Identify all the places in your home that are potential danger zones for your grand-children, and childproof them.

➤ Provide plenty of games and toys to keep your grandchildren occupied and con-tented in "safety zones."

➤ Teach safety rules and insist the rules be followed.

➤ Pay special attention to safety where pets are concerned.

➤ Have information and first-aid supplies available in case of an emergency.

Safety in the Great Outdoors

Okay. You've covered all the sharp corners on your tables and cabinets, and your cleaning supplies are safely stashed on the very top shelf of that locked closet. Whew! I guess it's okay for the grandkids to visit.

Uh-oh! It might be all right in here, but what happens if they want to play outside? Outside...that magic world of your backyard and beyond, just waiting to be explored. You can't keep your grandkids in the house all the time, that's for sure. So, we'll need to consider how to make your outside property as safe as possible.

Fenced-in yards and decks are a great boon to grandparents. You still need to keep a close watch, but you won't have the constant worry of them running out into the street or tromping down your neighbor's prize irises. Big yards require a lot of upkeep, but they sure pay off when the grandkids come to visit. Let them race around playing ball or tag for an hour or two, and they probably won't mind settling down a little later for quiet time. Not only will a rest be good for them—it will be just what you need after a morning of running, chasing, and catching.

If your own outdoor facilities are limited, check out nearby school or public playgrounds. Many communities have installed new playgrounds where safety is a top priority. Unlike the old metal play equipment, the climbing equipment and other toys on these new playgrounds are make of wood. The ground is covered with wood chips or other material to lessen the chance of injury from falls, and all corners are rounded. Just make sure the equipment is suited to the ages and skills of all the grandchildren you have along.

The kids also would enjoy a trip to a pretty park with lots of open room for running. Keep an eye out for potential trouble, though. Large dogs running loose or groups of older kids who seem to be looking to start a little trouble all bear close watching.

This chapter looks at half a dozen subject areas that relate to the great outdoors and the things it holds that appeal to everyone: infants, toddlers, children, young adults, and grandparents.

Hartt to Hartt

One beautiful summer day, we put both toddlers in a twin stroller and were happily walking them four blocks to the playground. Many people were out enjoying the day and our grandsons waved at them all. People returned the waves and smiled. But two rough looking men walked toward us who did not respond to Max's wave. "Are those bad guys, Grandma?" he asked.

"We don't know them well enough to say," I replied. But I thought then how difficult it is to alert young children to possible dangers with strangers, yet at the same time train them to be outgoing and friendly— and not afraid.

Water Baby: The Lure of Pools and Ponds

If it's water, kids will find it. They're drawn to water like paper clips to a magnet. Doesn't matter if it's an Olympic-sized pool, a garden fountain, or a puddle in a parking lot, they will zoom in on it and be completely powerless to not get at least some part of themselves in it. The care you'll need to take, of course, depends on the nature and size of the body of water in which they'll be playing. You can sit in a chair and relax while you watch those grandchildren, who are old enough, splash around in a tiny pool in your backyard. A full-sized swimming pool or pond will require much more attention. Remember that swimming normally involves sunshine, which involves sunscreen.

Be sure to apply lotion (of the parents' choosing) to your grandchild and have her put on a hat with a visor. If the parents don't give specific sunscreen instructions, use a sunscreen with an SPF of at least 15. The SPF indicates the time one can stay in the sun without getting burned. For instance, if your grandchild would normally burn in 10 minutes, the use of SPF 15 will allow her to stay in the sun for 150 minutes without burning. However, if she is in and out of the pool, reapply even waterproof sunscreen every half hour. Try to avoid lotions containing PABA, because it can irritate sensitive skin. And remember, don't use sunscreen on babies under six months.

Hartt to Hartt

One day, while at the lake with his grandparents, a boy of 11 decided that if all those little kids could swim, so could he. He reasoned that if he got into the water, he could figure it out. He jumped off the diving board into deep water, and came up gasping and struggling for air. Fortunately, there was a lifeguard on duty who rescued him. His grandparents were shocked that he would have done such a thing. Strict rules were put into place and the boy was enrolled in swim lessons.

Water Safety Rules

It is very important to insist that children always follow the rules while swimming. Pools are fairly easy to supervise. Small children require close watching, though, both in the pool and around it. Many accidents have occurred when a child tried to retrieve a toy that had fallen in the pool and then fell in also. Infants and toddlers should never be allowed in any part of a pool by themselves, including "baby" pools. Just as in a bathtub, a youngster can easily slip under and drown. Don't depend on flotation devices such as inner tubes or water wings to keep kids afloat, either. These articles are good additions to, but not substitutions for, adult supervision.

Ponds, lakes, rivers, streams, and oceans are more challenging to supervise than pools and require great vigilance when small children are around. You know how quick the trip is from the dock to the water when a five-year-old leans down to look at the minnows! Never let your grandchild go in the water without making sure he knows the rules and is willing to follow them.

The first and foremost rule is: Each child must demonstrate sufficient swimming ability before being allowed to go in the water. Other rules include:

➤ Swim only within an area specified ahead of time.

➤ Young children or inexperienced swimmers should use approved flotation devices or life preservers. Never use an adult life jacket on a child, they can actually force him backward so his head is under water. Always use life jackets when boating.

➤ If allowed to swim for any distance, the child must do so only with a buddy.

➤ Don't run on a slippery dock or floating raft.

➤ No pushing.

➤ Never dive into unknown waters. Diving into shallow water can cause great injury, including paralysis.

➤ Beware of submerged rocks and sharp objects on the bottom.

➤ Avoid swimming near diving boards.

➤ When swimming off a beach or in a stream, make sure you know the location, direction, and force of currents and riptides.

Hartt to Hartt

We wanted to take our grandchildren sailing while they were visiting with us at our vacation spot. We felt it wouldn't be safe, however, because there were no other adults to handle the lines and for us to do so would leave the children unattended on the boat. As an alternative, we put the children in life jackets, lifted them aboard the boat while it was tied up at the dock, and let them scamper in and out of the cabin while we watched. It was great fun, but finally the three-year-old put his hands on his hips, looked up, and asked, "Grandpa, doesn't this boat ever go?"

How Does Your Garden Grow?

Gardens contain many things that kids love. Dirt, for instance. What fun to dig holes and fill them back up with dirt! Other attractions are colorful flowers (it's delightful to pull them out of the ground!), vegetables ("Look Grandpa, I picked a tomato but it's still green!"), butterflies, bugs ("Grandma, is this a grub?"), worms, birds, pine cones, squirrels or chipmunks, garden hoses and tools, pots, odd smells, and sometimes great gobs of mud.

Letting your grandchildren "help" in your garden is a great gift to them. Not only is it fun, it could be the start of a lifelong interest. It also will help them to understand how plants grow and that their food does not originate from the supermarket. Developing an appreciation for nature at a young age may lead your grandchildren to all kinds of wonderful adventures later in their lives. Just be sure to tell them you expect to be invited along!

If your garden contains decorative pebbles, you may find they are as much fun as sand to shovel into a bucket and dump out again. This is not for very small children, however, who might put pebbles in their mouth and stuff them in their ears. Garden hoses can be enormous fun to play with, too, but keep the pressure low and prepare to get wet. Be sure your grandkids are wearing old shoes and clothes whenever they're playing or "working" outside. Much about being a kid is messy business, and you don't want to send them home in a ruined outfit.

Danger Zone
It's a good idea to be extra safe by keeping the really dangerous things (extremely sharp tools, automatic grass trimmers, and insecticides and herbicides) on a very high shelf or in a locked cabinet inside the shed or garage. It's very easy to leave a door open for a minute, and that's all it takes for a catastrophe to occur.

Also, warn your grandchildren against eating anything from your garden or yard unless you give it to them. Many pretty flowers and leaves can cause problems if ingested, and vegetables or fruits may contain pesticides. Point out any plants such as poison ivy, oak, or sumac, which could cause allergic reactions, too.

A-Choo! Pollen and Allergies

Continuous sneezing, runny nose, and itchy eyes can turn the most exciting outdoor adventure into a real drag. If your grandchild suffers from hay fever or other allergies, you know how miserable she can feel. Generally, hay fever and other minor allergies are more of a nuisance than anything else. Children sometimes outgrow allergies, though they might retain an "allergic tendency." Always tell the child's parent if an allergy seemed different or worse than usual while the child was in your care. Severe allergic reactions should be reported to your grandchild's doctor immediately.

Danger Zone
Anaphylaxis, a very severe form of allergic response, can be life-threatening and requires immediate attention. It can be brought on by a reaction to an insect bite or bee sting, a drug, or food. Call 911 or your local help line or take your child directly to an emergency room if he shows signs of extreme dizziness, profuse sweating, difficulty with breathing, or complete or partial loss of consciousness.

There are many sources of allergens. Most are proteins, ranging from common food proteins such as egg whites to invisible and unexpected ones such as fungus spores or fleas. With hay fever, the culprit is pollen. If the allergy occurs in the fall, it is likely that the allergen is one of the molds that forms on plants as they die down and on root crops brought in for winter storage. Some common causes of hay fever and related allergies are:

➤ *Pollens.* Pollen from any plant may trigger an allergy attack. Grass pollen, abundant in early spring, is a common culprit. Tree pollen (in the air in the spring) and ragweed pollen (abundant in the fall) also are common allergens. There tends to be less pollen in the air in the morning than later in the day, so encourage your grandchild to play outside early in the day.

➤ *Household dust.* House mites, also called dust mites, are a major cause of perennial allergic rhinitis. Its symptoms are very similar to those of hay fever, but they occur all year long instead of seasonally. Keeping your house as free from dust as possible, having the heating ducts cleaned, or installing filters on your heater may help.

➤ *Dogs and cats.* Those said to be allergic to dog or cat hair are actually affected by dander. Dander is tiny flakes of dried saliva that cling to the hairs shed by the animals. If there is cat hair on a sofa, the animal does not need to be present for an allergic reaction to occur. Avoidance of areas containing animal hair is the best prevention.

Don't Mess with Mother Nature

The great outdoors is great, but it's not without its perils. Teaching grandchildren to respect nature and to be able to cope with its whims will be a great help to them throughout their lives. The National Safe Kids Campaign, an educational campaign developed by the American Association of Advertising Agencies as a public service, makes several recommendations on how to cope with Mother Nature and her many challenges.

Lightning

If you get caught in a thunderstorm, take shelter in a building or car, and avoid open fields, isolated trees, parking lots, and small bodies of water.

Dehydration

When the temperature climbs, small children can become quickly dehydrated, particularly if they aren't used to the hot climate and have not been drinking a lot of liquids. Get in the habit of taking cold water on bike rides and keeping bottled water in the car. Don't substitute soft drinks, since many of them contain caffeine and sugar, which speed dehydration.

Toxic Plants

Learn to recognize toxic plants that are prevalent in your region, such as poison ivy, oak, and sumac. At the first indication of contact or sign of itching, flush the affected skin and wash with dish soap or rubbing alcohol. Anti-itch lotions and creams are good things to keep handy no matter where you go. If you are caught without them, try vinegar or a paste of baking soda. Severe cases of poison may require a doctor's attention.

Things with Stings

Keep your eyes open for yellow jackets, hornets, and wasps, and move away from them if you see them. Avoid wearing perfumes and other scented products that tend to attract these pests. Look down at the ground, too, and skirt small sandy mounds that may indicate the presence of fire ants in regions of the country where they are known to live.

Warn children to be extremely careful when eating or drinking outside. Wasps, particularly yellow jackets, are attracted to food and sweet drinks, and a sting inside the mouth is very dangerous. Such stings can trigger severe allergic reactions. If the person who has been stung develops hives, swollen lips, abdominal pain, is drooling or having trouble breathing, or feels a tightness in her throat, it is imperative to get her to an emergency room as quickly as possible. If there is a known allergy to stings, an insect-sting kit should be taken on all outdoor outings in the event the person is stung again. Be sure your grandkids know what bee and wasp nests look like and how to avoid them.

Bugs that Bug You

There are all kinds of bugs that make outdoor living less than perfect. Chiggers, mosquitoes, ants, and flies all contribute to general peskiness. Of a more serious nature are ticks, which carry diseases such as Rocky Mountain Spotted fever, encephalitis, and Lyme disease. If your grandchildren have been playing outside in a region of the country known for ticks, a thorough "tick check" is a must when they come in. Bath time is a good time to look for ticks, as they can be anywhere on a child's body.

If a tick has imbedded itself, you can remove it by carefully grabbing it with tweezers and pulling it slowly and evenly. Deer ticks, a primary carrier of Lyme disease, are tiny and hard to see; so check carefully. There are some repellents available that claim to be effective on deer ticks.

Danger Zone
Also associated with hot weather hazards are fireworks. Fireworks cause many injuries every year, despite being legally regulated in most states. Limit your grandchildren's experiences with fireworks to viewing them at well controlled and authorized community events. Resist the temptation to bring home seemingly innocent fireworks such as sparklers or black snakes. They all require fire to light.

Hartt to Hartt

In New Jersey, where we live, it is illegal to buy or sell fireworks. However, sparklers are not considered fireworks and can be purchased. Marilyn bought some one Fourth of July as a treat for our two-year-old grandson. He was inside, watching through a window when Marilyn started lighting the end of the sparklers. The very first one scared him enough to make him run into the living room to his parents, shouting, "Grandma's playing with fire!"

Keeping the Reins Behind the Wheel

It's your car. And when the grandkids are in it, it's your responsibility to transport them safely. There are few places where it is more important to make sure that kids obey the rules than in a car. You simply can't afford to be distracted or have your passengers unsafe. The following rules will help keep your passengers safe, and you in control.

> **Great Grandparenting**
> When your grandchildren are a little older, but still likely to get restless and whiney during a too-long trip, introduce them to games they can play in the car. A favorite car game is compiling lists of out-of-state licenses. Another, for older children, is "highway poker," using license plates to build poker hands. Automobile associations, such as AAA, often publish instructions for highway pastimes like these.

➤ Young children must always ride in the back seat. Never allow them in front!

➤ Ban loud, sudden noises that could startle the driver.

➤ Seat belts must be kept fastened at all times.

➤ No pushing on or kicking the seats in front of them.

➤ All body parts must be kept in the car at all times.

➤ The volume on portable radios and tape or compact disc players must be kept low.

➤ No waving or gesturing to drivers or passengers in other cars because this could distract other drivers.

An automobile is no place for high jinks, that's for sure. It's far too dangerous. Make sure your grandchildren know you are serious about this. If they don't listen, explain that they will now have to miss an outing or two that entails a car ride.

Rights and Wrongs on Bikes and Trikes

Learning to ride a bicycle is one of the rites of passage of childhood. Helping your grandchildren master wheeled vehicles of all kinds can be great fun. By the time the grandkids are 10 or so, they'll no doubt know far more than you do (unless you happen to be a cyclist yourself) about bikes. So, listen carefully and you might learn how mountain bikes differ from conventional bikes or why three-speed differentials are mandatory if you are training for the Grand Prix in the Pyrenees.

Meanwhile, there are some practical considerations to keep in mind before you sit your grandchild on a bike.

Size and Dimensions

When borrowing or renting a bike, make sure that the length to the pedals, size of the wheels, and contour of the seat are comfortable for your grandchild.

Whee! on Wheels

Look Mom, no hands! Look Dad, no feet! Look Mom and Dad, no teeth! The more chances some kids can take on their bikes, the happier they are. This old quip raises the issue of bicycle safety, which should be stressed before you set your bike-riding grandkids loose in your neighborhood. They'll be more comfortable, and you'll be less nervous, if everyone understands and follows the rules. We encourage the following guidelines:

➤ *Always wear a helmet when biking.* Helmets are required for children in many states, but they should be worn regardless of the law. A properly fitting helmet is the best defense against a head injury in the event of an accident. Insist that your grandkids wear helmets, even if they're just riding around your block. Helmets and protective pads also are a must when in-line skating.

➤ *Make sure all bikes are properly equipped* with good brakes, properly inflated tires, reflectors, chains that are free of rust and well-lubricated, and functioning gears and shifts if the bikes are to be used on hills.

➤ *Keep hands on the handlebars* (your own, that is—no linking up with another cyclist).

➤ *When it's necessary to ride on a road with car traffic,* ride single file, next to the curb, on the right side.

➤ *Do not cycle at night unless the bike is properly equipped with a light and fluorescent patches* or reflectors that glow in the dark. A reflective vest should be worn for night riding.

➤ *Warn all bikers to be alert* for bumps on the road, sharp stones, fallen branches, and other hazards that could cause spills and bruises.

➤ *Train young users to keep their bikes clean* and wipe them off thoroughly if they have ridden through water or in the rain.

Hartt to Hartt

If you enjoyed riding bikes at some point of your life, you might want to renew the interest. Some friends with older grandchildren have made it something of a hobby to learn more about bikes and other wheeled vehicles. They ask their grandkids to tell them all about the latest state-of-the-art developments. This not only lets their grandkids know how interested they are in the grandkid's activities, it also gives the grandparents some fascinating information on how biking and biking equipment has changed. There are several biking magazines and some interesting books on the subject if you are interested in learning more.

Driveway Safety

Even your own driveway, front yard, or sidewalk can be dangerous places for your grandkids to bike, skate, or play. It makes sense that most accidents occur in the places where kids spend most of their time. You can't assume that they're safe just because they're close. It's very tempting for a small child to chase that runaway ball out into the street, and it's just as likely that he'll forget to look both ways before he does. Make sure kids understand the following tips when playing in your yard or driveway, even if your street is not heavily traveled:

➤ *Always stop completely before entering the street* from the driveway or sidewalk.

➤ *Look both ways* for cars before heading into the street.

➤ *Don't chase after balls* or other toys that roll into the street. Ask an adult to help you.

➤ *Be alert for times of heavy traffic in your neighborhood.* These could be in the morning or late afternoon when people are going to and returning from work, or when school lets out and teens are driving home.

➤ *If you see a car or truck that looks as if it's going to turn into the driveway,* quickly get off the driveway onto the grass.

> **Great Grandparenting**
>
> You can easily make a BE ALERT—CHILDREN AT PLAY sign to place at the end of the driveway or in any other conspicuous place where passing drivers and bikers will see it. Some towns supply such signs, or you can obtain them through a mail-order company. They come in bright colors and fold easily for transport to other locations where your grandchildren will be playing.

➤ *Never wrestle or push anyone on the hard driveway surface.* Be especially careful near the end of the driveway, where somebody could get pushed out into the street.

➤ *Be careful of water or oil* on the driveway that could be slippery.

The Least You Need to Know

➤ Recognize the potential dangers of water. Teach children water safety rules and insist they follow them.

➤ Evaluate your yard and neighboring playgrounds, woods, and fields. Are they places where kids can expend their energies safely?

➤ Look for the source of the problem, and take remedial action if grandchildren have fits of sneezing or any other symptoms of allergies.

➤ Summertime brings outdoor fun, but also certain hazards. Consider the things you need to be wary of in your location and climate.

➤ Maintain tight discipline at all times when driving small passengers in your car.

➤ Train the young to think of bikes and even trikes as vehicles that require proper training, use, and maintenance.

Chapter 8

Discipline: Ironing Out Generational Points of View

In This Chapter

➤ Minimizing generation gaps

➤ Keeping nostalgia in its place

➤ Letting parents be leaders

➤ Handling disagreements with an open mind

➤ Good guidance for bad kids

If it sometimes seems to you that the world is moving too fast and you're in danger of being left behind, don't despair. You're not alone. Everybody feels that way sometimes, especially in these days of microprocessors, kilobytes, megabytes and the World Wide Web, two-income families, job sharing, e-mailing, day caring, and mini-vans.

Society has changed a lot during the past 30 or 40 years, there's no question about it. Child-rearing methods and philosophies have changed along with everything else, and sometimes it's hard to accept new ways of doing things. Kids today grow up more quickly. They seem to know more earlier—or at least they talk about it more. They plug in to computers by the time they start kindergarten and, thanks to *Sesame Street* and other educational shows, some of them can count in Spanish nearly as early as they can in English. They're more street wise and savvy. You're not sure it's all for the best, and sometimes you wonder about your son's or daughter's child-rearing methods. When you think about the way you were raised, and the way you raised your kids, you're likely to be really struck by two things: The boundaries between the generations are much looser today than they ever were, and the avenues of communication are open much wider.

Kids and child-rearing methods have changed, but so have grandparents. Grandparents don't sit quietly on porches anymore, watching their grandkids play in the yard. Sure, grandmoms still make cookies, but the baking is likely to be squeezed in after a day at the office. Grandpa is just as likely to be planning a scuba-diving vacation as he is planning a trip to the corner hardware store. Grandfather and former president George Bush showed the world recently that he still has the right stuff when he parachuted from an airplane. Golfer/grandfather Jack Nicklaus still awes fans on the course with his golf swing. Grandparents are working, traveling, throwing parties, going to college, taking up watercoloring, and starting businesses. They're enjoying life to the fullest, and they want to share it with their grandkids.

It's sometimes difficult to distinguish parents from grandparents. Today's grandparents are much more athletic, liberal, and active than the elders of the pre-World War II era. They're taking care of themselves with proper diet and exercise, and medical advancements have brought cures for conditions that once would have been debilitating.

Despite greater similarities between the generations, though, generational viewpoints often conflict. You must be prepared for the give and take of situations in which there are differences of opinion, especially when it involves child raising.

"That's Not the Way We Did It in Our Day!"

While it seems sometimes that things change too fast, rest assured that there are other things that never change. The sun rises and sets every day. The phone always rings at dinner time. Summer always follows spring. And, older people, when considering the manner in which younger people operate, will always say (or at least think to themselves) something like this:

"What's this young generation coming to?"

"Sometimes I can't even understand what these kids are saying!"

"If I'd acted that way when I was little, my dad would have paddled my behind!"

"Young people these days wear the strangest getups. Why do they want to look like that?"

The grandparents who will best be able to relate to their grandkids and appreciate them for who they are—not how they look or sound—are the ones who can go along with the times. Ask yourself this question: Would you really want everyone in your family to be the same? Wouldn't it be strange, not to mention boring, if everyone wore the kind of clothing you wear, used the same language you use, and liked all the same things?

It's important to accept that differences are not "bad" or signs of moral decay. Kids who dress in odd clothing are expressing themselves. They have something to say and they say it with their clothes, hairstyles, music, and language. They say it through the television shows they watch and the books they read. Your children did the same thing, and, guess what—you did too!

Think back and it's a sure bet you'll remember your own parents rolling their eyes and shaking their heads over something you did. As long as there are different generations, there will be generational differences.

It's sometimes difficult for older people to understand why young people (especially if those young people are their grandchildren) adopt habits and lifestyles and choose friends and activities that seem alien. Remember, though, that as a grandparent, being judgmental is neither your job nor your privilege. If your grandchildren have something to say and are saying it through their dress or music, perhaps you'd do well to listen.

Avoid making judgments or generalizations that pit your generation against theirs. They most likely are already experiencing some conflicts with their parents at this point. If you lend them support and understanding, you have a good opportunity to bond and get closer to them instead of alienating them. Talk to your grandkids about their parents. Tell them about the clothing they wore during their "hippie" days, and share a laugh. But, be respectful when talking about your kids. You don't want to create dissension between any of the generations. When you report back to the parents about the time you spent with their children, mention the good things that happened. How encouraging it will be for your grandkids to hear themselves being praised to their parents!

The lesson here is to be positive and open minded. If you simply must remark, "That's not the way we did it in our day," or "When I was your age, I was never allowed to do that," say it with a sense of humor and understanding, not disapproval.

Hartt to Hartt

We like to look back on our own lives and reflect that *our* grandparents must have found it difficult to understand some of the things we did. We used childish slang and wanted to wear outrageous outfits. We remember that a lot of times our grandparents gave in to our whims, mainly because they liked to spoil us. In turn, we make it a practice to look kindly on some of the things about our grandkids that we simply don't fathom. We spoil them in return, and enjoy doing it.

Discipline? Let Parents Call the Shots

Your two grandchildren, ages eight and eleven, are coming for the weekend. Last time they visited, they gave you a mighty hard time about going to bed. They also fibbed to you, telling you they're allowed to watch "Awesome Saturday Night Ghost Stories" on TV. You later found out that show is strictly forbidden because it gives them both night-mares. You've been thinking about how you'll handle these kinds of problems if they arise again, and you've decided on some rules you'll set and some punishments you'll impose if the rules aren't followed. Okay, bring on the grandkids. You're ready for them.

If this sounds like something you might do, you may just be heading for trouble. Disci-pline can be one of the most sensitive areas for intergenerational relationships. Before you take charge, whether at your house or at your children's home, you need to find out the parents' feelings about discipline and what punishments are appropriate for certain actions.

You might think that a good dose of soap is the best cure for a smart mouth. Your daugh-ter and son-in-law, however, might be horrified by that idea. It is best to know how the parents normally handle particular situations and adjust your own strategies. One expert in family relationships said it is vitally important for grandparents to defer to parents in matters of discipline. Your job as a primary caregiver is done, the expert said, and the baton has been passed along to your child. Trust that your child learned well and has the good judgment to raise his children in similar fashion.

When in Doubt, Discuss

If you have a problem with how your child and his or spouse are disciplining (or not disciplining) their children, it's within your rights to talk to them about it. Experts advise talking to your son or daughter, since you are coming from a common background regarding discipline. You can discuss how it was when he or she was growing up, and to what degree things today are the same or different.

If it was common practice for you to place your son on a "naughty chair" when he disobeyed, ask him what he thinks about that as a punishment for his own son. Ask your child to explain his or her theories on discipline, and try to understand. Her philosophies might be different, but not necessarily wrong. Don't let the discussion turn into a matter of pride or a contest about who's right or wrong. Remember that you and your child have the same goal in mind—successfully raising your grandchild.

When you discuss discipline matters with the parents, keep the following points in mind:

➤ Be mutually clear about which rules are rigid (no "Awesome Saturday Night Ghost Stories"), which are flexible (bedtime is at 8:30, but 9:00 might be okay), and which can be left up to you to select ("Grandma, may I have another cupcake?").

➤ Discuss the fine line that divides strictness on the one side and spoiling the child on the other. Where do the parents stand?

➤ When more than one grandchild is involved, find out whether different grandchildren are held to different rules, and which kids are likely to abide by the rules and which are going to try to put something over on you.

➤ If there are certain rules or restrictions you want your grandchildren to observe when they are at your house, even though the same rules might not apply at their house, make it clear to the children and parents that the rules will be enforced, and why.

Once you, the parents, and the grandkids all understand the rules and the reasons for them, you'll be ready to go ahead with that visit.

> **Great Grandparenting**
> Once you feel that you understand the attitudes and expectations of the parents, try to arrange for more time to enjoy your grandkids without their mother and father present. Many grandparents say they are more relaxed when they are alone with their grandkids, and they enjoy the closeness and bonding that occurs.

Talking Across the Generations

Parent: "Our kids wouldn't be so hard to control if your mother and father didn't spoil them all the time; they act like little monsters when they come back from a visit."

Grandparent: "These grandkids are acting like little brats, but there's nothing I can do about it. That's their parents' problem."

Grandchild: "I'm always getting picked on for doing something wrong when I didn't know it was wrong. Maybe if Mom, Dad, Granny, and Grandpa would talk to each other occasionally, we would all know what's going on."

The sentiments expressed in the previous three statements are classic examples of lack of communication. If expectations are not discussed, a person can't know what is expected. You may not be able to resolve all the conflicts that surface (and that become even more acute when a second, or even third, set of grandparents are involved). But, what you must do is stay in close touch with each other and support each other in your efforts. A united front among adults is extremely important when dealing with children. As we pointed out earlier, parents and grandparents share a common goal of raising a child or children to be happy, healthy, and responsible adults.

You can take these positive steps to stabilize communication among the generations:

➤ *Constantly promote the concept of the total family,* to which all three generations belong.

➤ *Have open discussions* about acceptable behavior and rules.

➤ *Take into account the differences in locales and situations* before you try to set hard-and-fast rules.

➤ *Be sensitive to stressful situations,* such as single-parent households, or homes in which there may be four or five children suddenly thrown together as stepbrothers and sisters. Situations like these may call for special rules and behaviors.

➤ *If you have free time, take classes on child development* so you can provide sound advice to parents. Many such classes may be offered at local colleges.

➤ *Look at the situation from the standpoint of the grandchildren,* and make sure you understand their goals and needs.

➤ *Rather than being judgmental, work together* with the other generations to solve problems.

➤ *Be aware of, and honestly admit, your own anxieties or bewilderment* if you are not sure about a conflict of interests or ideas.

➤ *Arrange for more frequent get-togethers at times and places where you can communicate freely with each other,* and openly discuss family predicaments and rules of conduct.

➤ *Never let anyone in the family tell you that grandparents have no say in their grandkids' upbringing.* It is understood that parents are the primary caregivers and make most of the child-rearing decisions. But, if you are involved with your grandkids, then you are involved with their upbringing.

What to Do When You Disagree

Life would be a bowl of cherries, as the old song says, if no one ever disagreed. But you'd better be realistic because life's just not like that. Sooner or later (and it probably won't take too long), you and your daughter are going to disagree about something, such as whether or not your granddaughter should be made to finish her turkey before she starts in on the oatmeal cookies that she loves. Your daughter thinks it's silly to insist that the little girl eat everything on her plate. After all, why should we force her to eat food she doesn't want? You, on the other hand, believe that it makes very good sense for your granddaughter to finish her dinner before she starts dessert. Besides, it's good discipline to teach her the rules and see that she follows them.

One of the marks of smart grandparents is that they are flexible and willing to look at both sides of a question in order to resolve a conflict or disagreement. Below are some clearly unsuccessful methods of dealing with disagreements between you and your daughter:

➤ *"I'm older and wiser."* Age is not the determining factor in who gets to run things. If so, Bob Dole would have been named president over Bill Clinton without the benefit of an election, and the oldest person in the office, not the one with the best qualifications, would get to be the boss.

➤ *"You don't know how sensitive the child is."* When the dispute is laid at the feet of a grandchild, you're simply avoiding the communication problem you and your daughter are experiencing. If your daughter suggests that her daughter should be able to have the cookies because there's going to be a nasty scene if she doesn't get them, don't snort in disgust. Point out that this is a good time to take a constructive step and ease the child away from a bad habit. And, consider that your daughter may be trying to avoid such a scene because she's embarrassed for you to see it, or may be trying to spare you any discomfort it might cause.

➤ *"You don't know this kid like we know her."* Parents may claim that because they have a more intimate knowledge of the child, they know what is best for her. Perhaps your daughter has been through this turkey-vs-cookie scene many times before and knows how the child will react if made to eat the meat. Again, she may be trying to avoid a scene and keep things pleasant. In reality, she's avoiding dealing with a problem.

➤ *"You don't have to live with this kid."* This statement may cause a grandparent to shudder if you think it means that the parents are caving in to the whims of their child in order to avoid dealing with the consequences of imposing a punishment. If that is precisely what the parents are doing, they're in for a long, long haul with this child.

➤ *"All the kids are allowed to do that."* Parents may think that grandparents are out of touch with current parenting mores, while grandparents might think their children are too lenient or should be stronger and not go along with "the crowd."

➤ *"Look, you used to make me finish everything on my plate and I had a weight problem until I moved out of the house!"* Blaming another generation for something in the past might be tempting, but is not useful.

➤ *"I always hated it when you did that, and I can't stand to see you let my granddaughter do the same thing!"* Again, bringing up a past conflict will not solve the problem at hand, unless you can apply to the current problem the solution you used to fix the conflict the first time around.

When disagreements occur, as they inevitably will, the only way to solve them is through meaningful, respectful, well-intended, and sincere discussion. If the matter is upsetting to you or your daughter, wait until a little time has passed and you've both gained some perspective, then try talking about it again.

Hartt to Hartt

When she was a teenager, Marilyn set a rule for herself: As a parent she would always say "yes" to her children's requests unless she could think of a sound reason to say "no." And even a "no" might leave the door open to a compromise. While questions such as "Aw, do I have to wear a seat belt?" would certainly be answered in the affirmative, questions such as "May I stay up an hour late tonight to see that new TV show?" would be open to discussion. When Marilyn became a mother, she didn't always find her self-imposed rule easy to follow. But, she tried.

Playing "No Favorites"

All grandchildren have something special about them. For most grandparents, it's not hard to find what those things are. That sweet, shy smile, the way he runs up and gives you that big, special hug every time he sees you, or that great sense of humor she displays. It might be the ability to learn quickly, musical talents, or skill in sports. When children are noticed and commended for their particular gifts, they grow up feeling special, without feeling that other children are favored.

If you see your son or daughter treating one of your grandkids in a manner that you perceive to be unfair, what should you do? You know that the parents are in charge and it's not your job to second guess them. In this case, however, you really think that your grandchild is coming up shorthanded. Here are some suggestions:

➤ Watch and listen to the child you feel is being treated unfairly to see if you can get a feeling of his perception on the matter. Perhaps you're seeing something that doesn't exist. Or, perhaps he has a plan for dealing with the problem. Be careful that you don't make matters worse by setting the grandchild up as a victim in his own eyes.

➤ Watch the grandchild who seems to be favored to see if she displays any sense of superiority or inclination to use her favored position to make the other child feel bad.

➤ Avoid any fault-finding discussion with the parent in the presence of the grandchildren.

➤ Invite both siblings to visit you, or take them on an outing long enough for you to judge whether the friction is real or imagined.

➤ If you really do detect dissension, discuss it with your son or daughter, and describe what you've noticed.

➤ If the parents do not change the ways they deal with the children, do whatever you can to build up the injured child's esteem and self-confidence. Point out his strengths and tell him what you like about him. Help him with schoolwork or in other ways that might improve his performance and make him feel good about himself. Make him feel loved and secure by telling him things about the extended family of which he is a part.

➤ Remember that tender loving care and hugs and kisses go a long way toward making youngsters feel they are equal to their siblings when it comes to being cared for and appreciated.

Hartt to Hartt

We got an emergency call one morning from our children, both working parents. One of our grandsons was sick and they both had busy days at work. Of course we would watch him for the day. We were tempted to take his mind off his discomfort by buying him a toy as a little surprise, something he could play with at our house and on the way home. But, we decided against this tactic when we realized his brother might feel neglected by not getting a toy, too. Fortunately, we had kept Granny's Toy Box well stocked, so we had plenty of interesting playthings to take the child through an entire day of bed rest.

Refereeing Fights

When you have two or more grandchildren together, especially if they're siblings, you can bet that sooner or later their joyful noise and laughter will degenerate into bickering, followed by screams and tears. This, unfortunately, is standard behavior for kids. But, what do you do if one child always seems to be the villain who starts the battle? Or when a child is constantly kicking, punching, or scratching so that you have to threaten dire punishment and trot to the bathroom for Band-Aids?

Your first strategy is to develop an "anti-battle" program:

➤ *Avoid touchy situations.* Kids are more likely to be hostile to each other when they are tired, bored, hungry, or left alone with no supervision. Avoid these situations whenever possible.

➤ *Make sure that what appear to be serious scuffles are not just playful, rowdy romps* before you stop the action.

Danger Zone
If you suspect your grandchild might have a really nasty streak, watch for these signs: bullying, purposely harming another child and then lying about it, going into tantrums when scolded for bad behavior, picking on younger or weaker children, and goading others into retaliating in the presence of an adult so your grandchild can gloat when the other child is punished. If you observe these signs frequently, talk to the parents—the child may need some professional help.

➤ *Simply break up the activity and get the kids to do something else.* Once you ask "Who started it?" or try to find out which child is most at fault, you're in trouble.

➤ *When you hear too much bickering, tell them you're sorry they're not getting along together, but you know they can work it out.* Relate that as soon as they do, they can come out to the kitchen for some cookies or another treat.

➤ *Suggest a different activity* if there aren't enough toys to go around.

➤ *Be firm in classifying yourself as the boss,* making it clear that you'll send those who are unruly to their rooms if they don't play by your rules.

➤ *Praise your grandkids when they act in a responsible manner,* particularly when they do something that shows consideration for others.

➤ *Don't let yourself get tricked into starting an argument.* When children argue with you, you'll often find that they are simply modeling your own manners.

Setting Rules

Although in most cases grandparents should defer to parents when it comes to setting and enforcing rules, things are a little different when the grandkids are at your house. You certainly are entitled to set guidelines for what goes on in your home. Here are some sensible guidelines to follow:

➤ *When taking over responsibility from the parents, ask them to tell their children clearly that you are in charge and must be respected.*

➤ *Try to keep the rules at your house pretty close to the rules your grandchildren are expected to follow at their house.* For instance, if they're not allowed to walk to the corner store by themselves at home, don't let them do it while they're at your house. There's no point in confusing them with inconsistency.

➤ *Make sure your grandkids understand basic rules from the start.* For example: no eating in the living room, no playing in the street, or no jumping on the beds. Don't let them manipulate you later on by saying they didn't know they weren't supposed to take that double-dip chocolate ice cream cone into the living room with the white carpet.

➤ *Don't throw so many rules at your grandkids all at once that they become overwhelmed and don't remember any of them.* Rules concerning bath time and TV time probably can wait until the situation arises.

➤ *If your grandchildren are older, discuss the reasons for your rules and make sure they understand them.*

➤ *Be consistent,* and don't get into situations where Grandma is strict and Grandpa lenient, or vice versa.

➤ *Avoid making rules you can't enforce or threats that have no meaning.* If you have no intention of keeping your grandson home from the zoo because firm plans have already been made and can't be changed, don't threaten him with that as a punishment. And, unless you plan to be with them constantly for the entire time they spend at your house, don't tell them they're not allowed to say anything remotely nasty to the other. It's next to impossible to enforce such a rule.

➤ *Keep your sense of humor* and occasionally let young children get away with something you can all laugh at.

> **Great Grandparenting**
> Rules make a child feel safe. Imagine a youngster trying to cope with a day lacking clear limitations. May I play outside? May I turn on the TV? When do we eat? Am I allowed to get food out of the fridge myself? Can I play with the kids next door? Grandparents must be honest about what's acceptable and what's not.

Rules are necessary and good, but don't get carried away. After all, you want to have a good time with your grandkids, not spend every minute policing them. Expect respect and good behavior from them and give them the same from you. You'll all get along just fine.

Bending the Rules

The secret of intelligent discipline is to decide when to let things slide. Together with the parents, you can actually work out a list of rules, some of which are firm and some of which are flexible. It might look like this:

Setting Rules

Negotiable	Not Negotiable
How long grandkids can watch TV	Must wear seat belts
Clothing grandkids can wear	May not cross the street outside alone

continues

continued

Negotiable	Not Negotiable
Selection of chores to do	Must brush teeth
How much food grandkids must eat	No hitting and kicking others
Playing with pets	No teasing the cat
Staying in bed late	No going out after dark

Words That Work

You should speak with authority when you give an order that, if not followed, will result in a punishment. But, whenever possible, give choices so that your grandchild is not backed up against a wall with no way out. Almost any grandparent has stories of defiance. One tells of an eight-year-old boy who said, "When Granny orders me to do something, I want to do just the opposite."

> **Great Grandparenting**
> You may want to sound off if you're impatient, particularly if you're running late. If you find yourself constantly pressed for time when with your grandkids, try giving them more time to do the things they need to or want to do. Don't overschedule activities so that you end up hurrying through one to get to the next one. If you're patient, you'll get more cooperation and model better self-control for your grandchildren.

If you're having problems getting your grandchildren to listen to your instructions, perhaps your lingo isn't on target. Not only your tone of voice, but the way you say something can also make the difference between resistance and compliance. Consider, for example, these kinds of choices when you want to avoid a power struggle with the youngest generation:

Don't say: "Unless you brush your teeth right now, I'm not going to let you watch TV."
Do say: "Sure you can watch TV—just as soon as you finish brushing your teeth."

Don't say: "How many times do I have to call you to come in for lunch?"
Do say: "Come on in, kids, I've just fixed the kind of lunch you really like. Surprise!"

Don't say: "If you don't put your seat belt on, we won't go."
Do say: "Okay, we're all ready to go, as soon as you've buckled up."

When Punishment Rears Its Ugly Head

There probably has never been a child who at one time or another did not require some well-deserved punishment. Many child specialists say it is best to use natural consequences as punishment for inappropriate actions. If a child throws her toys around when she gets angry, one eventually will get broken. If a bicycle is left outside instead of being put back in the garage as instructed, it may be stolen. Homework that is ignored at home will not be ignored by the teacher who is expecting it the next day in school.

If natural consequences are not your cup of tea and you feel punishment is necessary, specialists say it should be immediate, and applied directly to the act for which the child is being punished. For instance, it makes no sense to tell your five-year-old grandson that he'll watch no TV that evening because he pulled the cat's tail that morning. By evening, he certainly will have completely forgotten the tail-pulling incident. On the other hand, if your granddaughter goes into the neighbor's yard after being told repeatedly not to, a reasonable punishment would be to immediately take away her outside play.

Punishment is meant to encourage a change for the better in a child's behavior, not to give you satisfaction. Avoid saying something such as, "See, I told you so—if you hit your little sister, you have to go to your room!"

Psychologists say that it's natural for grandparents (and parents) to occasionally feel angry, resentful, and guilty over things their children or grandchildren have done. It is the way you express those feelings that is important. Screaming at a child might scare him, but he'll hear only your tone, not your words. Hitting a child lets him know you're bigger and stronger than he is, but nothing about what he did wrong. Kids have a lot of perils to worry about these days. It's a scary world for many of them. Their home (and your home) should be a safe and secure place, not another place for fear and distrust. If you feel that you are not capable of handling your anger and you have been, or feel you could be, physically abusive to a grandchild or other member of your family, you should seek professional help at once.

Here are some specific tips to help you handle crime and punishment:

➤ *Scolding should not be humiliating to a child or presented in a nagging, sarcastic manner.* Words can hurt as bad as a slap, and can cause lasting damage. Be as unemotional as possible when you correct a child's behavior. It is the words you want her to hear, not your tone.

➤ *Reward, as well as punish,* specific behavior, focusing on the conduct itself and not on whether your grandchild is "good" or "bad."

➤ *Teach the policy of self-control,* so kids grow up realizing they have responsibility for their own actions and are not being controlled by you. Teach them about appropriate and inappropriate behavior and ways to vent anger or other emotions they might be feeling. For instance, a child feeling anger could punch a pillow or take a run around the block instead of hitting a smaller child or throwing something

Danger Zone
When you have more than one grandchild in tow and are about to punish one for some infraction involving the other(s), such as hitting or seizing a toy, make sure you have the facts straight. If you didn't actually see the incident, don't let the older or more aggressive child con you into believing a falsehood.

➤ *While physical punishment is sometimes tempting, experts say it is not productive.* The American Academy of Pediatrics opposes hitting a child for any reason. Think about it—if you hit a child because he hit his sister, what message does that imply? Use punishment that is meaningful, but not emotional on your part. Time-outs seem to be generally acceptable punishments, and they are beneficial in that they give everyone time to cool down and gain some perspective on the situation. Other punishments might include the loss of a privilege (if there is a logical connection to the offense) or having the child acknowledge and apologize for poor behavior.

➤ *Be understanding and lenient* if you suspect that unsuitable behavior is the result of a child's physical illness, feelings of stress, or being in an unfamiliar environment.

➤ *Acknowledge the state of your own emotions* if you are upset, undergoing stress, and likely to be overly sensitive to a child's behavior.

The subject of punishment is complex and often controversial. Before imposing punishment, you should know how the parents would handle the same situation and try to remain consistent. Talk to parents before the grandchildren come to your house, and see if there is any behavior that might be anticipated. If so, ask the parents what punishment they would think appropriate and try to use something similar, if necessary. If the parents' punishment seems much too harsh, talk to them about it. Don't do anything that makes you uncomfortable, such as imposing corporal punishment because that's what the parents advocate. If you can't reconcile this kind of issue with parents, maybe you need to postpone the visit. Keep in mind that these discussions should all occur out of earshot of the grandchildren.

Be prepared. Avoidance can be the best policy. If you know that behavior problems crop up every time your grandkids are in a restaurant, the obvious solution is to eat at home. If two siblings fight constantly, invite them to visit one at a time. Not only will you avoid incidents at your home, you'll give them both a break from their daily routines.

Above all, make it clear to each child that you expect good behavior and will not tolerate anything but. When bad manners surface or an infraction occurs, treat the problem quickly, unemotionally, and to a degree consistent with the nature and extent of the misbehavior.

The Least You Need to Know

➤ Respect the generation gap as something quite natural in life; don't try to equate what you used to do with what is appropriate today.

➤ Take your cue from the parents in all matters relating to discipline and rules.

➤ Talk with the parents when you're confused about rules or think the rules should be changed.

➤ Anticipate that you and the parents will disagree on some disciplinary matters; talk about these matters openly.

➤ Be sure you know what kinds of punishments are acceptable in the eyes of the parents.

Chapter 9

SOS!!
Emergencies

In This Chapter

➤ Preparing for emergencies

➤ Coming to the rescue: handling minor upsets

➤ Putting unsafe medications out of harm's way

➤ Avoiding the spread of germs and the like

➤ Dealing with things that spark fright in the night

You've taken a big step and invited your three grandchildren, ages four, five, and seven, for a long weekend at your house. Yep, Thursday night to Monday morning. It's gonna be great! This will give your daughter and son-in-law that much-needed mini-vacation, and you'll be able to do some real bonding with your grandkids. Sure, you've had the grandkids overnight before, but it was just one at a time. Well, it will probably be easier to have all three. They'll entertain each other—right? It will be a nice, relaxed time for all.

Wanna bet? It's practically a given that the four-year-old will fall from her bike, scrape up her knee and elbow, and go into fits of hysterics. The seven-year-old will swallow his bubble gum and have a bout of choking, and the five-year-old will wake up in the night screaming that a giant spider is in the bedroom. All of a sudden the nice, relaxing week-end is anything but! Don't worry. In this chapter, we'll show you how to handle almost any emergency.

Be Prepared!

Anticipation is the key word when it comes to handling accidents. Before an emergency has a chance to occur, follow the old Boy Scout rule: Be prepared!

These should be the most important rules in your plan of action:

➤ Know where the parents will be at all times. Have an address and phone number at which you can reach them.

➤ Make sure you're aware of any chronic health or medical problems the children have, such as allergies or fainting spells. Make sure you know what kind of medications or treatment these problems require.

➤ List emergency phone numbers for your doctor's office, a local pediatrician, the poison control center, the hospital, the police and fire departments, and the emergency number (911 or its equivalent). (See Chapter 6 for a list of important phone numbers you should keep by every phone in the house.)

➤ Get the children's parents to write and sign a note giving you permission to authorize medical treatment for your grandchildren in the event of an emergency. Include the children's insurance information and social security numbers.

➤ Childproof your home (be sure to read Chapter 6).

➤ Have a basic first-aid kit handy.

➤ Obtain a first-aid guide, familiarize yourself with its contents, and keep it with your first-aid kit.

Taking these steps will help you to avoid your worst enemy in case of emergency: *panic*. When an emergency occurs, you have to be able to decide quickly and calmly whether to handle the problem yourself, try to reach the parents, or get professional help.

Hartt to Hartt

A family member never leaves her children in our care without also leaving a list of doctors and phone numbers. She operates on the premise that "anything that can go wrong will go wrong." At first we found this attitude to be worrisome, but soon we realized that her list is really a comforting safeguard. The more ready we are for emergencies, the more relaxed we are with the children when in our care.

Think of it this way: We all get annoyed when we carry an umbrella and the predicted storm never arrives. But, think how smug we feel when a surprise shower hits and we're the only ones around with any protection!

First Aid in a Flash

You're in the park with the grandkids and everybody is having a great time. They're using the swings, climbing on the rope ladder, and coasting down the sliding board. Twenty minutes later, the five-year-old has a scraped knee and the seven-year-old a splinter. You're going to have to head home to treat the wounded.

It's comforting to know that most injuries grandparents encounter will be of this sort—your basic little cuts, scrapes, scratches, and burns. Over the following pages, we'll show you how to handle these and other everyday mishaps, and discuss some more serious ones as well.

Cuts and Bleeding

A minor cut (one with little bleeding or with bleeding that stops on its own after a few minutes) requires very little treatment. Bleeding will carry dirt out of most wounds, so you just need to clean around the cut. Using cool water, wipe from the edges of the wound outward, using a clean gauze or cotton pad for each swipe. Small cuts heal best when left uncovered, but, if the child insists on a Band-Aid, it's okay. Just remove it as soon as possible to promote healing.

If blood is spurting from the wound or flowing so heavily that it can't be stopped by pressing a gauze pad firmly over the cut for several minutes, you are facing a medical emergency. The loss of as little as half a pint of blood is considered severe bleeding for a child. Apply pressure on the wound with a clean cloth or bandage, and get your grand-child to a doctor or the emergency room quickly.

A puncture wound, usually caused by stepping on something such as a nail, is trickier than a simple cut. It's very liable to become infected, because any germs are carried deep into the tissue, and there is little bleeding to carry them out again. A deep wound (especially one made by something dirty or rusty) should be seen by a doctor. Antibiotics and a tetanus shot might be necessary.

Insect Stings

Insect stings can be nothing more than a nuisance, or they can be life threatening. If your grandchild is stung by a bee or wasp, calm him down. Tell him you know it hurts but the worst is over and the pain will soon stop. Run cold water over the affected area, or use an ice pack. If you have a spray or lotion, go ahead and use it if he'll let you. If you can see a stinger, scrape it out with a knife or fingernail. But, never use tweezers to pull out a stinger because you could squeeze more venom into the wound.

If your grandchild has an allergic reaction to a sting, you'll need to get medical attention quickly. Symptoms of such a reaction might include severe swelling of areas other than where the sting occurred. Severe itching, with or without hives; stomach cramps; wheezing or coughing; vomiting; dizziness and unconsciousness are other symptoms of a severe reaction.

95

If the child has gotten into a nest of bees and has been stung many times, be on the lookout for an allergic reaction. Remove the child's clothes and wrap him in a cold, wet sheet to relieve the pain. Be ready for a trip to the emergency room.

Very rarely, a child reacts to a sting or stings with general collapse. He'll become pale, sweaty, and faint, and unable to function. This is called anaphylactic shock, and is a full-scale emergency.

There are only two poisonous spiders found in the United States: black widow and brown recluse (also called fiddler) spiders. If your grandchild is bitten by a spider and you live in an area where these spiders are found, pay close attention to the wound. If any symptoms occur, get medical assistance quickly.

In the same family as spiders are scorpions. Scorpions are found in the Southwest portion of the U.S. Scorpion bites are extremely painful and can be very dangerous to children.

Animal Bites

If your grandchild is bitten by cat or dog that belongs to someone in your neighborhood, confirm that the animal has been immunized against rabies and other diseases. If this is the case, treat minor bites and scratches the way you would a cut, keeping a close watch for any signs of infection. Consult the child's doctor to see if a tetanus shot is recommended. If the domestic animal that bites your grandchild is not known to you, or if the child is bitten by a wild animal, try to catch and contain the animal (without risking a bite yourself), so it can be checked for rabies. Call your local police or animal rescue organization if you require assistance. This is especially important if the animal was aggressive and attacked the child for no reason, or if you saw other signs of rabies such as foaming at the mouth or strange behavior. If you suspect your grandchild may have been bitten by a rabid animal, consult a doctor immediately. It is important to begin treatment quickly.

Burns

Even minor burns, including sunburn, can be extremely painful. Soak the affected area in cold water, or hold it under cold, running water, for ten minutes or until the pain lessens. Don't use ice on a burn because it can damage tissue. If blisters form on the burned area, don't break them. If clothing rubs against the blisters, cover them with a loose bandage. Do not apply any cream or ointment to a burn, and never treat a burn with butter. (That old-time folk remedy will only make matters worse.) If a burn covers more than a half a square inch of skin, it is not an emergency, but should be shown to a doctor. If the burn covers a portion of skin that is as large, or larger than your hand, it is potentially very serious and the child should be taken to the hospital immediately

Nosebleeds

Nosebleeds generally are not serious, and can be easily treated. The sight of blood may be upsetting to your grandchild, so reassure her to keep her calm. Sit her up, leaning her forward over a basin or the sink. If the bleeding continues for more than two minutes, pinch the nostrils firmly together for two to five minutes to allow a blood clot to form. Have the child refrain from blowing or picking at her nose for at least several hours. If you can't get the bleeding to stop after about 20 minutes, call a doctor.

Fainting

Fainting spells may occur as a result of heat, overexertion, stress, or hunger. Keep your grandchild lying down, with feet slightly elevated, in a room where there is good air circulation. Most spells last only a minute or so. If your grandchild is unconscious or seems to be very groggy for more than two minutes, call for help. Be sure to report any incidences of fainting or feelings of faintness to the child's physician.

Choking

If you suspect your grandchild has something lodged in his throat, treat this as a critical emergency. If he can't speak, cough, or breathe, and appears bluish, you should open his mouth and put your finger in to the back of his throat to see if you can hook the object and dislodge it. If not, you will have to use the Heimlich maneuver (described in first-aid guidebooks). Be aware that a different version of the Heimlich maneuver is used on babies or very small children.

If the child is having difficulty breathing but is able to speak or cough, let him cough to see if the object clears. You may put him across your forearm or knee so that his head and chest are lower than his legs and hips, and pat him on the back, between the shoulder blades, to assist. Always have a choking victim who has been given the Heimlich maneuver checked by a doctor. Damage to internal organs occasionally occurs.

Poisoning

If you think your grandchild has been poisoned after ingesting a household chemical, pesticide, cosmetic, or a toxic plant, try to determine what the poison was and how much was ingested. Call the poison control center or hospital (these numbers should be posted by each phone) immediately, and follow the instructions you are given exactly. You may be told to dilute the poison by giving the child water or milk, or to induce vomiting to eliminate the poison. Do not induce vomiting unless instructed. Keep Ipecac syrup on hand in case it is necessary to induce vomiting.

The most common symptoms of poisoning are drowsiness, vomiting, seizures, or flushing. If you suspect poisoning, call the poison control center or get the child to a hospital as quickly as possible.

Sprains and Strains

If a child cries out in pain and clutches an ankle, knee, or wrist, suspect a sprain or strain. These can be extremely painful, and normally involve swelling and bruising. The injured area should be treated with cold water or an ice pack, and then wrapped firmly with an elastic, or Ace, bandage to prevent swelling. (But don't wrap so tightly that you cut off blood circulation.) Have the child avoid putting any weight on the affected area for a day or two. If the pain continues or worsens, call a doctor or take the child to a hospital emergency room. What you think is a sprain could actually be a broken bone.

Neck or Back Injury

These injuries are very serious and help should be summoned immediately. Don't move the injured child unless it is necessary to get her away from a dangerous location. Try to reassure her while waiting for help to arrive.

Fingertip Injury

Childhood is hardly complete without smashing a fingernail or two in a door or gate. While fingertip injuries are quite painful, they are not generally serious. Apply ice or a cold cloth, and give him some Tylenol or another doctor-approved pain reliever, if necessary.

Head Injury

Most bumps and knocks on the head are not serious, although if there is any sort of cut or scrape, it will bleed like crazy and give you quite a scare. If the child is crying and complaining, but otherwise seems normal, don't worry too much. But, if he seems dazed or otherwise out of sorts, make him lie down for a while. If he goes to sleep, that's okay, but keep a close eye on him. If he becomes very pale, or his breathing is unusually rapid or rasping, try to wake him up. If it is difficult to wake him, call a doctor. If any of the following symptoms occur, call a doctor immediately, or take your grandchild to an emergency room: vomiting, bleeding from the ears, nose, or mouth, headache, blurry speech, clumsiness, unevenly sized pupils, or failure of the eyes to move together when you ask him to follow your finger as you move it in toward his nose.

Asthma Attack

If your grandchild has asthma, or has had symptoms of asthma, be sure you're prepared to deal with an attack. Be assured that asthma is not unusual among children, and most of them outgrow it, but be aware that the attacks can be extremely frightening. Asthma attacks can be triggered by many things including animals, pollen, dust, fumes, vigorous exercise, an overreaction to an infection, extremes of heat or cold, and emotional distress. Symptoms include rapid or constricted breathing, a repeated short cough, and tightness of the skin stretching over the ribs.

If your grandchild suffers an attack while in your care, help her to find a comfortable position in an area with plenty of fresh air. Be sure to remove whatever might be causing the attack (a cat, dog, cut flowers, or any other allergen-producing object.) Administer whatever treatment has been prescribed (such as an inhaler), while remaining as calm as possible. You don't want to further raise the anxiety level your grandchild is feeling by acting panicked or afraid. If the attack does not subside, call a doctor or go to the nearest emergency room.

If a first asthma attack occurs while the child is in your care, you must make sure it is, indeed, an asthma attack. This will require a visit to a doctor or emergency room. Try to keep the child as calm as possible.

Vomiting

Vomiting can be distressing to a child but is seldom serious. Some children vomit quite often for different reasons: at the beginning of an illness, from overexcitement or nervousness, from motion sickness, or for no apparent reason. Make your grandchild as comfortable as you can, and reassure him. Keep handy a container into which he can vomit, but keep in mind that, if he's feeling sick, the sight of the container might make him feel even worse. When he's finished vomiting, give him a glass of water to use to rinse his mouth, and maybe a little ice or a small amount of liquid to drink. Wipe his face with a cool cloth, and keep an eye on him.

If vomiting continues, you need to be on the lookout for dehydration, especially if he also has diarrhea. Signs of dehydration are: decreased urination, crying without tears, sunken eyes or cheeks, and dry mucous membranes (feel the inside of the mouth to check).

Notify a doctor if you see any of the following: a coffee-ground type of material present in vomit, a large amount of bright red blood in vomit, bile (bright yellow or green liquid), the child's stomach is distended and hurts when you touch it, or a decreased level of alertness.

Stomachache

Stomachaches are tricky because they can mean nothing at all, or they can signal a very serious illness such as appendicitis. You need to decide whether or not to call a doctor based on the following criteria: severity of pain, duration of pain, general illness of the child, and other symptoms such as fever, nausea, constipation, or vomiting.

If the pain seems very intense and has lasted for more than a short time, it is best to call a doctor and make sure it's nothing serious. Use your best judgment, but don't take any chances.

Fever

Fever can be an indicator of a great variety of problems. It accompanies serious illnesses such as meningitis, appendicitis, and pneumonia, as well as ear infections, respiratory tract infections, flu, or tonsillitis. If your grandchild's temperature reaches 102° F. or above, you should call a doctor. Keep the child as comfortable as possible with cool washcloths, and ask the doctor to recommend a fever-reducer such as children's Tylenol. Since aspirin has been linked to Reye's syndrome, a serious disorder which often is fatal, NEVER give your grandchild aspirin unless instructed to do so by a doctor.

A high temperature in a child five years old or younger may trigger convulsions. If this occurs it will be extremely alarming, but unlikely to cause any lasting harm. These febrile convulsions very often are major seizures, during which the child may become unconscious, twitch violently for two to three minutes, then slowly regain consciousness. She will be irritable and may complain of a headache. Shortly after, she will fall into a deep sleep, usually awakening several hours later and seeming to be quite normal. If such a convulsion occurs while your grandchild is in your care, lay her on her side. Don't attempt to restrict movements, and don't force anything into her mouth to keep her from biting her tongue. Doctors say tongue biting is rare and an object placed in the mouth is likely to do more harm than good. Take the child to a doctor as soon as possible following a convulsion, but try to avoid such an episode by controlling the child's temperature with a fever reducer.

Leg Cramps

A common ailment for many small and preteen kids are leg cramps, also called growing pains. These cramps are most common at night, but can happen anytime throughout the day. They can be frequent and quite painful at times and disruptive to everyone's sleep. Doctors recommend stretching the leg muscles and tendons, as in the runner's stretch, to prevent these cramps. If cramps do occur, gentle heat from a heating pad, hot water bottle, or warm bath can help minimize the pain.

CAUTION Danger Zone
In almost all cases, your instincts will warn you when an accident is life threatening or critical. Telltale signs are: acute distress, severe pain, unconsciousness, inability to move part of the body, fever, convulsions, an ashen look, cold and clammy skin, severe agitation, and either a weak or rapid pulse. In these cases, don't wait to see whether there is a change for the better—seek immediate help.

Warning Signs

While most of us are not qualified to diagnose illness, we all should be aware of different warning signs that could signal a problem.

➤ *Waking at night or difficulty falling asleep.* This could signal an illness, or it might be that the child is worried about something, is having a bout with nightmares, or is too hot or cold. If she wakes at night and is distressed, try to comfort her and find out what is causing her to awaken. Avoid giving the child anything containing caffeine (cola, tea, coffee, or chocolate), and make sure her room is quiet and peaceful.

➤ *Persistent crying.* Crying that doesn't stop signals a problem of some sort. Check for fever or other signs of illness. If the child is too young to tell you why he's crying, check for obvious things such as diaper rash or the possibility that he's hungry. If the crying continues and the child seems distressed, consult a doctor.

➤ *Signs of blood in urine or bowel movements.* Blood in excrement is a symptom of several serious illnesses. If your grandchild ever passes blood in this way, call a doctor immediately.

➤ *Skin rash.* A rash can signal an allergy, illness, or infection. Or, it could simply be a reaction to heat or something itchy. Keep an eye on it. If it is accompanied by a fever, vomiting, headache, sensitivity to light, or pain when bending the head forward, consult a doctor immediately.

➤ *Headache.* Headaches in children are seldom a symptom of anything serious, but can be distressing to a child. They usually are brought on by stress, just like in adults. If a headache lasts for more than one day, or if your grandchild suffers from frequent headaches, it's a good idea to consult a doctor.

➤ *Coughing.* Any cough that lasts for more than two weeks should be reported to a doctor. If your grandchild's cough is accompanied by a fever and abnormal breathing, it could signal an infection such as bronchitis or pneumonia. Coughing also can be a symptom of asthma, choking, or a disease such a whooping cough. Or, it could simply mean the child has a cold.

➤ *Listlessness.* If your grandchild is moping around, irritable, and just not himself, he might be in the early stages of an illness. Or, he might just be tired, getting over a cold or illness, or having a bad day. If listlessness continues for more than a day or two, it's probably a good idea to see a doctor. If the child is having difficulty sleeping or has headaches or is losing weight, definitely put in a call to a physician. Ask the child if he can tell you how he is feeling.

➤ *Disruptions in eating patterns.* Kids change their food preferences the way adults change their shoes, but real disruptions are worth a second look. If a child who has been a "good eater" suddenly stops eating or shows no interest in food, be alert for an oncoming illness. If there is no apparent physical reason for her loss of appetite, consider the possibility of depression or another problem. If she has been eating as much as ever and has been no more physically active than usual, but is losing weight, see a doctor immediately. The weight loss could signal diabetes or a thyroid problem.

Drs. Grandpa and Grandma

Caring for a sick grandchild can be a terribly demanding job. Sick kids can get pretty grouchy and demanding. Once they feel a little better, they get bored and impatient. But, caring for a sick grandchild also can give you the opportunity for quiet time together. It's an opportunity to show your grandchild how much you care about him.

Try to make the experience pleasant, but don't shower the child with so many treats and toys that she can't wait to get sick again. Read a book or look at a magazine together. Watch a family show or video while you snuggle on the couch. And remember to always report to parents about symptoms the child has had and any medicine you've given.

Deadly Drugs and Medications

Suzie is taking one of those pesky antibiotics for her latest ear infection, and you're going to have to give her the medicine. You know she's going to fuss and carry on when it's time to open up, and you're tempted to just let it slide for a dose or two. Don't! It is very important that a child takes all medicine prescribed by a doctor. Even if she's feeling better, a course of medicine such as an antibiotic will be most effective if taken in its entirety. Before giving your grandchild medicine, be sure you know:

➤ What the medication is

➤ Why it is being taken

➤ What reactions it may cause, if any

➤ How often it needs to be taken

➤ When it should be taken

➤ How it should be taken (with food, on an empty stomach)

➤ Any items that will react adversely with the medication (other medications, certain foods)

➤ The exact amount to be taken

Catch Their Attention—Not Their Colds

If you tell your grandkids to put on a jacket when they go out so they won't catch cold, you might as well save your breath. Everyone gets an occasional cold—most people within the first year of life. Kids are very susceptible to nasal viral infection between the ages of one and three, but then have a bit of a respite as they gain immunities. They'll usually get more colds again when they start school and are introduced to new types of viruses. Most people acquire more immunity as they get older, and colds become fewer and less severe. But don't expect them to ever end completely.

Caused by one of about 200 viruses, a cold can make life miserable for a few days. There's not much to do but wait it out, although over-the-counter cold tablets, cough syrups, and nasal sprays can offer some relief. Just make sure to follow the recommended dosages and don't give any medicine to very young children, under two years, except on the advice of a doctor. A child with a bad cold should stay at home and rest (for the sake of others as well as the child). Make sure his room is comfortable and avoid the tendency to overheat it. A cool-mist humidifier might make it easier to breathe and keep him more comfortable.

In small children, watch for signs of earache along with a cold. Respiratory infections often travel along the Eustachian tube and cause middle-ear infections. Earaches are painful and should be treated with antibiotics.

Despite opinions to the contrary, you can't catch a cold from sitting in drafts, going without a hat, or getting your feet wet. You can get one from being sneezed on or from ingesting germs from your hands. It is always a good idea to wash your hands frequently and thoroughly with an antibacterial soap, especially when there is a cold in the house.

Although there is no real cure for the common cold, you can make a grandchild more comfortable by:

➤ Providing small portions of nutritional foods that he likes. Chicken soup, the traditional remedy for colds and a host of other illnesses, serves a valuable purpose in treating a cold. In addition to providing good nutrition, the hot liquid helps to clear nasal passages and makes breathing easier. So go ahead and make a pot.

➤ Creating diversions to take the child's mind off a sore throat or stuffy head.

➤ Offering plenty of fruit juices, water, and other liquids.

➤ Reducing stress and anxiety, factors that can actually cause or increase coughing or headaches.

➤ Being attentive and caring.

A bad cold is no fun, but it's an unavoidable part of life. Prepare yourself for a few days of grouchiness while your grandchild is not feeling well, and remember that this too shall pass.

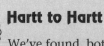

Hartt to Hartt

We've found, both as parents and grandparents, that there's not too much you can do to keep colds from invading your home. We try to get our grandkids in the habit of using their own towels, washing their hands, and staying away from each other if they have a cold. We also keep tissues handy in the house, car, and play areas to avoid wiping noses with hands or clothing. Those packages of pre-moistened cloths are also useful for wiping noses and cleaning hands. Other than these things, we pretty much just cross our fingers and hope for the best.

Nightmares and Bogeymen

Nightmares signal that your grandchild is anxious about something, and this is perfectly normal. Think about possible sources of anxiety: a new house or school, a new baby in the house, even a vacation that has broken her routine can result in anxiety that surfaces during the night. Nightmares often come in phases. Your grandchild may have one every night for two weeks, and then have no more for six months.

Many children experience a variation on the nightmare when first going to sleep. As she begins to doze off, something that bothered her during the day takes hold in her mind and results in this phenomenon. It is believed that these "twilightmares" often arise directly out of something the child has heard or seen on TV. You'd be wise to monitor her viewing carefully. If you suspect your grandchild was disturbed by something she overheard or saw during the day, do what you can to allay her fears and reassure her.

Great Grandparenting

Your grandchildren may resist going to bed if you try to rush them because you're tired and ready for sleep. When this happens, it's time for a compromise. Tell them they don't have to go to sleep, but they must get into their own beds to read, color, or play with a toy. You might allow them to listen to some bedtime music or play with flashlights. This way, they'll be relaxing and getting ready for sleep, and you get some quiet time for yourself.

Another variation on the nightmare is night terrors. Much rarer than nightmares (thank goodness), night terrors are exactly what they're called—terrors. Most children will never have these, and it is even rarer for them to occur often. It is not understood why they occur, but, if your grandchild has one of these, you will find her in a state of neither sleep nor wakefulness. She will not know where she is or what she's doing, but will be terrified of some imagined horror. She may not know you're there when you enter the room, or she might involve you in her terror. Put the lights on and do what you can to comfort her with reassuring words, but don't try to reason. She won't understand. If the terror subsides and she goes back to sleep without ever fully waking, don't attempt to wake her up. If she remembers anything about it in the morning (which she probably won't), just say she had a bad dream.

The goal is to prevent nightmares by addressing anxieties. Try to talk to your grandchild about things that might be upsetting her, and let her know she is loved and cared for. Make bedtime as calm and pleasant as possible, and avoid having her get overly tired. Know, however, that since we can't always know what a child's anxieties are, nightmares probably will occur from time to time. The number one rule, when they do, is to get to your grandchild quickly. Having you there will reassure her greatly, and she'll likely go back to sleep. If she is allowed to become fully awakened by her own screaming, she will be all the more frightened and sleep will be difficult. Leave a small light on in the room, if desired, and assure your grandchild that she is safe in your house and you are there if she needs you. A familiar song might help her to go to sleep.

If you give in to the temptation to climb into her bed and sleep with your grandchild, or take her back to your room for the night, remember that many experts recommend against this. Doing so could set up a behavior pattern that will be hard to break. If you do sleep with the child, either in her bed or yours, make sure she understands it's just for one night, and don't repeat it the next night. Her parents will not thank you if they come home from their mini-vacation to find out their six-year-old expects to bunk in with them that night!

Hartt to Hartt

When our grandchildren occasionally tell us they are afraid at bedtime, we assure them that all is well, but ask what we could do to make them feel safer. Leave the hall light on? Put a night-light in the bathroom? Have the door open instead of closed? Put a special bear or doll in bed with you? We don't advocate lying down beside a child until sleep comes, because it could easily become a habit. But we let each child explain his or her fears, and we counter each one with a simple explanation. We'll open the closet door, check under the bed, and look behind the shades to make sure there are no monsters in the room. The children are reassured by this, and it shows them that we understand their fears and don't belittle them.

The Least You Need to Know

➤ Anticipate that where grandkids go, cuts and bruises are sure to follow. Be prepared.

➤ If you don't already have them on hand, buy a first-aid kit and a medical guide, and get familiar with them.

➤ Know when to treat an injury yourself, and when it's time to see a doctor or go to an emergency room.

➤ Take a sensible approach to treating and coping with the most prevalent of all ailments—the common cold.

➤ Take steps to prevent or minimize nightmares and fears of the dark in young children.

Part 3
Memorable Pleasures with the Grandkids

The things you plan and do during your visits with the grandkids can be memorable for both generations.

It's fun to line up events and activities that you all can enjoy together, but sometimes it's hard for grandparents to know what kinds of plans will appeal to everyone, and be worthwhile and rewarding as well.

This part of the book explains how to find and plan all kinds of activities: those that are recreational, educational, environmental, and festive. Plus, it gives you pointers on where and how to get reliable help and information in advance, if you need it.

Chapter 10

Planning Visits

In This Chapter

➤ Establishing special times for special visits

➤ Planning activities that everyone will enjoy

➤ Are you really ready for this?

➤ Relating to your grandkids

➤ Setting and enforcing house rules

➤ Is one-on-one the way to go?

Time spent with your grandkids should include activities that you all will enjoy. You may not be keen to put on in-line skates and knee pads and zoom around the neighborhood, but neither will they want to sit at the dining room table and learn to play bridge while snacking on mixed nuts. You've got to find some common ground.

Think of things that you liked to do when you were the ages of your grandchildren. Come on, you can think of some. After all, it wasn't that long ago! Maybe you can introduce them to some games you played when you were a kid. Grandkids often are fascinated with what people did back in "the old days." And, in addition to teaching them a new game and having a good time together, you'll be nurturing a sense of heritage—of things passed along from one generation to another.

Use your own ideas, and take some from those included in the following chapters. A little preparation can make for a smooth visit that everyone will remember fondly. Imagination and enthusiasm are essential if everyone is to have a good time, so don't hold back on either. Just relax, and enjoy yourself. We too seldom take time to play and remember all the simple things that are good in this life. Let your grandchildren help you to do that. In this chapter we'll show you how to plan and prepare for a special visit.

Mark Your Calendar

Keep a record of dates that are important to both your grandkids and you. That makes it easier to plan times for visits, as well as to create "themes" for events that might take place. Perhaps the grandkids like to stay over at your house the night before the Fourth of July holiday because your community has a big holiday parade. Or, maybe it's a tradition to have each grandkid sleep over the Saturday before his or her birthday. Wouldn't it be fun to make a special "Just for Fun Holiday" that you and your grandkids observe each year by spending a special day together? Always check with parents before setting a date with your grandkids. Otherwise, they'll be disappointed if the plan doesn't work out.

Once you've determined the dates that you'll get together, send postcards reminding your grandkids of upcoming events. Kids appreciate cards or notes as much as you do, even if they sometimes forget to acknowledge them. Your note will further increase their anticipation and get them excited about the visit.

Pre-Visit Preparation

Where to go and what to do…there are tons of things you can do with your grandkids that are sure to please. Think about places near your home where you'd like to take them. That great park with the swans on the lake. The museum with a real mummy in the Egyptian room. That new playground with the soft ice cream stand right next door. The theater that specializes in shows for kids. Time is sure to be more of a problem than opportunity, so you've got to get organized.

Make a file of all the places you want to go and things you want to do. Gather suggestions from your newspaper's entertainment section, your neighbors, friends, and any other available sources. Once you've got some ideas, make a casual list of everything and anything you can think of that might interest your grandkids. For instance, are any of them at the can't-get-enough-of-dinosaurs stage? Or do they love a hike in the woods? Roller skating? Ice hockey? Trains? At this stage, don't try to arrange it in any orderly fashion, but make your list as complete as you can.

When you've got your file of "Neat places to visit and things to do with the grandkids," and your "Things my grandkids like to do" list ready, you can compare them against each other and see what matches you come up with.

You might get lucky and find out that your local museum will be having a dinosaur exhibit on the weekend your grandson is visiting. Or that, not only is the old-fashioned steam engine railroad going to be running that Saturday two weeks before Christmas, but Santa Claus himself will be riding on it.

Here are some issues to keep in mind as you begin to brainstorm fun projects and plan excursions:

➤ *Scout the territory.* If you want to plan trips to places you haven't been to, it might be a good idea to check them out in advance. That way, if the so-called animal farm turns out to be a couple of squirrels and a goat with a junky gift shop as the main attraction, you won't waste your grandkids' visit by going there. You get the picture, right? You don't necessarily have to visit all the places on your list, but at least make a phone call or try to talk to somebody who's been there.

➤ *Know your limitations.* Rule out any activities that would be too taxing for you or for little ones. A self-guided walking tour of a nature preserve sounds great, but if it necessitates three and a half hours of walking and you'll be taking a two-year-old, it's probably not a good idea. There is nothing like a fatigued and cranky toddler to negate all your good intentions.

➤ *Know your budget.* Plan only events and activities that you can comfortably afford. Don't despair if you have to cross something off your list because of a prohibitive price tag. There are plenty of inexpensive and free activities available. Your grandkids will remember the time you spent *with* them, not how much you spent *on* them.

➤ *Choose age-appropriate activities.* If you'll be entertaining grandchildren of different ages, make sure you plan activities that all of them will enjoy. Make sure to give "equal time" to all.

➤ *Think about what you'll need to take along on each outing.* The walk through the nature preserve, for instance, will require snacks. Probably several snacks. The trip to the museum may call for a camera, and you'll need a diaper bag for the train ride excursion.

➤ *Be prepared for anything.* Plan activities for rainy days, sunny days, indoors, outdoors, day, and night. Make sure you have a variety of ideas, so if the animal farm closes due to torrential rains, you can fall back on Plan B.

➤ *Get others involved.* Note which special activities are for just you and the grandkids and which might include other family members or friends.

➤ *Know what's involved.* You may want to organize your plans by labeling each activity with a code. For example, "O" signals an outdoor activity such as the nature preserve, while "I" designates indoor games at your house, the model train museum, the museum, and so on. An "E" will remind you that there are expenses involved, while "H" could label high-energy sports that will wear you out completely. These codes are just suggestions. Come up with your own so that you can choose activities quickly and easily.

111

➤ *Keep track of time.* If you have very young children, they're sure to get up early and be ready for action long before you are, especially if they know there is something special planned. If they are teenagers, don't make any plans that require getting out of the house before mid-morning. Once they're finally out of bed and have their hair just right, the wildflower walk at the museum will have ended.

➤ *Get your grandchildren involved.* It's all well and good to decide that you're going to have a whopping good time when your grandchildren visit, but you have to let them participate in the planning, too.

Talk to your grandchildren about their interests and find out what they'd most like to do. Tell them the various activities you have in mind and let them choose the ones they like best. It may help to show them snapshots and clippings of the places you have in mind.

Preparing the Premises

If you've already read Chapter 6, then you're familiar with the idea of childproofing your home. There are other things to think about, though, before your grandkids visit. In addition to considering the obvious questions such as "Where will they sleep?" you need to consider things such as providing room for indoor activities, stocking the pantry with kid-friendly foods, and checking your local cable listings to see if you can tune in to their favorite shows.

If you're planning indoor activities such as a craft project or a game night, consider the best place to locate it. The dining room table is a likely choice, but what will happen when you're ready to serve the macaroni and cheese, and the dried flower project you've been working on all afternoon is still spread out, nowhere near finished? And, you don't want the Saturday-night Monopoly tournament located too close to the room where Baby will be sleeping.

Speaking of craft projects and Monopoly games, if these are on the agenda, make sure you've got all the necessary equipment. Are you sure your second cousin returned the game when she borrowed it last spring? If so, did you check to make sure all the pieces are there? It's frustrating to sit down to start a game and discover the dice are missing. If you want to do a craft project, make sure you know exactly what you'll need and have it on hand. You don't want to waste time dragging your grandkids from craft shop to craft shop looking for unbleached muslin.

If you are an information addict who must watch local, national, and world news every night or you'll suffer from withdrawal symptoms, you might want to locate the kid's activity areas away from your TV. Some people get mighty testy when they can't hear what Peter Jennings is reporting, and you don't want to put a damper on your visit with your grandkids by getting cross or impatient with them about a little noise. If your house is small, could you adapt a space in the garage or basement for activities?

Most kids love videos, and there are many good ones for families to watch together. You could visit your local video store and pick out one or two for a movie night. If you're not familiar with recent good family movies, you might ask the clerk at the video store—he or she is sure to know what's popular. But, be sure to check the ratings to determine whether these (or any movies) would be appropriate for your grandchildren.

Include parents in your planning, and let your grandkids have some input, too, to assure that everyone has a great time.

Anticipating the Blues

We know that you're caring, doting grandparents who love your grandchildren dearly. But, that being the case, you still have to accept the fact that for the first few visits the grandkids might not be too crazy about spending the night at your house.

Don't take it personally. It has nothing to do with you. They'd be less than thrilled to spend the night in Cinderella's castle at this point. The first nights away from home without parents are tough for most kids, regardless of where they are.

Talk to parents before the visit and get some ideas on how to make the situation easier for your grandchild or grandchildren. Ask the parents to let each child pack a small bag with his favorite stuffed animals, a few toys, books, and any other necessities. This bag should be separate from the one containing clothing, pajamas, toothbrushes, and other necessities. It may help if the child brings a photo of his parents or his entire family.

Find out about any bedtime rituals, and use them at your house. Is there a favorite tape your grandchild likes to listen to? A favorite story that he likes to read every night? Does he usually take a bath? Watch a special television show?

If a grandchild gets homesick, all you can do is comfort him and try to distract him. Talk about the fun activities you have planned for the next day, or let him think of something special he would like to do. It's your call whether or not to phone his parents (if they can be reached). A chat with Mom and Dad might cheer him up—or the sounds of their voices might make him dissolve into tears. Try to make sure he gets plenty of sleep, as tiredness will only compound the problem.

Don't despair. You might hit the jackpot and get a couple of grandkids who love to sleep overnight at your house and never get homesick in the least. But, just in case, it's best to prepared.

Are You Ready to Cope?

Everything's ready for the grandkids' visit. Except maybe one thing—YOU! Be prepared. It may have been a long time since you had young kids in the house. Can you remember what it's like? They eat differently. They talk a lot louder than you do. They watch weird shows on TV. They get up really early. If they're teenagers, they get up really late. They pull things out of drawers and leave toys all over the place. They get out of your sight very quickly, requiring you to chase them to make sure they're okay. They fall down and cry, want lots of snacks, and whine when they get tired.

Of course, these are all sweeping generalizations that probably don't apply to your grandkids. Your grandkids no doubt will follow the same schedule you do and keep everything in its place. You can skip this section. It's for other grandparents who aren't as lucky as you.

If you do feel the need to read this section, don't let it scare you. Taking care of kids is like riding a bike. It will come back to you as soon as you climb into the seat. But one suggestion: Don't offer to take all three grandkids for a weeklong visit if you've never had even one of them sleep overnight before. You'd just be asking to be overwhelmed.

If you don't live near your grandkids, it might help to visit them a couple of times before they come to see you. Seeing how they live in their house will give you a good idea of how they'll live in yours. That will allow you to gauge how you'll have to adapt your habits to mesh with theirs.

> **Great Grandparenting**
>
> It might take you a day or two to remember just how tiring caring for kids can be. And don't forget how much younger you were when you did it the first time around! Pace yourself. Don't try to go to the park, pitch baseball, and take the kids fishing all in one day. You can't afford to be exhausted the next day when you promised to go boating!

This isn't saying you have to do everything just the way the grandkids do at their house. You're perfectly entitled to expect them to follow your policies. But, it will make for a more pleasant visit if you're all willing to bend a bit.

Once you've decided to invite the grandkids (or have been asked to invite them), ask yourself these questions: How long should I ask them to stay? How many should I have at one time? It probably is smart to start with a short visit, and maybe have just one or two grandkids at a time. If you live far away, however, a one- or two-night visit isn't practical and you might have to jump right in. You could start out by having only one grandchild at a time, or find a good baby-sitter to help out if you think that might be necessary.

No matter what you decide about the number of visitors or duration of the stay, make sure your grandkids know that you are the decision makers, and they'll need to follow your rules.

House Rules

If your grandkids ran wild on their last visit, refused to sit at the table for meals, and pitched fits when you asked them put away their toys—and that was with their parents there!—it's time to set some rules. You can be selective when you make them; it's better to have three or four important rules that are followed than 25 trivial ones that are ignored. But, make sure that rules are established up front and enforced consistently (although they may vary as the grandchildren get older or situations change). Communication is important. Let your grandchildren know from the start what the rules are, and that they're expected to follow them.

Experts agree that kids not only need boundaries, but they also want them. Knowing what the rules are makes kids feel secure and cared for. They are more comfortable when they know what they can and cannot do and understand your expectations. Because kids generally respect rules more if they have some say in establishing them, sit down with them when they first arrive and go over your house rules. Let them express opinions about the rules, but be firm about the ones that are important to you. It may be necessary to allow exceptions to some rules, but you should have the final say.

Of course, even if everyone agrees on the rules, this doesn't mean your grandkids won't test you sometimes by bending them. After all, they are kids. Here are examples of sensible rules you might want to establish and enforce when your grandchildren visit:

We sit down at the table for meals, and no one gets up until he has been excused.

No arguing, hitting, or kicking at the dinner table.

No jumping on beds, sofas, chairs, or other furniture.

No screaming.

Running, bike riding, roller skating, and ball playing are not allowed in the house.

We all respect family members who have special needs—for example, playing quietly when the baby is asleep or older people are resting.

Privacy is respected. No one eavesdrops when someone is on the phone, and no one enters a room without knocking first.

No playing in the flowerbeds or riding bikes on the lawn.

Once the rules are set, discussed, and understood, you can relax. That is, until some of the rules are broken and you have to administer an appropriate punishment. This is a touchy subject, and one that you would do well to discuss with the parents. What is considered appropriate punishment in one home might be considered extremely inappropriate in another.

Hartt to Hartt

Some friends of ours who have eight grandchildren (ranging in ages from 2 to 16) have a "House Rules Agreement" poster, which they keep on the refrigerator. The grandchildren, who all visit frequently, had a hand in deciding which rules were okay, which should be modified, and which were too strict. Some rules have footnotes to indicate which age groups are affected. All of the eight grandkids signed the agreement at the bottom. They all know what is expected of them, and the smallest children are especially happy to be included.

Mess Makers

It's impressive when you think about it. You spent most of a morning one day last week cleaning the den. You vacuumed, you dusted, you cleaned the baseboards. You even cleaned the windows. Everything was in its place and the room looked great. Enter the grandkids...five minutes into the visit and your order has been transformed into chaos. The card table has been draped with the blanket from the couch to make a tent. Cushions from the sofa are stacked into a miniature mountain. Two chairs lie on their sides to form a cage for Brownie Bear. And a roll of toilet paper has been spread across the floor to form a highway for trucks and cars that look as though they've just been in a major wreck.

Unless your card club is showing up that afternoon, don't panic. You should be happy, in fact, that your grandkids have such great imaginations and can entertain themselves without a lot of high-tech, sophisticated props. Their imaginary play will probably keep them occupied for a long time.

If you're concerned about objects getting broken, create a place in your house where it's okay to make a mess. You can use string to show which parts of the room are off-limits and which are open for play.

When the grandkids are done playing, make cleaning up part of the fun. Look around and determine what needs to be done, then play "chores." Write each necessary task on a slip of paper, put the papers in a hat, and let each grandchild draw a chore out of the hat. They'll like the game, and you'll like the results.

TV and Other Media

Some things are a lot more complicated today than they were when you were raising your kids. Sure, there was TV back then, but you had only eight or 10 channels—not 70! If you missed a show you wanted to see, you waited for the summer rerun instead of program-ming a VCR ahead of time to tape it for you. The most trouble you ever got into with magazines (well, other than that one your brother left under the couch by mistake) was with those photos in *National Geographic*. People didn't jog while using headphones to listen to a compact disc.

Times have changed, there's no question about it. Kids have the opportunity to access all kinds of information today—much of which you'd rather they didn't know about. This glut of available information is reason for concern, but not panic. Before your grandkids come to visit, talk to the parents about restrictions and rules they impose on their chil-dren with regard to TV, magazines, videos, music, and computers. Have the children participate in the discussion so they know the ground rules and can't try to get their way later by saying, "Mom and Dad always let me...."

The television is usually the biggest culprit in the "excessive exposure" department. Many statistics cite the vast number of hours children sit in front of the TV screen, watching instead of doing. Experts argue whether TV violence causes viewers to act in similar fashion, or to what degree it desensitizes viewers to real violence. Educators bemoan the fact that kids spend too many hours in front of the tube and too few hours behind a book. A family counselor worries that constant displays of violence on TV give children the impression that the world is more dangerous and hostile than in actuality.

These concerns may or may not apply to your grandchildren. But, if you feel that they're watching too much TV, or you don't like what they're watching while they're at your house, it's within your rights to turn off the set. Be ready for moans and groans, but they'll usually be short lived. If you offer kids a fun alternative to TV (a baseball game or trip to the zoo, for instance), they'll usually quickly forget about whatever they were watching.

Most people concur that television, when used properly, can be a valuable tool for educating kids and adults. Think of some of the wonderful shows you've seen about nature, history, and famous people. And, there is some good entertainment to be found, too. Watching TV with your grandchildren can provide many opportunities to view and discuss all kinds of subjects of mutual interest.

Beware, however, that unless you're watching a public station that doesn't use advertisers, it's next to impossible to shield young viewers from the persuasive commercial messages constantly beamed at them. One media specialist suggests that you give your grandkids a 10-minute "course" in TV commercials (which the parents will most likely appreciate, too). Some pointers to discuss:

➤ Exaggerated terms and claims, which often leave consumers disappointed when the actual product doesn't measure up

➤ The use of repetition to pound suggestions into the viewer's head

➤ Disclaimers (like small print) hinting that the products or services advertised aren't quite what they appear to be

➤ How camera angles and special effects make products look larger or more superior than they really are

➤ Dishonest claims

As you watch TV with your grandchildren, some commercials will just beg for comment, whether positive or negative. Ask your grandkids what they think about the product being promoted. Have they ever used it? Do they like it? Is the commercial sensible or exaggerated?

Television can be used effectively, but it should never be allowed to replace reading. Try a policy of "equal time," where grandkids may watch one hour of TV for each hour they spend reading a book. Studies show that the children who are read to, who have plenty of books available, and who see adults reading in the home are the ones who become good readers themselves. Take your grandkids to a public library and let them pick out some books. Spend some time there so they can get an idea of the thousands of topics they can learn about from reading.

The Internet

There's a seemingly infinite source of information on the Internet. Entire libraries can be accessed from your desktop. You can get weather facts, locations of space shuttles, and a vast amount of information you never even knew existed. It is fascinating, to say the least. Remember though, that your grandkids can access that same vast amount of information from the Internet as you can. While it can save them some trips to the library's research department, it also has the potential to give them information that is inappropriate, at best, and extremely dangerous, at worst. You've probably read horror stories of young girls who have been seduced and run off with men they've met "on line," and similar tales.

If you have a computer in your home with Internet access, ask the parents what their feelings are about their kids using it. Are they allowed to explore the Internet at their own homes? Are there areas that are off limits? There are ways to limit access to certain areas of the Internet, or block access completely if you or the parents wish to. Your grandchildren will probably be fascinated with all the available information, and understandably so. But, if you have any reason to believe that their explorations have progressed past a point that you're comfortable with, pull the plug on your computer and talk to their parents immediately.

Hartt to Hartt

When our grandchildren visit, we put out appropriate books and magazines and think ahead about what videos we'll rent. We also like to play classical CDs (at a comfortable volume). Reading books, listening to music, and watching movies with our grandchildren gives us opportunities to discuss what is contained in each, and to share our beliefs and interests. We feel that the kinds of lessons we want to teach our grandchildren will have more impact through the use of mixed media than through conversations alone.

Party Animals

The days of diapers are long gone. The tricycles and bikes with training wheels were replaced long ago by multi-speed mountain bikes and in-line skates, which appear to have become connected to your granddaughter's feet. The pigtails have been replaced by dangling earrings, and your phone rings constantly when she's in the house. Your little grandchild has suddenly and mysteriously grown up. She's a teenager!

It's common knowledge that raising teenagers can be interesting, to say the least. What do you do if it's become interesting at your house, due to the fact that during your granddaughter's visits with you, she's dating boys you don't approve of and staying out much later than you consider appropriate?

118

Discuss the situation with the parents, preferably well before your grandchild comes to visit. Insist that she follows the same rules concerning dating and curfews while at your house as she does at home. If you are uncomfortable with the rules her parents have imposed, because you think they are not strict enough, discuss your misgivings with the parents. If your granddaughter is unwilling to follow your guidelines, you'd better think about postponing the visit. If she's going to be dating from your home, ask her to let you know ahead of time who she'll be with, where they're going, and when she'll be home. Even though she's a teenager, she's still your responsibility while in your care. Try to meet the people she goes out with.

If a grandchild agrees to follow your rules before her visit, but then defies you once she arrives, you'll be in for a long haul. One expert advises that you deal immediately with small problems by imposing time outs or other appropriate punishments. Big problems, however, need to be dealt with in conjunction with the child's parents. If a teenager tells you she'll be in by midnight, then shows up at 3 a.m., for instance, you could suspend any more dates she had planned during her visit, and make sure she understands the matter will be discussed at length when her parents return.

Should You Go One-on-One?

As a recently retired grandfather, you've got some extra time on your hands these days. The money situation is okay, and you've been thinking lately that you'd like to do something really special with Pete, your only grandson. Pete is already 12, and he's getting involved in a lot of extra activities at school. Pretty soon he won't have much time for those fishing trips you and he have always enjoyed. You've been thinking about taking him up to Canada, hiring one of those planes that flies you into a remote spot, and doing some serious fishing. You hear there are bass up there you'll never see in your area. Pete would just love it. Wouldn't he?

Grandparent/grandchild vacation trips are getting more common. There are a number of commercial travel agencies that arrange intergenerational tours, cruises, dude ranch vacations, and the like. But, give this kind of venture some thought before plunging in. You'll need to ask yourself these questions:

➤ What is my objective?

➤ Is the money I spend any real indication of caring?

➤ Will a special trip force us into a one-on-one relationship for too long a period?

➤ Will my grandchild begin to miss his friends, parents, or siblings at some point during the trip?

➤ Will giving Pete this opportunity cause problems with other grandchildren? Will Pete's sisters resent the attention he gets because he is the only grandson?

A one-on-one visit or trip lets a child pursue his interests with a grandparent without interruption from parents or siblings. If it is likely to cause problems of any sort, however, you might do well to spend your time and money on short, more frequent visits with one grandchild at a time. Schedule activities that you both will enjoy.

If you decide to visit a resort or a family camp, select an environment that won't be too stressful or unfamiliar to your grandchild. While you might find it exciting to go somewhere with a foreign atmosphere, for example, your grandchild might be confused and uneasy.

Climate and weather are also factors to weigh carefully before planning any special trips. That mountain lake in the tour book might look picturesque and inviting. But what does the place offer for a youngster if it's rainy or cold most of the time?

Our advice: Take Pete on a mini-vacation and see how it goes. You can always build on it in a couple of years.

Hartt to Hartt

Many years ago, Marilyn's parents got the idea that a family vacation would be just the thing to help them get to know their grandson Paul. We decided to camp in Big Bend National Park, near the home of Marilyn's parents. We looked forward to the vacation, but nobody warned any of us about August there. The bugs were so thick that you couldn't eat outside without getting a couple in every bite you took. And, our visit to the Rio Grande was steaming! Marilyn's parents ended up renting an air conditioned motel room, where they slept. We all ate our meals there and used it to cool off. The lesson is to be sure you know what you're getting into before you go!

The Least You Need to Know

➤ Choose some dates, such as holidays or birthdays, that are important to you and your grandkids, and arrange for them to visit you on those occasions. Mark the dates on a calendar that you keep posted in a conspicuous spot.

➤ Determine in advance the kinds of activities you can enjoy together—rain or shine, day or night. Give everyone involved a chance to help plan the activities.

➤ Make sure you've considered ways in which you need to prepare for the visit. Is your home ready? Have you thought of the possibility that your grandchild will get homesick? Are you ready for the disruption of your routine?

➤ Set house rules and insist that your grandchildren follow them.

➤ Make sure that any one-on-one adventures for you and your grandchild are thoroughly investigated first and are in the best interests of everyone.

Chapter 11

WHO WANTS DONUTS?

YEAH!!

Food, Glorious Food!

In This Chapter

➤ What and when to feed your grandkids

➤ Creating suitable menus

➤ Making the kitchen a fun place

➤ Following sensible diets—without seeming to

➤ Coping with picky eaters

It's a rainy day and there's nothing to do. The soccer game was cancelled and cheerleading practice called off. The grandkids are amusing themselves by bickering and whining, and you're wondering how the heck you're going to get through the afternoon. Suddenly, a thought occurs. You're planning to make spaghetti and meatballs for tonight's dinner. You were going to get it ready after the soccer game while the kids swam at the neighbor's house, but that activity has been cancelled too. Well, as long as everybody's around and looking for something to do....

Break out the measuring cups. Find the oregano and garlic and defrost the ground meat. And don't forget the Parmesan. We're gonna do some cooking!

Kids of all ages love to help in the kitchen, and working there can provide all kinds of useful information and experience. It's a math lesson (measuring cups and spoons), a reading lesson (what does that recipe say to add next?), and a nutrition seminar (how much fat is in this ground beef?) all rolled into one. It's fun, too. Especially on a rainy day when sports are cancelled and the grandkids have tired of playing Monopoly before lunch.

In this chapter, we'll take a look at good things to eat and more. We'll also find out how to make the kitchen a place where kids can have fun, and why it's called the heart of the home.

What's on the Menu?

What are we having for dinner? When are we going to eat? These are recurring themes when the grandchildren visit, and it's best to have some answers before the questions arise. Mealtimes with your grandkids can be great. They give you a chance to sit and talk (even the most active kids usually will sit long enough to eat spaghetti), and find out what's been going on in their lives.

Mealtimes, however, require a bit of planning. It is best to have set times for meals and stick to the schedule when possible. Or, at least determine what works best for that day and let the kids know when meals will be served. Try to keep eating times close to the children's home schedule, and know what foods they like and dislike. It makes no sense to spend your time and money preparing salmon with Hollandaise sauce if only grandma and grandpa are going to eat it. The first spring asparagus might be a treat that you look forward to every year, but don't expect that the six- and eight-year-olds are going to share your enthusiasm!

> **Danger Zone**
> If your grandkids are vegetarians, do some reading about foods that combine to make complete proteins, possible vitamin and mineral deficiencies, and other issues pertaining to a vegetarian diet.

Likes and dislikes aside, you need to be wary of foods that can cause tummy upsets or allergic reactions. Some of these are pretty obvious: shellfish or cow's milk, for instance—but even grains, egg whites, strawberries, peanuts, and chocolate can trigger allergic reactions in some children. Ask the parents for a list of foods to avoid, and read labels. Some prepared foods may contain these ingredients and will cause allergic reactions. Be sure you have and follow specific instructions from the parents and/or the child's pediatrician about foods that might cause bad reactions.

"Can't We Eat Something NOW?"

When children are impatient for a meal, one of the following reasons might be the cause:

➤ You like to eat dinner at 6:30 or 7:00, but your grandkids sit down at their house at 5:00 sharp. It's now 6:10 and they're starving!

➤ You said the meal would be ready by 5:30. Of course, you didn't know then that your six-year-old grandchild would let the dog off its leash and you'd spend more than an hour chasing it around the neighborhood. It's now 5:30 and you're just starting to boil the water for the spaghetti.

➤ Little Bobbie didn't eat enough at the last meal. Who would have thought he would refuse a peanut butter sandwich because the jelly was strawberry instead of grape?

➤ You know that chicken à la king with your special sauce is their favorite dinner and they've been looking forward to it all day. It seems like you started preparing it soon after lunch, but it's 4:45 already and it's not anywhere close to being ready.

If the kids are really hungry and dinner is still an hour off, give them a healthy snack. A piece of fruit, some popcorn, or a few crackers and a piece of cheese will hold them over until dinner is ready. Or, think about letting them eat the salad that was going to accompany the spaghetti, or giving them a piece of the Italian bread that is part of the meal. That way, they're simply starting dinner early, not ruining their appetites with potato chips or a cookie. And, speaking of snacks....

Safe Snacking

One of the benefits of grandparenting is that you can relax a little bit when it comes to making sure the grandkids are eating their share of green, leafy vegetables and whole grains. Offer them a variety of nutritional foods and trust that they'll survive just fine. When it's time for snacking, try to provide snacks that they'll enjoy, but that also contain some nutritional value. Cut up some apples and put them on toothpicks or kebob sticks with mini-marshmallows in between the pieces. Consider graham crackers with a little peanut butter or string cheese with a pear. Be careful, though, about giving snacks such as grapes, raisins, and popcorn to small children. Foods of these sizes could present serious choking hazards to young children. And, there may be foods that parents don't want their kids to eat for other reasons. For instance, some parents are concerned about the use of pesticides and discourage their children from eating fruits and vegetables that have not been organically grown.

Some other suggestions for healthy snacks follow:

➤ Take the grandkids to the market and let them select tangerines, bananas, nuts, or small cheeses to munch on between meals.

➤ To give fruits more appeal, try freezing bananas, grapes, or apple slices.

➤ Put out small bowls of cut-up, uncooked, crunchy veggies, such as carrots, bell peppers, radishes, broccoli, asparagus, celery, and cauliflower. If they insist on a dip, try some low-fat or fat-free ranch dressing.

➤ Use a blender to make "smoothies," milkshake-like mixtures of frozen yogurt and fruits.

➤ Instead of sodas and sweetened drinks, offer plenty of fruit juices in colorful plastic cups with straws, sometimes mixed with carbonated mineral water.

Snacks can contribute nicely to your grandchild's nutritional needs if you make sure they're healthy. Avoid too many snacks that are high in fat, sugar, and calories, but low on vitamins, such as potato chips, French fries, cookies, and candy.

Happy Meals

If mealtime is one of the few times you'll be able to sit down and talk with your grandkids during their visit, plan to make the most of it. These guidelines will help you assure that meals are as relaxed and happy as possible:

➤ Plan to eat at a time that is convenient for everyone. Figure out when you'll have the fewest interruptions, and when the kids won't be restless and anxious to get out and play. Don't start lunch at 1:00 if the softball game is going to start at 1:30.

➤ Let your grandchild choose a favorite meal or side dish. If you're cooking for two or more grandkids, they can draw lots for meals or for different courses.

➤ Prepare a dish that is unfamiliar to your grandchildren but may intrigue them enough to make them want to eat it. Steamed clams dipped into a little melted butter just might become their new favorite food. If not, have something you know they like available, and enjoy the clams yourselves!

➤ Use show-and-tell to teach your grandchildren how to eat foods that need "special handling," such as artichokes, lobster, or chicken wings—it can be great fun.

➤ Let your grandchildren see you enjoy the food you've prepared and served. Even if it turns out that they don't like whatever it is that you've made, they're likely to give it a try if they see that you like it.

If you can teach your grandchildren to be open-minded about what they eat, you'll be doing them a great service. The world is full of wonderful foods. Kids who restrict themselves to hamburgers, French fries, and applesauce come up big losers in the culinary arena. But, don't make too big a deal about food or use it as a punishment or reward. Food is to be enjoyed, but not used to manipulate.

Hartt to Hartt

Our four-year-old grandson likes to pretend he's as enthusiastic as his grandpa about every one of our menu choices. But we never force the issue if we see him try a bite and then leave the rest. We believe that introducing children to new foods helps them overcome food prejudices and makes their visits to our home more special. Part of the excitement of coming to Grandma and Grandpa's house is trying foods that are new and different. We've found, too, that if children help to prepare a meal, they're more likely to try the food once it reaches the table.

The Joy of Cooking—Together

You spend the better part of an hour in the kitchen making healthy chicken nuggets for the kids' lunch—chicken breast meat, cut up and coated with a crunchy corn flake crust, baked in the oven to avoid fat from frying. The kids will love it, right?. Wrong! They love chicken nuggets, all right. But only if they're deep fried and served in a little plastic fast-food container with French fries on the side. Your healthy version remains on the plates as the kids start foraging for the potato chips.

Your intentions are undeniably good, but perhaps your execution needs some fine tuning. Next time, try consulting your grandkids before you start defrosting the chicken. If they turn up their noses, you know not to waste your time. By consulting them, however, you're likely to get them interested in helping choose their foods, and probably even in helping to prepare them.

Of course, if you don't enjoy being in the kitchen, then spending time there with your grandchildren probably isn't going to be much fun for anyone. But, if you like throwing on an apron and whipping up a new version of a tuna casserole, the kitchen experience can be a pleasant one for all.

Given free reign, most kids would happily plan a menu of potato chips for appetizers, a main course of French fries, and brownies with chocolate ice cream for dessert. If you set some guidelines, however, and help them to understand the nutritional values of food, they just might surprise you. Give them choices from the various food groups, and let them mix and match a healthy meal.

Encourage them to help as much as possible with preparing the food. Explain the value of the foods they've chosen and tell them how the foods grow or where they come from. If the apples are from Washington state and the potatoes from Idaho, show them on a map where those states are located. Getting your grandkids involved with preparing meals can be fun and rewarding for you, and a good learning experience for them. Make sure everyone who wants to be involved has a job to do, and remember there are a number of safety considerations for kids in the kitchen. Some things to keep in mind are:

> ➤ When assigning tasks, make sure they are age-appropriate. A preschooler can wash fruit, tear lettuce leaves for the salad, fetch vegetables from the refrigerator, and carry napkins and silverware to the table. Grade-school kids can cut up fruits and vegetables that don't require too sharp a knife. They can measure and stir ingredients for cookies, and even roll out the dough or drop it

> **Great Grandparenting**
>
> To keep young children away from the hot stove or knives and sharp utensils, focus their attention on other areas of interest in the kitchen. Show them where food is stored. Explain how and where the peppers and the apples were grown. Give them a little bit of cookie dough and a cutter and let them play at making shapes.

125

onto the baking sheets (just don't let them put the sheets into a hot oven without close supervision). Older kids can prepare a portion of the meal by themselves, such as a side dish or dessert. Get everyone to help with clean-up, too.

➤ Make planning the menu and shopping for the ingredients part of the fun for everyone old enough to help. The more involved you get them, the more pride the grandkids will have in the finished product.

➤ Explain the importance of selecting healthy foods: fresh fruits and vegetables, chicken, fish, and whole grains. Even three- and four-year-olds can understand the need for food that is "good for you."

➤ Make it a rule that an adult or responsible young person is always in the kitchen when youngsters are helping out. Establish ahead of time which parts of the kitchen are off-limits to certain age groups and which are okay.

➤ Familiarize young helpers with common kitchen tools and show them how to use them to pare vegetables, weigh and measure ingredients, retrieve pans from the oven, or roll out cookie dough.

➤ A fun game is to blindfold your young grandchildren before they come into the kitchen and let them guess what you're cooking, if something with a delicious aroma, such as bacon, popcorn, roast lamb, chicken soup, or ham. Children get a kick out of associating smells with different foods.

Many kids love to spend time in the kitchen while others couldn't care less. If your grandkids enjoy being with you while you cook, go for it. You'll have many happy hours ahead of you. If they balk at kitchen duty, don't force them. Maybe they're more interested in getting involved with a carpentry project or helping to fix the leaky hose on the washer. Keep food preparations fairly simple so that preparation doesn't become a test of everyone's patience and endurance. Above all, have fun. We live in a country where we are blessed with bountiful quantities and selections of food. We should use them joyfully.

Hartt to Hartt

We add to the fun in our kitchen by using it as a sort of craft studio where we can display and study the remarkable variety of patterns and colors in fruits and vegetables. "Don't you think these layers of circles are pretty?" we ask, cutting into an onion. We open a peach and explain what the pit is. We slice a pear in half to show the arrangement of seeds, or open a kiwi fruit, which has a particularly delicate pattern of tiny, dark seeds. The kitchen table is an ideal place to lay out crayons and sheets of paper on which our grandkids can copy the patterns or draw their favorite fruits and vegetables in color.

Diet Dos and Don'ts

You can tell kids everything you know about good nutrition, but if they see you polishing off a big bowl of Rocky Road with chocolate sauce and extra nuts each night it's going to be hard to get them to join the healthy eaters' club. Make healthy eating a family event, and try to get the parents involved too. Stress the positive benefits of good health (more energy, healthy skin and teeth), without turning food and weight into a moral issue.

There are some good magazines devoted to healthy eating—and many good books as well. Two books you may want to look at are:

➤ *Your Perfect Weight* by Mark Bricklin. This book from Rodale Press contains material from *Prevention* magazine, with chapters such as "Keeping You Kids Slim" and "One Hundred 100-Calorie Snacks."

➤ *Quick and Easy Menu Cookbook* by the editors of *Weight Watchers* magazine. Published by New American Library, this book contains low-calorie recipes for birthday cupcakes and chocolate cookies. And it promises that "children of all ages will love them."

Remember, kids love treats. Instead of denying them an ice cream cone after dinner, give them a cone of low-fat frozen yogurt. They may not even notice the difference. Some other healthy substitutions include:

➤ Graham crackers or ginger snaps instead of chocolate chip or peanut butter cookies. Read the labels to determine fat and calorie content.

➤ Baked potatoes or oven fries instead of French fries. To make oven fries, cut potatoes into wedges, spray with a baking spray such as Pam, salt lightly, and bake until brown and tender. Serve with ketchup.

➤ Whole-grain toast with jelly instead of doughnuts.

➤ Fresh fruit instead of pastries.

➤ Plain popcorn instead of potato chips.

➤ Lean ground beef instead of regular ground beef. The difference in fat content can be significant. Try making burgers from ground turkey meat, too, but ask about or check labels to see what you're buying. If the skin is ground along with the meat, it could contain as much fat as some beef.

➤ Skinless, baked chicken instead of fried chicken.

➤ Fig bars, juice Popsicles, or fruit instead of creamy desserts.

➤ Low-fat milk instead of whole milk and cream.

➤ Vegetable-based soups instead of heavy meat-based ones.

Good nutrition doesn't have to be something kids don't like. Let them find out that a healthy eating plan has room for treats and snacks, and teach them to enjoy preparing and eating good, wholesome food.

Surviving with Fussy Eaters

Two-year-old Sally refuses to eat anything except frozen peas and bread. Her five-year-old brother Robert loves cheeseburgers and ice cream, but trying to get him to swallow a vegetable is next to impossible. What do you do? Make her stay at the table long after everyone else is gone? Forbid him from going out to play because he didn't finish his cauliflower?

Relax! Sally could be eating worse things than peas and bread, and Robert won't grow up malnourished because of his cheeseburger stage. If you insist on punishing them for their eating habits, you'll merely reinforce their behavior by letting them know you think food is worth fighting over. The "clean plate club" is pretty much a thing of the past.

Experts recommend giving children plenty of choices of healthy foods, and letting them pick what they'll eat. Of course, it won't do to stock the cupboards with sugary cookies, cereals, and donuts, but if offered a variety of wholesome foods, a child will generally eat enough to meet his nutritional needs. And, if Robert is going to be eating cheeseburgers and ice cream, make sure the beef is the leanest you can find, and look for reduced-fat cheese. You may even be able to slip some finely shredded vegetables into the ground meat without him ever noticing. As far as the ice cream goes, try some low-fat or non-fat frozen yogurt and be glad he's getting good amounts of calcium.

If you have a picky eater among your grandchildren, don't despair. Most kids go through fussy stages, but none of them starve because of them. Here are some tips to make meal-time easier:

➤ *A little wholesome food will go a long way.* Some kids simply don't need as many calories as others. Give small portions of a variety of foods.

➤ *Avoid using food to punish or reward a child.* This sends a message that food is overly important. Don't insist that he eat everything on his plate, although you should encourage him to try everything.

➤ *Serve at least some foods that you know your grandkids like.* If you make your favorite meal and they won't eat any of it, chances are you won't enjoy it much either.

➤ *Try adjusting the meal hour or avoiding between-meal snacks or sweet drinks.* If children are reluctant to eat or just pick at their food, they may simply not be hungry.

Children should be encouraged to eat healthily and make good food choices, but dinner tables should not be used as battlegrounds. Treat food as something we need to have in order to grow and stay healthy, and something we should be grateful for. But don't make a big issue of the food they eat—or don't eat.

Hartt to Hartt

We learned about the problems of fussy eaters when we were relatively young parents. When our oldest son was five, we were worried because he was small. We took him to our pediatrician to let him hear firsthand that he should eat more wholesome dishes and fewer junk foods. To our surprise, the doctor was very casual about what our son should or should not eat. We were left to enforce our own rules about junk food—if we wanted to—but were assured that our son was within the "normal" height and weight range for his age. This experience helped prepare us for the low-key mealtimes we now enjoy with our grandchildren.

Norman Rockwell or Rocky Horror Picture Show?

We've all seen those Norman Rockwell paintings of families enjoying each other's company at tables laden with scrumptious-looking food. Everyone is pleasant and smiling. You can't imagine that anyone in those paintings is going to suddenly spill a large glass of milk, prompting peals of laughter from siblings and disgusted sighs from parents and grandparents. Certainly, nobody is kicking anyone else under the table or entertaining notions of launching some peas at his sister.

Dining experiences in your home probably won't be 100 percent Rockwell, but they don't have to be horror shows, either. Set some mealtime ground rules so everyone knows what is expected, and then relax.

➤ Discuss table manners and let your grandchildren know they are expected to be polite while at your table.

➤ Allow younger children to leave the table once they finish their meal and ask to be excused. Provide a quiet activity for them and enjoy your coffee in peace.

➤ Place an adult between children who are likely to get into kicking or elbowing matches.

➤ Recognize that you might have to serve as referee sometime during the meal.

➤ Pay attention to requests to pass things. Being ignored frustrates kids and leads to trouble.

➤ Don't allow the radio or television to interfere with mealtimes. It's important to have time to talk to each other and catch up on the events of the day.

➤ Create a calm atmosphere to encourage openness and discussion.

Memory Lane—The Family Meal

Most families plan important events around food. After all, it's part of nearly every occasion. Holidays, celebrations, and simple family get-togethers revolve around meals. There's nothing wrong with making food an integral part of family life. Many memories are hatched around the dining room table, or in the kitchen as a batch of cookies bakes in the oven. Children remember helping to decorate Christmas cookies long after the holiday has passed, and they get a real sense of accomplishment from putting icing on the cup cakes for their birthday parties. As grandparents, you have few better opportunities to communicate with your grandkids than while cooking or eating together.

So use your imagination, ingenuity, and sense of humor, as well as your experience in food preparation, to make memories for your grandchildren. If your heart is in your kitchen, it can't help but become the heart of your home.

The Least You Need to Know

➤ Remember to consider timing and schedules when planning meals. Kids used to eating at 5:15 sharp will not be happy campers if dinner at your house doesn't reach the table until 6:30.

➤ The kitchen is one of the best spots in your home for bonding. There's something about a kitchen that encourages conversation and closeness.

➤ Approach dietary concerns with an open mind, use good judgment to foster wholesome eating habits, and don't get too uptight about nutrition. Nobody ever got scurvy in one weekend!

➤ Don't force fussy eaters and grandchildren who won't clean their plates to eat everything.

➤ Plan mealtimes with the grandchildren so those times will be something you want to cherish, not hope to forget.

Great Games and Super Sports

You've barely gotten your hello hugs before the grandkids are out the front door to play. You hear the garage door open and know that within five minutes the driveway will be strewn with baseball bats and gloves, basketballs, skates, bikes, sidewalk chalk, jump ropes, and other play equipment.

Kids love to play, going from one game to another as the spirit moves them. When they play, they can be astronauts or outer space aliens. They can be meteorologists as they track storm clouds and set up rain gauges, or they can be bakers and bake shop operators at the sandbox. They can be Michael Jordan shootin' hoops on the front driveway, or Dan Marino throwing a touchdown pass in the side yard. They can be explorers, discovering a secret new route through your hedges and into your next-door-neighbor's yard. Or they can be pioneers, gathering berries and acorns to store for winter meals. The world is theirs when children play. They can be whatever or whoever they want.

The mess on the driveway might be a bit daunting, but don't discourage your grandkids from their play. Instead, watch them with wonder and marvel at their creativity and imagination. Pay attention to and encourage their games. If your granddaughter is pretending to be a newspaper reporter, maybe you could give her a notebook and pencil. When your grandson is done pretending to be a dolphin trainer, perhaps you can find a television show relating to dolphins or other sea life. Watching their play can give you insights into their interests.

Playing with your grandchildren can give you insights into other things as well. You'll learn whether they tend to be leaders or followers. You'll see if they are confident or awkward about their physical skills. You'll hear whether they are willing to cooperate with each other's ideas and wishes. And, playing with your grandkids can be a lot of fun.

When's the last time you took off your shoes and waded in the creek, pretending to be a naturalist in search of a rare breed of tiger? How long has it been since you set up an obstacle course in the back yard? Or had a 30-yard-run for a touchdown? Go ahead. Your grandkids will be delighted when you take off your shoes and head for the creek, and so will you. Being an adult doesn't mean you're not allowed to play.

In this chapter, we'll discuss many ways to enjoy fun times with your grandchildren, while encouraging them to be good sports.

Athletic Exploits

If you know your grandson learned to play tennis at summer camp and is gung-ho on the game, by all means schedule him some playing time at the local courts when he comes to visit you. If you play, hit with him or get some of your friends together for a doubles match. If you don't play but have always wanted to learn, ask him if he'd mind showing you some basics. If your granddaughter just passed Level II in her swimming lessons, encourage her to show you what she learned. If you don't belong to a public pool, perhaps you have a friend who has a pool you could use. Tune in on their athletic interests and plan activities around them.

Of course, you have to decide to what degree you'll participate in these outings. Playing a couple of sets of tennis or swimming a few laps is one thing, but skiing down the side of a mountain might be quite another. Be as active as you are comfortable being, but don't force yourself to do things because you want to impress your grandkids or be a good sport.

Here are some sports, fun activities, and fitness programs that grandkids typically enjoy and for which facilities are widely available:

➤ *Sliding, climbing ladders, swinging, and balancing at the local playground.* Young kids love trying out different equipment, so visit different playgrounds when you have a chance.

➤ *Bicycling and tricycling.* Many communities have special paths for bikers, walkers, or joggers. Or, use side roads that have little traffic.

➤ *Informal softball.* If you live in a neighborhood with lots of kids, encourage them to join your grandchildren for a game of softball. Just make sure the kids are approximately the same age or the teams are divided fairly.

➤ *Jogging or fast walking.* If you jog or walk for exercise, take the grandkids who are old enough to keep up along with you. Or, push a little one in a stroller while you get your workout.

➤ *Tossing a ball around at the beach or on the lawn.* It doesn't get any more simple than this, but throwing and catching a ball is always fun and can be done almost anywhere.

➤ *Calisthenics.* Do them indoors if it's rainy or cold outside.

➤ *Roller skating and in-line skating.* If this isn't your cup of tea and your grandkids need some help, you might be able to find a teenager around your neighborhood who's willing to assist.

➤ *Throwing a Frisbee.* This time-honored pastime is even more fun if you have a friendly dog who wants to play.

➤ *Jumping rope.* Teach your grandkids some jump rope rhymes and join in the jumping. It's great exercise.

➤ *Hiking.* Is there a state park or forest near your home? Jump on a trail and enjoy the great outdoors.

If all else fails, you can always roughhouse or play running and tumbling games with small grandchildren. This gives them some exercise and allows them to use up some of that seemingly endless supply of energy. Just be aware that little ones (usually between the ages of two and four) can become overexcited, and that sometimes leads to nightmares. Think about that before you growl and jump out from behind the big chair while pretending to be a bear. You might end up awake in the middle of the night, comforting a frightened grandchild.

Rules of the Game

When you entertain younger grandchildren, choose games at which they sometimes can win. It goes without saying, of course, that you should set the right example by being a good loser. Don't feel that you need to let the grandkids beat you all the time, though. They need to learn how to win *and* lose. Praise not only the winners, but the talents and efforts of all the players.

If you were one of those kids who was always picked last for playground games, you're sure to remember the humiliation that goes along with it. Be on the lookout for kids suffering from the same thing. Maybe you can make those kids be team captains and let them do the choosing. Or, put the names of all the players in a hat and choose the teams that way.

Hartt to Hartt

It doesn't hurt to keep an eye on the youngest players when there's a game in progress. Older kids caught up in the spirit of the contest sometimes forget they have distinct advantages over the little guys who can't run, throw, or hit as well. Also, encourage boys and girls to participate together in whatever games are being organized in the park or the back yard. Boundaries of boy's play and girl's play are practically indistinguishable these days. If your grandson balks at having his sister join in his game of hoops, remind him that he may someday play alongside a girl on his high school basketball team.

Great Grandparenting

If your grandchildren's ages vary, or there are kids of different ages playing whatever game is on at the moment, take a cue from golfers and invent some kind of "handicap" system so the younger children can compete more fairly with the older ones. Be sure to clearly explain how this handicap works and why it's being used.

If you're playing games with grandchildren of different ages, make it possible for all of them to excel in at least one aspect of the action. Kids love to win prizes, so now and then you could hand out a trinket or piece of candy, awarding the best sport, most improved player, or participant who tried the hardest.

If you decide to initiate or set up any kind of contest or competitive game for your grandkids, regardless of their ages, make sure you clearly establish the rules in advance. Having everyone on the same page as far as the rules go will result in fewer arguments, complaints, and tears. It also will get you off the hook from having to make calls that could be interpreted as signs of favoritism. When you play or watch games of their choosing, be sure you know the rules they use before the game starts. It not only will help you to understand what they're playing, but you might also be called on to be referee. Some essential rules you'll need to know are:

➤ How to score

➤ Time limits for the game, or winning score that ends the game

➤ How to play

➤ Number of teams and participants

➤ Prizes to be awarded, if any

➤ Person who will be the referee or judge

➤ Handicaps, if any

➤ Equipment or outfit needed

Don't get too hung up, though, on organizing games and setting rules. The important things are for your grandkids to have some fun, get some exercise, and learn how to get along with other kids. Let them have some freedom to organize their own games and see what they come up with.

Getting the Right Gear

It's so easy when they're little. A baseball game in the yard entails only the essentials. All you need are a whiffle ball and bat and a couple of markers for bases. Enjoy it while you can. As kids get older, their gear gets much more involved. All of a sudden they need four different pairs of shoes for various sports (heaven forbid you would wear your track shoes to a soccer game!), protective equipment, and various and assorted uniforms.

Established Sports

If your grandchild is playing on a team, her coach will tell her exactly what equipment she's required to have. Proper equipment is necessary to protect players from injury, as well as to satisfy team or league regulations. Even young children's leagues these days are into equipment. Take a look sometime at what junior ice hockey players are required to wear. When properly equipped, they look like miniplayers from the New York Rangers! Whether your grandkids are into individual sports such as biking or in-line skating, be sure they have, and use, the proper equipment. Here are some examples of what they'll need for different sports:

➤ *Biking:* Helmets are required by law for children in some states, but every biker should wear a helmet to guard against head injury, especially if riding in traffic. Knee and elbow pads wouldn't hurt for just-learning riders. Older kids who might be riding at dusk or at night will need a bike light and reflectors. Special biking shoes and clothing are available for serious riders, but not necessary.

➤ *In-line skating:* This extremely popular sport—made even more popular by participants like Tipper Gore and JFK Jr.—requires some protection. Knee, wrist, and elbow pads are recommended, along with a snug-fitting helmet. Don't let your grandkids out on skates without the gear. The Consumer Products Safety Commission reports that in 1994 there were 73,000 trips to emergency rooms across the U.S. due to in-line skating accidents.

➤ *Football:* Even mini-mites wear all the gear. This includes a helmet, football cleats, shoulder pads, mouth guard, hip pads, and elbow pads.

➤ *Baseball and softball:* glove, shoes, bat, and ball.

➤ *Field hockey:* shin pads, mouth guard, and spikes.

➤ *Street hockey:* In almost any neighborhood, you'll have a cul-de-sac or wide section of street taken over by kids playing street hockey. Participants wear in-line skates, and the game can get pretty rough, depending on the temperament of the players. In addition to skates, sticks, balls, and nets, shin guards, helmets, gloves, and mouth guards are recommended.

⚡ Danger Zone
CAUTION

Don't let your grandkids talk you into letting them participate in any sport without the proper safety equipment. It doesn't matter whether or not they wear fancy biking shorts, they've got to wear a bike helmet. Improper or faulty equipment, or failing to use proper equipment, has been the cause of many accidents and injuries.

➤ *Basketball:* Because basketball is not (officially) a contact sport, no special equipment except shoes is required. This goes for organized and unorganized play.

➤ *Swimming:* Unless your grandchildren are very small, the only equipment that might be needed for swimming is goggles and a bathing cap. Small children and non-swimmers, of course, require flotation devices, which should also be used for boating.

➤ *Golf:* If your grandchild is taking up golf and you're buying the necessary equipment, get ready to open your wallet. In addition to the clubs and bag, she'll need shoes, tees, balls, and a glove.

➤ *Tennis:* A racket, a can of balls, and a good-fitting pair of tennis shoes are all that's required for this sport.

Once your grandkids (and you) have the proper equipment, you'll be ready to roll, swing, shoot, or score. Experts say that wearing the proper gear can help your performance. You're more relaxed, they say, and not so worried about getting injured.

Parental Permission

If you're wary about whether or not your grandkids should be playing street hockey with the neighborhood gang, consult their parents. Your grandson might assure you that his in-line skating skills are good enough to get in the game, when, in fact, he wouldn't be able to keep up at all and could be putting himself at risk for an accident. Parents should be the ones to judge what sports your grandchild can play when visiting you. Be sure they send along the proper equipment for whatever is on the agenda.

Second Opinion

All your granddaughter has talked about for weeks is the parasailing course she took while she was at the beach on her vacation. She can't wait to do it again. She'll just die if she can't go soon. Parasailing is just the most awesome thing she's ever done. She's even suggested that you should try it—because it's so awesome.

While you're happy that she's sharing her interests with you and even a little flattered that she suggested you join her, there's one big problem. You have no idea what parasailing is, much less why it's so awesome. Your granddaughter just assumes that you know what she's talking about, and you don't want to have to ask your son about it. What to do?

Well, you could head for the beach and ask someone to point out a parasailer. Or, you could confess all and have your granddaughter explain it to you. You could do a little research at your local library or browse around on the Internet until you locate information on this mysterious sport. You might call a sporting goods store and ask if anyone there could explain it to you, or you could continue to bluff when your granddaughter talks about it. Here's a hint: If you choose to bluff, just don't agree to join her for an outing before you know what you're talking about!

The point is, it's always a good idea to be informed about the things your grandkids are really interested in, and you shouldn't be afraid to ask a lot of questions to find out. They'll be flattered at your concern, and you'll get closer to them as you share their interests.

(By the way, parasailing is a sport that requires a person to be hooked up to a contraption that is sort of like a kite, and then to be pulled by a boat across the ocean or bay until he becomes airborne. He then "sails" above the water.)

Safety in Numbers

If your grandchild is about to embark on an adventure without you, make sure he's in good company. Find out the specifics of the planned outing, and make sure you're comfortable about it. Will the hiking club's trip be chaperoned, for instance? Does the friend with whom he's going boating know enough about boating so they'll both be safe? Have you met the friend? Is he reliable? Is there a lifeguard at the beach where they're planning to surf? Know where he'll be and who he'll be with. And make sure your grandchild and his friends realize that if an accident occurs in an area where assistance is not immediately available, it's best if someone stays with the victim while another person goes for help.

Keeping in Touch

If your grandchildren are going to be playing ball at a nearby field, hiking on a local trail, or biking around your neighborhood, make sure they have your phone number and emergency numbers such as police and ambulance. Establish a curfew time in advance, and tell them to call if they're going to be late (just as they would call their parents). If the child scrapes his knee, twists his ankle, sprains his wrist, or is otherwise injured during a game or activity, consult the first aid section in Chapter 9.

> **Great Grandparenting**
> Whenever possible, at least one grandparent should attend sporting events in which one or more grandkids are involved. Take lots of pictures, show enthusiasm during the game, and praise your grandchild afterwards for a win—or for a good try.

Fun and Games

Team sports and other athletic endeavors are great for kids, there's no doubt about it. They teach cooperation, improve coordination and stamina, and are fun. There are other activities, however, that are just as healthy and as much fun for kids. All it takes is some imagination and ingenuity. Here are some ideas:

➤ Organize a treasure hunt indoors or outdoors. Make it simple for preschoolers by hiding large objects in easy-to-spot places. Or, get more imaginative for older children: Create a "pirate map" loaded with hints about where the booty is located.

➤ Get a copy of a handbook on American sign language and teach little ones who are learning the alphabet how to spell their names with signs.

➤ If you have a few tricks up your sleeve, teach each grandchild a magic trick or card trick suitable for his or her age. Then let each child perform the trick in front of the rest of the family.

➤ Have a contest to see who, in 20 minutes or so, can collect the most different-colored leaves, stones, pods, or anything else in quantity and variety near or in your home. (This game is not recommended for younger grandchildren, who might choose to put the collected objects in their mouths. It also won't work if someone has an allergy such as hay fever.)

➤ Hold a storytelling contest in which the most imaginative or funny story wins.

➤ Hold a "crazy picnic" where an actual picnic would be quite unlikely to take place, such as your attic, cellar, or the back of your station wagon.

➤ Hand out copies of a world map and play "travel"; let each grandchild select a place to go, and mark the route from your house to the place. Afterward, ask your grandchildren to explain why they picked their destinations and what they expected to find there. This game gives you a wonderful opportunity to discuss other cultures and geography—as well as learn a little bit more about your grandchildren's hidden interests.

➤ Let children enjoy body painting, by drawing on one another with foaming bath paints and then turning the hose on themselves.

➤ Set up an obstacle course in which players earn points for running down a marked line past a moving sprinkler without getting wet.

➤ Show everyone how to make invisible ink by dipping a paintbrush or toothpick into lemon juice or vinegar and drawing or writing a message on a piece of paper. When the paper is placed against a light bulb, the secret messages will mysteriously appear.

➤ Make a big "fish tank" with a scatter rug or bathroom rug. Have the kids draw fish on heavy paper, cut them out, and attach paper clips to them with glue or tape. Make "fishing poles" from sticks with string and refrigerator magnets taped to the ends. When the fish are scattered on the rug, "go fishing" and see who can "catch" the most fish in five minutes.

➤ Explore treasures in the attic with your grandkids.

➤ Pull out some old photograph albums and have your grandchildren try to guess the identity of the people in the pictures.

➤ Introduce children to dancing, which can become a tradition, as well as part of a fitness program. Even infants and toddlers can participate while being held in your arms, in cadence to a waltz or polka.

> **Great Grandparenting**
> You can plan a joyful—and useful—diversion for grandchildren ages six and up by entering them (along with yourself or another adult) in a charitable walk for a worthy cause. Check the local newspaper or ask your church, local charities, or chamber of commerce about upcoming walks.

As you can see, the possibilities for play with your grandchildren are limited only by the boundaries of your imagination. Even a walk around the block can be made special by looking for unusual objects or counting the number of red cars parked in the driveways.

Games We Used to Play

Play used to be much less organized than it is today. Think back on when you were a kid, or when your children were young. Organized sports didn't start as early in childhood. Games weren't so competitive, and you had only one or two pairs of all-purpose sneakers. Share with your grandchildren some of the games you used to play and how you would amuse yourselves. Show them a special tree you used to climb, or your favorite fishing spot. They'll be fascinated to hear your stories and picture you as someone who was once the same age as they are. Here are some games that might bring back memories:

➤ *Kick the can* is a game that goes back many years and requires nothing more than a can, which is kicked as far as possible by one of the players. The person who is "It" has to bring the can back to its original place, while the others all hide. The "It" person then has to find the hiders, but if one of them darts out and kicks the can without being tagged, the process starts all over again.

➤ *TV tag.* If the person being chased can think of the name of a TV show and yell it out before he's tagged, he gets a reprieve from being "it."

➤ *Pick up sticks.* Slender, plastic sticks of different colors are dropped onto the floor, and then picked up, one by one, without touching any of the other sticks. When the player moves a stick other than the one being picked up, her turn ends.

➤ *Cat's cradle.* A game for two players in which one player creates intricate patterns with a long, continuous piece of string that is stretched tight in the other player's hands.

139

➤ *Capture the flag.* Each member of two teams has a handkerchief or scarf. The object is to capture all the handkerchiefs of the other team without getting tagged while doing so.

➤ *Ringalevio.* After each member of one team has found a hiding place, the other team goes in search of its opponents. Captured opponents are brought to a "den," which is guarded by a den warden. Members of the hiding team can try to rescue their captured teammates by running into the "den," shouting "Ringalevio," and taking the teammate out of the den with them. All this must occur before the den warden tags the rescuer.

If the descriptions of these games bring back memories, go ahead and teach some of them to your grandkids. For complete rules on these and other children's games, both current and time-tried, look for a copy of *Hopscotch, Hangman, Hot Potato and Ha Ha Ha, A Rulebook of Children's Games.* The book is written by Jack Maguire and published by the Fireside division of Simon and Schuster.

Exploring the Exciting

Is there something exciting and adventurous you've been wanting to do for a long time, but for one reason or another just haven't gotten around to it? Perhaps you've been meaning to do that whitewater rafting trip, or the overnight canoeing excursion. How about the deep-sea fishing trip you've been thinking about, or the two-day camping get away?

If one of the nation's most illustrious grandparents, former President Bush, could manage parachuting at the age of 73, even the sky's not the limit. If you have older grandchildren, now is the time to recruit them as accomplices on a grand adventure.

What's available? The following are just a few of dozens of adventures that older people and kids alike can enjoy at modest expense and in many locales:

➤ Kayaking along rivers, on lakes, and along ocean inlets and bays

➤ River rafting, which ranges from gentle floats down smoothly flowing rivers to shooting the rapids and whirlpools

➤ Scuba diving along underwater reefs or snorkeling in clear waters

➤ Camping by packhorse, and cooking breakfast at dawn along mountain trails

➤ Hot-air ballooning over the countryside with two or three others

➤ Spelunking—exploring deep caves and caverns—with a guide who will take you safely to any lengths and depths you desire

➤ Whale watching from small boats in the open ocean, and getting close enough so you can almost touch them

➤ Helicopter-hopping for high-mountain skiing—doing it yourself or just going along for the ride and the view

➤ Cruising in an old-fashioned schooner, reminiscent of the way people traveled in the last century

➤ Participating in an archaeological dig in which you may actually find and classify valuable objects from antiquity

➤ Going aloft in a motorized hang glider or ultralight plane, where the piloting is done for you but you're free as a bird

These exotic adventures may or may not be for you, but they're fun to think about, aren't they? Even if your idea of an adventure is taking a picnic to the park, make the most of it. The time you spend having fun with your grandchildren is priceless.

Raising—and Praising—Good Sports

As much as we want our grandkids to do well in their athletic endeavors, we have to realize there's more at stake than the win-loss column. It's far more important that the grandkids learn good sportsmanship than it is that they complete a perfect season. They must learn how to win gracefully. They also must learn to lose. We are a competitive society, where we're taught to strive to be the best. We need to teach our kids that second or third, or even last, is sometimes okay—that as long as they've done their best and had a good time doing it, then the game was well played.

You can set a great example every now and then by playing a game that a grandkid can win, and being a good loser when he does. If your grandchildren see that you've had a good time and don't mind losing, they may not feel as frustrated or resentful when they fall short of the winner's circle. We do children no favors by teaching them that winning is the only goal. We need to instill a healthy competitive spirit in our grandchildren, but not to the point of where they see losing as a calamity.

> **Great Grandparenting**
> Let your grandkids see true sportsmanship by renting a videotape of some Special Olympics events. If you've never seen a Special Olympics games, it is a heartwarming and uplifting experience. People with various disabilities compete in athletic events, with the understanding that to win is good, but to not win is fine, too. Everyone wins because everyone has a good time. There is laughter and happy tears, and everyone watching gets a real lesson in sportsmanship.

The Least You Need to Know

➤ Make sure everyone knows the rules before you start a game.

➤ See that your grandchildren have the right clothing and equipment for the sports they play.

➤ Revive some of the classic games of days gone by and let everyone enjoy the fun.

➤ Praise good sportsmanship. Instruct your grandchildren to be good losers, as well as courteous winners, in competitive sports and games. Remember that they are instructed by your example as well as your words.

Chapter 13

All Around the Town

In This Chapter

➤ The fun of eating out

➤ Enjoying the big screen

➤ Meeting the animals, one by one

➤ Roller coasters and Ferris wheels

➤ Shopping spree glee

➤ Initiating sensible rules

Many neighborhoods are microcosms of the greater community. You have homes with people of all ages living in them—from babies to the very elderly. You might have a grocery store, a church, a school or two, and a park. Some neighborhoods are more diverse, with apartment buildings, restaurants, nursing homes, and shopping centers. There probably are a great many aspects of life within a few blocks of where you live. We often take the things we see each day for granted, passing by the homes and buildings without really thinking about who and what are inside of them.

It's never too late to take a good look around your neighborhood and larger community, and your grandkids are the perfect ones to accompany you. Kids are extremely curious, and always anxious to see and learn new things. By exploring your neighborhood together, you and your grandchildren will have fun and get a better feeling for all that lies beyond your doorstep. This chapter explores some of the ways in which you can use your neighborhood and your community to broaden your grandchildren's perspectives of the world around them.

Neat Treats and Eating Out

Somewhere in the realm of restaurants is a compromise between fast-food joints and the kind of places you go when you want to dress up a little and enjoy a nice dinner and a glass of good wine on a Saturday night.

Unless your grandkids are older, able to sit still for an hour or more at a time, and appreciate good food, there is no reason to take them to your Saturday night spot. It's just asking for trouble and nobody will have a good time. Besides, most kids will vote for fast food every time. It's understandable, really. They've known since they were two years old that the place across town with the golden arches not only has tasty French fries and milk shakes, but you get a toy with your meal and when you're done eating you can take off your shoes and jump into a pit filled with colorful plastic balls.

It's a pretty sure bet that if you spend much time at all with your grandchildren, sooner or later you'll end up ordering a cheeseburger with the works at one of these popular places. If your waistline can't tolerate the cheeseburger, fries, and milk shake diet, don't despair. Most fast food places offer healthier alternatives to burgers and chicken nuggets—salads, grilled chicken sandwiches, soup, and baked potatoes (hold the sour cream, please). Besides, most nutritionists say if you normally watch what you eat and get sufficient exercise, an occasional cheeseburger is perfectly okay. Just skip the secret sauce and don't make it a habit.

If possible, don't let your grandkids get too firmly entrenched in the burger, fries, and cola habit, either. Childhood eating habits evolve into adult habits, and a diet overloaded with fat, salt, and sugar is bound to cause trouble down the road. Fast food, with its extremely high fat and calorie content, is surely partly to blame for the growing number of overweight kids in our country. Of course, few six-year-olds travel on their own to the nearest fast-food place and order up a couple of burgers and shakes to go, so.... fast food has its place, as long as that place isn't your dining room table too often.

This leaves us to figure out something in between fast and refined. Fortunately, there are many new restaurants cropping up that are a couple rungs up the ladder from fast food and do a good job of catering to kids.

TGI Friday's and Applebees are just two examples of national chains that cater to kids. They provide balloons, special menus, fun drinks, and crayons. Getting your food takes longer than in a fast-food place, but there are many diversions and the waitstaff generally goes out of its way to keep little ones happy. Older kids and adults like these restaurants because they offer a lot of choices, and little ones can still get their hamburgers. Nearly all these restaurants offer high chairs and booster seats, and some even provide baby food for the youngest members of the family.

Far more families dine out regularly nowadays than used to be the case. If mom and dad both get home from work at 6 p.m. feeling tired and rushed, and there's nothing on the stove, it's a big temptation to run down the road for a little dinner instead of dealing with it themselves. Restaurant staffs recognize this and make their establishments as family friendly as possible.

Hartt to Hartt

We've found a great alternative to the limited menus and too-familiar atmosphere of fast-food restaurants—diners. They offer wide menus, including breakfast at any time of day, at prices rivaling those of the fast food places. The diners we frequent have vending machines with a variety of little prizes, which fascinate any child able to drop a quarter in the slot. Even teenagers can enjoy a diner, since many have jukeboxes with a wide selection of popular music.

You and your grandkids might also enjoy a trip to a regional museum or craft exhibit hall that has a restaurant or cafeteria. They can make your dining excursion even more interesting because there's something to see as well as to eat. If there's a gift shop on the premises, (as there usually is), you may want to establish in advance that each grandchild will be given a specified amount of money that can be used to buy something, or take home for the piggy bank.

When you have grandchildren in their teens who live nearby, dining out is a great opportunity to spend some special time with them. Set up a date in advance, since teenagers' schedules these days rival those of major corporate executives. Your grandchild will appreciate being singled out for a "grown-up" outing.

Pick a restaurant, or let her pick one, that is quiet enough so you'll be able to talk to each other comfortably. Teenagers often are more open with grandparents than with parents about things they're feeling or problems they might be having. Psychologists say this is because grandparents are less threatening to teens than parents are. Grandparents are not as likely to judge, and can detach themselves more from the child's situation than can a parent.

So, pick your kind of place and put the kids in the car. Dining out with your grandkids will be a memorable experience.

A Night at the Movies

Ahhh, the big screen. There's something almost magical about sitting in a darkened movie house, munching on buttery popcorn and staring up at that huge screen. You get a real feeling for the scenery, the people, and the action when it's all bigger than life and right in front of you. Even in these days of video stores, when we can rent and watch three movies a day in the comfort of our own living rooms, the big screen can be very appealing.

It's natural that you'll think about taking your grandchildren to see a movie. You want them to have the theater experience, complete with the popcorn and Raisinettes. You look forward to seeing their expressions as they intently watch the film, and to talking about it with them afterwards. Besides, taking in a movie is enjoyable for you as well as them, and it sure can be a lifesaver on a rainy Saturday.

Be forewarned: Movie outings can be quite different from the serene vision you have of your grandkids quietly watching the film as they willingly share a box of popcorn. If your grandchildren are very young, they might not be able to sit through the whole movie, no matter how much they like it. Some kids just aren't programmed to sit down for more than 20 minutes at a time. Or, they may be able to sit still, but not keep quiet. There are few things more annoying when you've paid big bucks to see a movie than having the kids behind you jabber away all through the last half hour of the film.

Other problems you could encounter when going to the movies are long ticket lines, inadequate or remote parking (especially on weekends), overpriced tickets (you might want to cash in a CD before you take a bunch of grandkids to a movie, especially if you're planning on buying popcorn, too!), the glut of junk food available in the lobby, previews that might not be exactly what you want your grandkids to see, and a small grandchild who gets scared or upset over some aspect of the film.

You can avoid or minimize these disagreeable hurdles by following these tips:

➤ Select a theater with adequate parking. If you can't park close to the entrance and there's more than one adult along, drop off the grandkids and an adult at the door and find a spot wherever you can.

➤ Go to a matinee or early evening show that is likely to be less crowded.

➤ Go on a weekday rather than the weekend, and preferably closer to the beginning than the end of the week if you can. Movies tend to be less crowded at these times.

➤ If you are budget-minded, check the theater listings for discounted shows or special prices for seniors and kids. Many areas have second-run theaters that feature not-brand-new movies at prices much lower than first run.

➤ Take along your own snacks if you're not into movie theater popcorn (it was cited as a very unhealthy snack by the food advocacy group Center for Science in the Public Interest, and it is expensive). A small bag of pretzels for each child, or some grapes in a sandwich bag would be healthier choices and still give kids something to munch on. Check first with the theater management, though. Many have policies against bringing your own snacks.

➤ Most previews have the same rating as the featured movie. For instance, if you take your grandchildren to a G-rated movie, the previews should be rated G as well, however, you could wait in the lobby until the movie credits start to roll, provided the theater isn't crowded and you're certain there'll be seats open inside when you go in.

If you misjudge a movie and it turns out to be too scary or intense for your grandkids, simply get them up and leave the theater. They might be reluctant to tell you that they're uncomfortable, because they don't want to be labeled as babies or spoilsports. As the adult, it's your call whether the movie is appropriate or not for your grandkids to see. If you do leave a movie, perhaps you could substitute another treat: a cone at the ice cream shop or a trip to the video store for a movie that everyone can enjoy.

Hartt to Hartt

Our youngest son and his wife took our pre-school grandsons to a made-for-kids movie. They assumed the movie content was appropriate for little ones, since that's who it obviously was aimed at. The "bad" guys were fascinating to the grandkids, and since seeing the movie, they've acted out its violent parts many times. The movie's central character had a tragic ending that upset the boys, and they've asked their parents several times if something bad might happen to them, too. Their parents had been looking forward to taking the kids to the movie, but were upset at the results. Next time, they'll do a little more homework beforehand.

A Day at the Zoo

Just about everybody loves animals, especially children. So if there's a zoo nearby, plan a visit. This kind of trip is particularly valuable if your grandchildren have never had a close-up view of elephants, giraffes, zebras, bears, and tigers.

We use the term zoo in a very broad sense. Zoos can include animal farms and parks, aquariums, aviaries, bird and animal sanctuaries, wildlife refuges, and other places where animals can be seen in native or simulated habitats.

Danger Zone
To preserve the natural-habitat look, many zoos and wildlife parks use moats instead of bars and fences, and some are not entirely tumble-proof. Tell your grandchildren they are never to try to touch or feed the animals. You and your grandkids will do well to maintain a healthy respect for the size, strength, and speed of all animals.

Many modern zoos, aquariums, and wildlife parks show animals in natural-habitat exhibits. These duplicate the animals' true environments as closely as possible, even to the plant life, trees, rocks, and earth underfoot. Visitors can actually see entire habitats, such as the African plains or the arctic tundra. These places can provide exciting, educational opportunities for kids, as well as a lot of fun.

Plan your zoo trip in advance. Too many people simply pack the kids in the car, take them to the gate, and rush on through for a helter-skelter tour that is tiring and inevitably boring. Without any guidance, small children quickly lose interest and are more attracted to the candy stands, toy animals, and soda machines than to the elephants and tigers. To assure that your zoo trip will be a success, take these tips from a "Zooper Granny" who has made no less than 20 enjoyable trips to man-made wild animal habitats:

➤ Make a trial run before taking your grandkids to the zoo. Use a zoo map to make notes of your impressions.

➤ Visit all the exhibits, and rate each one on the map for its potential interest to your grandchildren.

➤ Make notes of the time required to see each exhibit without having to rush.

➤ Plot your route, indicating exhibits you'd like to skip (but keep in mind that a child might want to stop at one or two you are passing by).

➤ Figure out how to bypass the more commercial elements that may divert little eyes, such as vending machines and gift shops.

➤ Plan on making rest stops. Also plan to have lunch at a time when the canteen or cafe won't be crowded.

➤ Get a colorful folder or zoo map for each grandkid to look at before your outing.

➤ Borrow a few books about wildlife parks, zoos, and animals before your trip. Share the books with your grandchildren.

➤ Consider renting a video on wildlife and habitats to watch with your grandchildren, either before or after the zoo trip.

➤ Tell your grandchildren about the exhibits and let them choose the ones they most want to see. If the zoo is large, you may not be able to cover it all in one visit, so knowing what they want to see will help you plan the trip.

➤ Schedule your visit for a weekday instead of a weekend, if possible.

➤ Try to arrive early and leave early. You may need to leave sooner than you've planned if the grandkids get tired or restless.

➤ Encourage the children to ask any questions they might have if they see one of the keepers taking care of an animal. These dedicated workers know the animals as individuals and can tell you their ages, what they eat, where they came from, and what makes them healthy or sick, happy, or sad. It's fascinating to watch a keeper communicate with an animal.

➤ When you return home from the zoo, talk to your grandkids about which animals they like the best and why. Try to give them some additional information about their favorites, and encourage them to do some reading about them. If you enjoy photography, take some photos of each grandchild in front of his or her favorite exhibits. Put the best ones in frames and present them as mementos of your trip.

Great Grandparenting

If no zoos or wildlife parks exist within easy driving distance, you can often find other kinds of animal habitats that would appeal to children—at least the younger ones. These include farms, large pet shops, humane societies, and botanical gardens, which often have native animals, birds, small reptiles, and fish to add action and interest to some of the plant exhibits.

Early visits to zoos and wildlife parks can be the start of a wonderful relationship between your grandchildren and nature. Children should be taught early in life to respect wildlife, and to become familiar with animals and their habitats as a means of better understanding the world around them.

Other Educational Outings

Okay. We've been to restaurants, the movies, and the zoo. Where else can we take the grandkids? Relax. There are plenty of choices of places to visit that you can feel good about and your grandchildren will enjoy. Look for programs that are instructional, mentally stimulating, creative, and out of the ordinary, as well as fun. Here are a few suggestions to put you on the right track:

➤ Historical landmarks or buildings with architectural significance

➤ Plays and musicals, whether contemporary or classic

➤ Art exhibits and showings

➤ Festivals or fairs that feature crafts and activities of other times or cultures

➤ Outdoor tours of nature preserves, geological formations, or endangered environmental settings

➤ Anything with animals, such as dog shows or equestrian events

➤ Archaeological digs and restorations

➤ Scientific displays

➤ Re-enactments of historical events or activities of the past. National parks and historic sites often have people in period costumes doing things like blacksmithing and candle making

➤ Musical presentations, chorale groups, and symphonic arrangements that differ from the music with which your grandchild is familiar

Be careful to select programs and performances that are suited to your grandchild's age and interest level. If your grandson eats, breathes, and sleeps trucks, take him to the exhibit of antique trucks that will be at the fairgrounds this weekend. If your granddaughter is wild about ponies, take her to the horse show. But don't insist on taking your grandkids to something in which they have no interest, just because you think it would be educational. You'll simply end up alienating them even more from whatever it is you're trying to encourage.

Hartt to Hartt

When Max was three, he developed a keen interest in dinosaurs. His father and grandmom took him to the local museum. There was sand to play in, and a rabbit and snake that you could touch! Max liked everything he saw, and the dinosaurs were the best of all. But most amazing was the discovery he made at the foot of the escalator: a life-sized tyrannosaurus Rex. Seemingly on cue as the escalator descended, Mr. T-Rex moved his head and let out a great roar. Max stood for several minutes, looking up at and talking to his new friend. When it was time to leave, he asked if he could stop by to say good-bye. Now about to turn five, Max is asking for lots of dinosaur books for his birthday.

Rollicking Adventures: Amusement Parks

The Wildcat. Greezed Lightnin'. Texas Cyclone. The Beast. No, these aren't the names of wild animals or natural disasters. They are some of the world's most spine-tingling roller coasters. Teenage grandkids or even younger ones might beg you to take them to an amusement park to ride on something that twists them sideways, turns them upside down, and soaks them with water. Should you or shouldn't you?

The amusement park decision depends primarily on your mental fortitude. Seeing small grandkids on big, scary rides can be extremely disconcerting. Certainly, the big headline rides at major theme parks and local, permanent amusement parks are well engineered, continuously inspected, and safe for any rider who follows safety instructions. The same might not be true, however, for the rides—even seemingly mild ones—at those country fairs and carnivals that appear out of nowhere on Wednesday and are gone without a trace before you wake up Sunday morning.

So if your grandchildren pester you to go, what do you say? Whether you're cautious or adventurous, your first response should be, "Let's ask your Mom and Dad." If it's okay with them, then it's up to you to decide.

If you do decide to amuse them at a park, here are a few tips to make your trip fun and safe:

➤ Beware of water rides when you have little ones in tow. Small children might scoop up the water (which is likely to be pretty dirty), or they could fall in.

➤ Watch out for rides that jerk and yank the rider around; they can cause serious neck and muscular injuries. And make sure your grandkids follow the rules about keeping their hands inside the ride at all times.

➤ Know where the first aid station is located before going on a single ride—just in case.

➤ Buy each child an allotment of tickets in advance in order to avoid using up a week's worth of grocery money on rides and other amusements. Make it clear that each child can choose any combination of rides until the tickets are used up. Or, look for discounted tickets to the larger parks. Grocery stores, banks, and schools sometimes offer dollars-off coupons.

➤ Tell the children that you will determine which rides they can and cannot go on, depending on their ages and physical capabilities. Always follow the park's guidelines concerning size and age.

➤ Take along your camera. Amusement parks can be great backdrops for amusing pictures.

If you go to an amusement park, be ready for a long and tiring day. Once kids get inside the gate, they'll want to make the most of it. Many parks provide picnic areas and lockers if you want to take your own lunch along, and many have free water or musical shows. Take advantage of these offerings. Sitting to watch a dolphin show is a great respite for kids and adults who have been roller coastering and Ferris wheeling all morning.

Amusement parks can be great fun. Just be sure everyone observes the rules. If it's a hot day, a backpack with some plastic bottles of water frozen the night before and placed in a plastic bag to avoid leaking will be welcomed. Take some pretzels or crackers along in case somebody starts asking for lunch when you've barely finished your second ride.

> ### Hartt to Hartt
>
> We love to take our kids to amusement parks because we get to act like kids right along with them. But an amusement park is one of the most expensive places we go with our grandkids, no matter how hard we try to watch what we spend. We have a large and a small park nearby, and our grandkids were starting to expect that every summer visit would include a trip to at least one of them. We solved our problem by making it clear that a trip to the big park would be the main event of the summer, and we'd skip the small park. We mark the date on the calendar and anticipate it all year long—just like Christmas!

Shop 'Til You Drop

Some kids love to shop, while others hate the thought of it. If your grandkids are in the affirmative category, you can include them on your shopping trips or even schedule special trips with them. Most grandparents love to buy for their grandchildren, so shopping can be a real treat for both of you. Just make sure the kids understand ahead of time what type of items will be considered for purchase, and warn them of any price limitations you plan to set.

It might be fun to head to a hobby store to buy materials for a project you'll work on together the next day, or to the video store to choose a movie you'll all watch together that night. Many communities now have "dollar stores," in which most of the items are sold for $1. These stores offer a great many things that kids love (toys, knickknacks, and gadgets). Give them a dollar and let them choose what they want. Just leave plenty of time; it may take a while for them to make their choices. Most kids also love the escalators and elevators found in department stores, and malls often have special events that kids like. Of course, a stop by the pizza or ice cream stand will go a long way toward making your mall trip a hit!

Before taking grandkids into a store or mall, make sure they understand that they must stay by your side. It is very easy to lose sight of small children in crowded store aisles. Tell them what to do just in case one of them does get lost. For older children, designate a place where you'll meet in the event you become separated. Younger kids should be instructed to seek out a cashier, sales person, or security worker to help them. Make sure they know who these people are.

Some children tend to get wild when they get into a store, so it's a good idea to do a little preliminary training. Try playing "department store" at home by walking through rooms and showing your grandchildren how to look but not touch. And just to be safe, keep them all away from the china and crystal department!

If your grandchildren dislike shopping, don't force them to do it. It will make for a miserable time for you and for them. Unless something is desperately needed at the moment, don't make an issue out of a shopping trip.

When you get to the store, be specific about the area where you're going to shop rather than wandering all over. It's a good idea to have a list of items you're looking for. Let your grandchildren help you make out this list and suggest what would be fun to buy.

Making New Friends

When your grandchildren come to visit, you naturally want them to meet your friends and neighbors, and have your friends and neighbors get to know them. You're proud of your grandkids—how well they're growing up, how nice their manners are—and you want other people to be able to see this, too.

Don't overdo it. Children are sensitive enough to get quite uncomfortable from too much attention and fawning, and they may get the impression they've been invited mainly so grandma and grandpa can show them off a bit. They might even look upon your friends and neighbors as silly characters and snicker at them behind their backs.

You certainly want to cement relationships and motivate your grandchildren to be friendly and outgoing. The best way to do this is to let them meet people in a natural, casual way.

Relatives

If you have other family members who live nearby, by all means let them get acquainted—or better acquainted if they've met before—with your grandchildren. You might invite them for a picnic or potluck supper. Just keep it low key and don't make a big deal about it.

Neighborhood Kids

Introduce your grandkids to neighborhood children their age. For the first couple of visits, make sure they have something to do together. Supply a board game, take them swimming at the beach, or get a video they'll all enjoy. Shy children, who may appear tongue-tied if forced to carry on a conversation, often become very animated and outgoing if there's some kind of action to beguile them.

Older Children

Don't risk a mismatch and possible conflict by thinking that you can bring children of different ages together in some kind of mutual hobby or pastime. This works only if the older child is engaged as a sitter and will be supervising some activity for a brief time.

Your Doctor

If a young grandchild needs medical attention for any reason, don't make an issue of it. Simply say, "I have to go to the doctor and you can go along with me. Maybe she can look at that rash on your arms that has been itching so badly." In that way, the doctor will not seem like a threat, but just a friend of granny and grandpa's.

An Educator or Coach

If the visit is long enough that you decide to give your grandchild swimming or tennis lessons while she's at your house, make it a point to introduce the instructor as a friend who is going to be helpful. Often, youngsters balk at the idea of taking lessons, feeling that they have to work rather than play, or be graded and perhaps fail. If you make the coach or instructor seem more like a friend than a teacher, your grandchild may be more excited at the thought of taking lessons.

Hired Help

If you happen to have somebody around the house—working in the yard, painting the garage, or fixing the porch steps, for example—your young grandchildren may be curious about what's going on (sometimes to the point of being pests). Let them ask a few questions about the job if they want to, but quickly divert their attention to something else, such as a ride in the car or a walk to the park.

Waiters and Waitresses, Barbers and Trash Collectors

> **Great Grandparenting**
>
> The old saying, "Actions speak louder than words," is one you probably learned as a child. You now are in a position to teach the same sentiment to your grandchildren. While what you say is important, it is your own behavior that will have the biggest impact. If they see you being rude or impatient with a sales person, they might emulate your tone of voice and body language.

Children are likely to get special attention at restaurants, at the barber shop, or just around the neighborhood. Teach them to be polite, respond to someone who speaks to them, and not giggle or make silly remarks about the person they're meeting. Teach your grandchildren that every occupation is important to society, and briefly explain what workers in various jobs do. You should let your grandchildren see you being friendly and courteous to a variety of workers: the gas station attendant, sales person, letter carrier, and delivery person. While you are concerned about how your grandchildren act in public, remember they're watching you for indications of what their behavior should be.

The Least You Need to Know

➤ Make eating in restaurants both a pleasure and a learning experience. It can be a good way to help grandchildren learn how to eat a variety of foods, and can make them more aware of their manners, too.

➤ Ensure that movie-going is a happy experience by checking the nature of the film and planning ahead of time.

➤ Before taking small children to a zoo or wild animal farm, visit it yourself and come up with a plan for a future trip there with your grandkids.

➤ Plan a trouble-free trip to an amusement park by getting permission from the parents first and observing all safety rules once in the park.

➤ Make a shopping trip fun by letting your grandchildren help plan where to go and what to buy, but don't force them to shop if they don't like to.

➤ Introduce your grandchildren to neighbors and other people in your life in a natural, relaxed way.

Chapter 14

Enjoying Mother Nature

In This Chapter

➤ Creatures of streams and wetlands

➤ Birds, butterflies, and other things that fly

➤ Secrets of the forest

➤ Oddities of nature

➤ The joys of gardening

It might be yucky. It might be icky. But, if it crawls around the yard, through the garden, or under the porch, kids just have to check it out. If it runs or hops, so much the better. It can be a shocking sight to see a little boy standing transfixed as a bright orange sala-mander crawls up one arm and down the other, but he'll think it's great. Frogs are held in such high esteem that they can't be left outside, but must be brought in the house to be examined and shared. A sunfish from the local pond is as thrilling a catch to a child as a giant sailfish is to a deep-sea angler. A baby bird left untended by its mother underneath a tree requires round-the-clock care, and a rabbit in the backyard might be something to talk to or even give a name to.

Kids seem to have an innate love of nature. Just look at their books. How many of the ones they like the best are written about animals, bugs, or fish? How many of their favorite videos feature mischievous dogs, cats, dolphins, or pigs? Take a kid to a creek and let him look for minnows, tadpoles, and crayfish, and it's practically guaranteed he'll come home happy (and wet). Watching a worm's slow progress as it crawls across a sidewalk after a rain has made many a child late for school, and even a garden slug is a thing of, well…fascination to kids.

Fostering your grandkids' interest in nature, or nudging them toward a greater interest is easy. Given the opportunity, nearly all children will respond with curiosity and delight to the world around them, particularly if you present it in a positive and interesting way. If you already have an affinity for nature, you will love sharing it with your grandkids. If you don't know much about nature, or the mere thought of toads and lizards is enough to send you running back to your needlepoint or woodshop, this chapter will give you some workable suggestions on how to make flora, fauna, and the animal kingdom enjoyable for both you and your grandkids. Who knows, it might even transform you into an amateur naturalist.

Seeking Strange Creatures in Wet and Boggy Places

Many people pass a pond, lake, or marsh every day with little appreciation for the complex life cycles existing within. In Henry David Thoreau's *Walden* (his account of two years spent in relative isolation in a cabin on the shore of Walden Pond, near Concord, Massachusetts), he writes "A lake is the landscape's most beautiful and expressive feature."

The seemingly still waters of a pond or fresh-water marsh form a miniature world that may not be high on your "must see" list, but is fascinating to children and a wonderful example of nature's intricacies. These habitats, known generally as wetlands, are natural wonders. Their plants provide food, security, and housing for a variety of fish, tiny shellfish, amphibians, insects, and spiders. Once left pretty much to the whims of real estate developers, wetlands are now—for very good reason— protected and heavily regulated.

Inhabitants of a typical pond might include frogs, tadpoles, dragonflies, diving beetles, newts, snails, ducks and geese, three or four species of small fish, clusters of frog's eggs, caddis flies, snakes, and many kinds of larvae. Among the most common plants are water lilies, grasses, ferns, and countless roots that poke their way underwater to nourish the vegetation along the banks.

Entire life cycles can be observed within a watery space no larger than your living room, constantly changing with the seasons and the variations in weather from periods of drought to spells of heavy rains.

If you like the idea of pond exploration and have a suitable pond nearby, by all means plan to visit it with your grandkids. Look it over before you take them to make sure there's a place with firm ground where they can stand and probe into the water with a long-handled net. You all might be very surprised at what you find.

Watching Winged Wonders

If wetlands aren't your cup of tea, look upward instead. No matter where you live, you'll be able to find a variety of birds to captivate your grandchildren. Go to your library or bookstore and get copies of children's books describing the kinds of birds native to your environment. Study them with the children and make a list of the species you're likely to see when you explore the surrounding woods and grasslands. It won't be long until they're pointing out the differences between finches and warblers, nuthatches and chickadees.

> **Great Grandparenting**
> Carefully scoop up some pond water and pour it into a bowl. Look at the water through a magnifying glass after the sediments fall to the bottom. You'll see delicate weeds, insects, larvae, and other tiny water creatures. Show your grandchildren how to use the magnifying glass to inspect them more clearly. This is a great way to teach your grandchildren about nature and, perhaps, interest them in science, too.

You often have to go no further than your backyard to see a robin's nest filled with bright blue eggs or a mother wren feeding her young. A bird house, even a small wren house, is great fun because it allows you to watch the birds busily flying in and out with materials gathered for building their nests. A walk in the park might give you opportunity to see a dozen different kinds of birds, and if you can get into the woods, the possibilities are even greater. If you're lucky enough to live near areas well known for bird watching, such as a sanctuary near the beach or an area along the migratory paths of hawks and other raptors, take advantage of the viewing and also of the knowledge of other bird watchers or staff people.

When observing birds in flight, ask each child to describe their flight patterns—soaring, gliding, diving, darting, or circling. Have them notice which ones like to fly alone and which prefer to fly in flocks.

Try to correctly identify the species you're watching, using a book or picture cards if necessary. Once you're all sure what you've seen, mark your sighting in a notebook; see how many entries you can accumulate during the children's visit. A couple of decent, but fairly inexpensive, binoculars will go a long way toward making your grandchildren feel like real ornithologists. Consider giving sturdy, reasonably kidproof ones for a birthday or holiday gift.

If your grandchildren are old enough, schedule a bird-watching expedition for dusk. Birds are busy at this time of day, and, if you're lucky, you might spot an owl or some bats coming out for dinner. Older grandchildren also may want to expand their searches and observations to bees, butterflies, dragonflies, moths, and even flying squirrels if these are commonly sighted near your home.

In conjunction with your bird watching, visit a nature museum or aviary where your grandchildren can study birds in more detail. Some parks and forests sponsor programs on birdwatching or other topics concerning birds.

Hartt to Hartt

In the spring, we like to play the "nest building" game with our grandchildren. We take a mesh bag (such as the kind that onions come in) and tie it to a low-hanging tree limb. The children weave short pieces of yarn, string, grasses, cloth ribbons, and strips of newspaper into the mesh—not too tightly, but just enough so that they stay in place. Then we watch. In a matter of hours, birds ready to build nests will fly off with everything we've made available. It's fun later on to try to find nests made from some of our "building supplies."

Exploring the Woodlands

Woods are meant to be explored, and even a small stretch of woodlands will reveal some amazing wonders of nature. A walk in the woods is a great way to explore local animal and plant life, and it's a relaxing form of exercise for you and your grandchildren. Before you go, fill a backpack with a magnifying glass, pocket knife, glass jar, scissors, tweezers, and a pad and pencil.

Here are some things to look for and do as you walk along a woodland trail:

➤ If you see marching ants, track them to see where they go.

➤ Poke the soft core of a rotting log on the ground, and observe the tiny inhabitants who quickly crawl out to see who's invading their home.

➤ Look for a spider web that appears to be unoccupied. Toss a speck of leaf gently against the center of the web, and watch how quickly Mr. Spider appears from nowhere.

➤ If you find a tree stump that has been sawed, have the grandchildren count the rings they see. Teach them that the number of rings determines the age of the tree when it was cut.

➤ Similarly, to determine the age of a pine tree, count the number of circles of branches from bottom to top. A circle is grown each year of the tree's life.

➤ Cut some needles from a pine tree. Scrape them and have the grandchildren feel the sticky substance inside. This is what nourishes evergreens during the winter, even in the coldest weather.

➤ If you walk in the woods after a fresh snowfall, look for animal tracks; have the children sketch the tracks, life-size, on the pad. Later you can identify them with the help of an animal book or a scout handbook.

➤ Find a maple tree with seeds that have two wings and look like tiny helicopters. Play a game to see who can toss them in the air and make them "fly" the farthest.

➤ Did you know that big rocks are insect "apartments"? Turn over two or three and let the children count the number and types of insects under them. Most common are ants, centipedes, beetles, slugs, and caterpillars.

➤ Use the jar and tweezers to collect samples to bring home for further study.

Anyone with an appreciation for nature will understand the importance of respecting and preserving it. While nature is intended to be observed and enjoyed, it is never to be exploited or taken for granted. While pointing out the wonders of the wetlands and woods, teach your grandkids to appreciate the precarious balance between man and his natural surroundings. Explain how easily the balance of nature can be upset by the careless actions and thoughtlessness of humans. Tell them how oil spills and other forms of pollution, overdevelopment, mining, and other factors have put nature in an extremely compromised position in many areas of the country.

Remind your grandkids to leave natural areas in at least as good condition as they found them. This means no litter and no trampled or broken plants or branches. Request that they do not make any extremely loud noises to startle animals and birds, and tell them never to disturb animals' homes. If you turn over rocks to examine the insects under them, return the stones to their original spots instead of leaving them on the pathway. Observe, but never disturb, an animal in its natural setting, especially one with her young. Always make sure your nature spot is not private property where you could be chased off—or worse.

Flora and Fauna

If you think a tree is a tree and a flower a flower, you'll need another trip to the library or bookstore. But if you have a basic knowledge of plants, by all means go ahead and share it with your grandkids. Look at the different kinds of trees in your yard, park, or the woods. Do a quick count and see how many varieties you can find. Look at the differences between the slender birch trees and the magnificent old oaks. If you're lucky enough to get into the woods in the springtime, take along a book identifying wildflowers and see what kinds you see. Jack-in-the-pulpits, violets, May apples, skunk cabbage, bloodroots, and wild lilies abound in many areas and are interesting to identify.

While you're teaching about plants and flowers, be sure to mention the not-so-friendly ones such as poison ivy, oak, and sumac and prickly plants such as berry bushes and nettles. You'll do your grandchildren a great service by teaching them early on how to identify and avoid these booby traps of nature. Make sure they know they should never eat anything they pick in fields or the woods (even berries) unless there's someone along who is qualified to positively identify wild foods. Under no circumstances should they ever eat wild mushrooms unless identified by an expert.

Camping Out

If you're thinking about taking your grandkids camping, you certainly deserve congratulations for your initiative. On the other hand, you might want to have your head examined. Camping is one of those experiences that can be really great—or really awful. A clear, starry night around a crackling campfire, enjoying each other's company and the sounds of the night before you crawl into a cozy tent to snuggle with your grandkids and enjoy sweet dreams is a memory to last forever. Unfortunately, so is that of rain dripping through your tent and onto your face at 3 a.m. as your grandson wakes up screaming from a bad dream, induced by too many s'mores and ghost stories around the campfire. While you may be able to find some humor in the latter scenario a couple of years later, it very likely could forever more squelch your desire to head into the woods. Before you think about camping with your grandkids, consider the following factors:

➤ Their parents' attitude toward such a venture

➤ Your physical condition and endurance

➤ The ages and capabilities of your grandkids

➤ The kind and amount of backpacking equipment you have, or would need to buy or borrow

➤ Your knowledge of camping (pitching tents, building fires)

➤ Your familiarity with the areas and trails you intend to traverse

➤ The weather and climate

Great Grandparenting

If you want to impress a grandchild with your knowledge of nature, play the "crocus game." When you find a crocus blooming with its petals open, cover it with your hat. These flowers are sensitive to light and dark, so after a few minutes, when you remove your hat, the petals will be closed tight. Then, as the sun reaches the crocus, the petals will open up again. Presto!

If you're an inexperienced camper, it's probably not a good idea to go out alone with your grandkids. Consider taking along a friend with more experience who could teach you the ropes. If you decide you're not ready for camping out in the woods, take some day hikes or pitch a tent in your backyard for a trial run. That way, when the rain starts dripping onto your face and your grandson wakes up screaming, you can simply move inside for a smooth finish to a rough night.

Beings You Wouldn't Believe

They're creepy. They're crawly. They're some of nature's oddest creatures. And, they're available for viewing to anyone who makes an effort to find them. Kids tend to be more intrigued and less put off by some of nature's oddballs than adults are, so give them a treat and introduce them to these weird and wonderful creatures. Some to look for are:

➤ *Praying mantises.* These strange-looking insects are long and slender, with spiny forelegs that often are held together, as if in prayer. If you find one, take some time to watch it, as they are quite fascinating. Their color lets them blend in nicely with their surroundings, where they lie in wait for prey. Moving extremely quickly, they grab their dinner (usually other insects, although some of the larger species have been known to munch on small animals) with their strong legs and devour it. These critters have some bizarre habits, such as the female eating the male after or even during mating. Praying mantises are protected in some areas, so warn your grandkids not to touch them or try to catch them.

➤ *Toads.* A close relative of frogs, the skin of toads is dry and warty looking instead of smooth and moist like that of their cousins. Many people think toads are ugly, and fear they'll get warts from handling them. Kids everywhere can verify that you don't get warts from playing with toads, and they're great fun to watch as they hop around. Toads are beneficial creatures, as they catch many kinds of annoying insects with their long, sticky tongues.

➤ *Bats.* The only mammals that actually fly, bats want nothing more to do with you than you do with them. They will not fly into your hair, nor attack you. It is a great experience to sit quietly by a lake at dusk and watch as bats come out for dinner. Starting with just a few swooping over the water to get mosquitoes, there soon will be dozens of them darting this way and that above the water. Some people are spooked by bats and can't stand to be near them, but consider the important role bats play in insect control. Some bats eat fruit, and these can be quite large. And, there is the vampire bat, which occasionally bites a human (usually when the person is sleeping) and sucks its blood. Generally, however, vampire bats prey on cows and horses. And a person bitten by a vampire bat will not turn into a vampire himself, although rabies would be a concern. Mostly, though, bats hang around (upside down) all day and mind their own business, catching bugs at night.

➤ *Walking sticks.* This strange-looking insect has no wings, and looks so much like a stick that it usually goes unnoticed. It has long antennae and moves very slowly. Either green or brown, they live on leaves and are quite harmless, though odd.

➤ *Spiders.* With the exception of the few that are poisonous, these are among the most wonderful and useful inhabitants of your backyard. Their ingenious webs catch many insects that spread disease and destroy flowers and vegetables. Watching them at work can be mesmerizing.

Great Grandparenting

Early in the morning when the dew is on the grass, have your grandchildren look for snails. If they find some, put them in a glass jar with damp soil on the bottom. They can watch the snails climb the sides. The snails will happily live there if fed leaves, petals, and dead insects, and they may even give birth. Make sure to ventilate the jar, keep it slightly moist, and out of the sun.

➤ *Daddy longlegs.* With their tiny bodies and long, long legs, plus the tendency to sometimes fall off a wall and onto people, these critters can be a little disconcerting. But their reassuring name and unusual appearance make them appealing to many children. Don't be alarmed if your grandkids like to have them run up and down their arms—they're harmless.

Nature, Nature Everywhere

Once your grandkids have discovered nature, they may want to do more and more study and exploration. Sea animals such as whales, sharks, and dolphins are very popular with many kids, and you may be able to locate an aquarium near your home where they could view some of these creatures. If you live near the ocean, consider a whale-watching expedition for older grandkids. Deer are plentiful in many areas (to the point of being a nuisance in some places) and can be viewed easily if you know where to look. State parks and forests sometimes rent cabins that are perfect for fledgling naturalists. You get the benefits of being in the woods and close to nature, with a little more comfort and security than tent camping. If you're very lucky, you'll be able to show your grandkids all kinds of critters—raccoons, skunks (not too close, please), deer, and various birds. Who knows, maybe even a bear will wander into camp!

Nature is all around us, and teaching children to appreciate and respect it is giving them a lifelong gift. Regardless of whether you're near the beach, mountains, lakeshore, desert, banks of a stream, or a park in a city, there are countless opportunities to explore and discover the world around us.

Hartt to Hartt

We have a vacation house on a lagoon where the yard is covered with pebbles instead of grass and there are very few hardwood trees. Our year-round house, on the other hand, is surrounded by gentle hills and small patches of woods with many different trees and shrubs. Our grandsons love to come to the vacation house and our "regular" house, because they know that, although different, each place offers chances to explore nature. There are ducks, herons, sandpipers, and lots of water and sand to play in at the summer house. The year-round house offers rabbits and squirrels, a variety of birds, and big trees to climb. Each expression of Mother Nature has its appeal.

How Does Your Garden Grow?

If you've got a plot of ground, you can have a garden. It can be a big area or small, sunny or shady, wet or dry. If you don't have a plot of ground, you can still have a garden. Herbs, flowers, and even vegetables can be grown in pots and boxes and provide the same satisfaction as an in-ground garden. If you're bound and determined, you'll get something to grow.

Beware, though. Gardening comes with a warning: Once you start, you may find it hard to stop! Your little plot might grow larger each year, giving you less and less yard for other uses. You may begin to spend more and more hours outdoors, forcing you to postpone polishing the silver or cleaning out the basement. You could get so hooked on gardening that you spend the better part of the winter scouring seed catalogues and planning your beds for the spring. Grow lights suddenly appear in your basement and you're planting your own seeds to get a jump on the growing season.

If you're a gardener, or a prospective gardener, plan to include your grandkids in your efforts. Little ones love to pull up weeds, sprinkle thirsty flowers, and pull the first red tomatoes from the vines.

In addition to providing you and your grandchildren with something to do together, learning about gardening will be educational and fun. It's a great opportunity to plant a seed, watch it sprout into a spindly seedling, mature into a full-grown plant, bloom, and then die with the first hard frost. A complete life cycle, there for the watching.

Schools have long recognized the educational value of gardening—hence those Styrofoam cups with the marigolds or sunflowers sprouting out of them that children carry home each spring. Nursing homes and rehabilitation centers also tap gardening as a means of recreation and therapy for residents. It is relaxing, rewarding, and beneficial.

Grandparents who don't have yards, or even patios large enough for boxes or pots, can look to indoor gardening as an activity to share with grandkids. Don't limit yourself to common houseplants. Plant a box of cooking herbs to put at a sunny window, or buy a lemon tree to coax into bearing fruit.

If you do have space outside and your grandkids visit often, consider letting them have their own little garden. If you show them how to prepare the soil, plant the seeds, and maintain their plot, they'll be able gardeners by the end of the season. Let them pick their own seeds or plants, but make sure that whatever they choose is suited to their garden site.

Sunflowers are great fun to grow. You can even make a sunflower house if you have enough sunny space in your yard. Plant sunflowers in a square, with morning glory vines next to each sunflower stem. As the morning glories grow, they'll climb up the sunflower stems. When they get high enough, pull the morning glory vines across the top of the sunflower square to the other side, creating a "roof" on the house. When the vines wither and the sunflowers droop, harvest the sunflower seeds for the birds (that is, if the squirrels don't find them first).

If your grandkids will be helping with your garden, the most important thing to teach them is which plants are weeds and which are plants you want. It could ruin your day to come out some morning and find them enthusiastically "helping" by pulling out all your prized columbines. Once they can identify weeds, let them go to work. Buy them each a cute pair of gardening gloves to keep at your house, and perhaps one or two kid-sized gardening tools. Some smaller watering cans are helpful too, because the large ones, when filled, get too heavy for small children to carry. Of course, even better than watering from cans is sprinkling flowers and vegetables with the garden hose. Playing with the hose is great fun on a hot summer day or evening. But remember that plants should not be watered while the sun is beating down, because the sun will scald them.

Once the garden matures, let the grandkids cut some flowers or pick some vegetables to bring into your house, give to a neighbor, or take home to their parents. This reward will reinforce the pride they'll feel for the job they've done.

Just a note on gardening safety: Keep all sharp tools away from small children, and make sure all pesticides and other garden chemicals are safely out of reach.

Once your grandkids have enjoyed a season or two of gardening with you, don't be surprised if they start showing some of the signs: a keen interest in the seed section at the local supermarket, a need to check out gardening tools in the hardware store, and a tendency to sit by the fireplace while the snow falls outside, browsing through seed catalogues.

The Least You Need to Know

➤ Use a nearby pond or marshy area as a marvelous learning laboratory for youngsters who are unfamiliar with wildlife or who want to learn more.

➤ Acquaint your grandchildren with birdwatching to heighten their powers of observation.

➤ Use a woodland as a down-to-earth classroom for teaching about insect and animal life.

➤ Teach your grandchildren that strange-looking creatures are often interesting and not necessarily harmful.

➤ Share with your grandkids the many joys and benefits of gardening, either outdoors or indoors.

Chapter 15

Happy Holidays

In This Chapter

➤ Having happy, stress-free holidays

➤ Creating new traditions

➤ Buying appropriate toys

➤ Avoiding spoiling your grandkids

➤ Making birthdays meaningful

➤ Planning for equal time with all

A grandmother's diary, December 23: "I've been especially looking forward to this Christmas and now it's just two days away. The whole family will be together for Christmas Day, at our house, of course. Janie, our youngest, and her family are even coming in tomorrow afternoon and staying over. I'm making beef stew and those flaky biscuits for dinner. Emily, the newest grandchild, is almost a year old now and just starting to walk. With that red, curly hair of hers she's going to look just so precious in that green, velvet dress I found (on sale, even!). I can hardly wait to get the camera out.

"I've gone to extra trouble with the decorations this year because I really want everything to be beautiful. Won't the grandkids love my nutcracker collection! Jack said I shouldn't put them by the fireplace because they'll get broken, but I think they'll be fine. The little ones will be too busy playing with their new toys to bother with the nutcrackers. I've got the grandkids' gifts all wrapped (I don't remember buying so much), the Christmas dinner menu is finalized, and I even know what I'm going to wear. Let the holiday begin!"

A grandmother's diary, December 27: "It's two days after Christmas and I'm still trying to figure out what went wrong. Oh, it was nice. But, it was so noisy, and I really didn't get a chance to talk to anybody because I was so busy trying to make sure everything went smoothly. Janie's plane was late, and by the time they got here on Christmas Eve the stew was stuck to the bottom of the pot and the biscuits were cold. The grandkids were completely wound up and two nutcrackers were broken before Christmas even got here.

"It was nice on Christmas Eve when the grandkids finally got to sleep (at almost 11 o'clock!) and Jack and I had a little time to talk with Janie and Steve. But, there were all those presents to put under the tree and we all knew we'd better get some sleep because Christmas morning would be starting very early.

"Jason and Emily were up at 5:57 a.m. and the day was underway. Between the presents Jack and I had for them and those their parents had shipped ahead of time, they sure had a load of toys. They rushed through opening them so fast, I can't remember what they had. I'm not sure they knew either. By the time the rest of the family came over at about noon, I was already exhausted. Everyone said dinner was good, but I hardly remember eating it.

"A third nutcracker got broken Christmas Day. (I guess Jack was right.) By about 6 p.m. the grandkids were fighting and whining. To make everything worse, Janie and Steve had a fight in front of everyone about Emily's behavior when she refused to put on the dress I bought for her. It was terribly embarrassing. I was never so glad in my life when I could finally get into bed that night. Next year we're going to do things differently!"

Special events and holidays are supposed to be joyous occasions, but all too often, they end up like the one described above. Holidays and other events often turn into stressful occasions, with everyone harried and wondering what went wrong. When you set extremely high expectations, like the grandmother whose diary we just read, you risk being disappointed. Few things turn out as perfect as we'd like them to be. Perhaps it would have been better to take some shortcuts. Have everyone bring something for dinner, or not worry so much about the decorations. And, yes, Jack was right about the nutcrackers.

If you can remember a birthday party that ended with three of the grandchildren in tears, or a Thanksgiving where your daughter and daughter-in-law argued about who-knows-what, or that night during Hanukkah when your lovely dinner was ruined because the oven didn't work properly, then you know firsthand the stress that holidays can induce. This chapter explores some of the holidays that your grandchildren love (and you want to love), and how to maximize the fun and joy while minimizing the stress.

Half-Time Holidays

As much as we look forward to holidays, they can turn into very long days. If it is feasible, you might want to consider a family get-together that lasts for only part of the day. Be imaginative. How about an Easter brunch instead of starting with an egg hunt at noon and ending with dinner at 6 p.m.? Or a special birthday breakfast for the 10-year-old twins? A shorter time together is likely to be more relaxed and fun. Participants will be less tired, and you'll know that you'll have time to clean up and regroup when the celebration ends.

If half-time holidays are not practical because your family is spread apart geographically, you'll need to be creative. When you're planning to visit your son and his family for four days at Christmas, you might want to consider staying in a hotel or motel instead of his home. Of course, you'd want to spend as much time as possible with your son and his family, but you would have the option of leaving when everyone gets cranky and tired. This arrangement also gives your son and daughter-in-law some "down time" with their kids.

If your son and daughter-in-law insist that you stay with them, try to separate yourself from them and your grandkids from time to time. Take a walk or read in your room for an hour to let them regroup. They'll have things to discuss that don't involve you, and they may feel that they're boring you if they must talk about such things in front of you. Be helpful, but not hovering. Help out the parents by taking the kids off their hands for a while. Perhaps take them sledding or ice skating, or for a drive to look at Christmas lights.

If everyone comes to your home for holidays, make your expectations clear ahead of time. Perhaps you'll arrange to prepare dinner for everyone each night, but leave it up to your children to fix breakfast and lunch for themselves and the grandkids. Make sure you have plenty of easily pre-pared foods on hand and let everyone have what they want. That way, you won't be spending all day in the kitchen, or doing other things you don't want or need to do.

You won't enjoy the holiday or the chance to be with your family if you're resentful about all the time and effort it requires. If you simply don't feel up to having the "big holiday" at your house this year, make your feelings known. Traditions change, and sometimes it's necessary to start new ones. Let a daughter or son take over Hanukkah this year, with the understanding that you'll have Thanksgiving at your house next year. It's not fair to anyone if you force yourself to host the holiday events and then end up grouchy and miserable.

Great Grandparenting

Make holidays more memorable, and more anticipated, by reminding your grandchildren of the happy times on that day in past years. Throw in a bit of humor and remind them of the lighthearted calamities that took place, such as the time the puppy ate the birthday cake. Perhaps you could make a photo album of past celebrations of a particular holiday to share with them.

When Your Traditions Aren't Theirs

Almost every family has some time-honored traditions. Maybe you have a special candle that you light at each person's birthday, or a special Thanksgiving meal that hasn't been changed for 40 years. Maybe it's a Fourth of July picnic started by your grandparents and now in its fifth generation, or the Easter egg hunt in your backyard that you initiated when your children were toddlers. Traditions can be cherished rituals that give a family depth and character. Someone called them "the fingerprints that identify your family from others." But, as your children start their own traditions with their spouses and kids, conflicts could crop up if you're not willing to be flexible.

You might be disappointed when your daughter tells you she and her family won't be coming for Christmas Eve this year because they're going to the candlelight service at their church. Instead, try to be grateful that she and her family are starting their own tradition, which will be meaningful to them for years to come. Perhaps they'd be delighted to have you join them, and a new tradition will be started.

If you can't help but feel a little left out, plan some special things with your grandchildren and create your own traditions. Take the kids ice skating earlier in the day on Christmas Eve. You might start a new tradition, or at the very least, you'd earn some points with the parents for giving them some time to finish some last-minute preparations or errands. Here are some other examples of unique traditions. These were mentioned by members of several families during a round-table discussion:

> A grandmother takes each granddaughter shopping for her first formal dress and then out to lunch. Just the two of them.

> The grandchildren in one family sleep at their grandmother's house every year on the night before the Fourth of July. On the morning of the holiday, they watch a parade and then help their grandmother make a special lunch, which their parents come to enjoy with them later.

> To mark a special birthday, one set of grandparents takes their grandchild shopping for a gift the child has particularly wanted.

> In one family, each grandchild who becomes a member of a school athletic team is presented with a special sports cap during a celebratory cookout or dinner. The cap includes the grandchild's initials and team logo.

> One grandfather opens a savings account for each of his grandkids when they reach the age at which they can add and subtract.

> Grandparents start a travel savings account for each grandchild on his or her 12th birthday. The money is earmarked for a special trip when the child turns 16.

> Birthdays and other holidays in one family are celebrated by letting each grandchild choose a subscription to a magazine of his or her choice.

Traditions, while important in giving your family a sense of identity, don't have to be rituals that have been passed along for generations, and they don't always have to stay exactly the same. If they don't work anymore, they should be adapted so that they do. As the family grows and changes, traditions must do the same. Teach your grandchildren your traditions, but don't be upset if they don't follow all of them. Knowing that the traditions are there will give them a sense of security and belonging.

Religious Rites

Religious holidays have the potential to trigger conflicts about traditions, most often when parents and grandparents are of different faiths. They also offer the opportunity for a family to grow together as the generations learn to understand and appreciate what is sacred and important to each of the others. All faiths and traditions should be treated with respect.

If your family includes members of varying religious faiths and you're trying to figure out how to include all of them in a celebration or observance, take heart. It can be done. One solution is to allow parents and grandparents to call the shots on those holidays that are the most meaningful to them. For instance, if your son-in-law is Christian and you're Jewish, arrange, if possible, to spend Christmas at his house or wherever he and his family will be celebrating. In turn, have him and perhaps his parents or other relatives join you at your home during Hanukkah to participate in some of your traditions. This serves to enrich the holidays for both families, while bringing family members closer together. (For more information about religious issues, see Chapter 19.)

Hartt to Hartt

We recently were made aware of a shocking example of clashing religious traditions, and of grandparents who defied all proper bounds of mutual respect. These grandparents arranged, under false pretenses, to have their grandchild, born to a Christian-Jewish marriage, baptized while he was in their care. Understandably, the baby's parents and other grandparents were hurt, angry, and saddened by the actions of these thoughtless grandparents. In the end, the grandparents lost all contact with their son, and their grandchild as well.

Toy Story

You can't turn on the television or open a newspaper between Thanksgiving and Christmas without being bombarded by toy ads. Your mailbox is overflowing before the middle of November with catalogues filled with every sort of intriguing toy and gadget that you can imagine. Many girls love American Girl dolls—beautiful dolls fashioned after girls

Danger Zone
If you or the parents have apprehensions about certain kinds of toys, such as guns, swords, bows and arrows, or dolls that are too realistic, put them on your list of "taboo toys" and don't buy them for your grandchildren.

from different periods in American history, with every accessory you can imagine. Legos are always popular, or does your grandson prefer Playmobiles? How about a trampoline for the yard? Or a tabletop vanity; real-action car wash; tool bench with real, kid-sized tools; a talking watch; or a painting set?

Where do you start when looking for a toy to buy your grandchild for a special birthday or holiday? A trip to the toy store can be as overwhelming as browsing through a catalogue. The computer game Myst? Turbos? Big Bad Beetle Borgs? Game Boy? Big Brother Ken? Baywatch Barbie? What *are* all these things?

A rule of thumb when buying toys for your grandchildren is to keep it simple. A set of blocks for a preschooler or some art supplies for a pre-teen encourage children to use their imaginations and be creative. If you are buying for older children, let them tell you what they want, or maybe even pick it out themselves. Remember though, that some toys never seem to go out of fashion. Dinosaurs, dump trucks, and baby dolls are always popular with those in the appropriate age groups. However, before going out and buying toys for any age group, find out what your grandkids already have at home. Even simple toys are not inexpensive, and you don't want to buy something they won't use.

Here are some other toy ideas, organized by age group.

Toddlers and Preschoolers

Small children with active imaginations will find hours of fun with these selections:

➤ Building blocks

➤ Stuffed animals

➤ Colored clay or processed dough

➤ Finger paints (non-toxic) and paper

➤ Child-oriented musical instruments

➤ Toys that roll or have sound effects

Don't be surprised when your little grandchildren start spending a lot of time with these simple toys. They provide a welcome contrast to Beanie Babies and *Star Wars* action figures.

Gradeschoolers

Here are some ideas for gifts for children ages six through 12:

➤ Construction sets

➤ Simple games of skill and imagination, such as card games, Monopoly, or Scrabble

➤ Cars and trucks

➤ Paint sets

➤ Kites, planes, and other things that fly

After you buy some of these things for your grandchildren, offer to teach them how to play with or use the toys. Teaching them how to play Monopoly, for instance, is likely to result in a fun afternoon for you and them.

Teenagers

You may need to consult with parents before investing (please don't take that word lightly) in gifts for teenagers. Don't make the mistake of giving them something that is "out," or beneath their age level. Here are a few suggestions:

➤ Games of skill and chance, such as chess or card games

➤ Musical instruments

➤ Skateboards or in-line skates

➤ Books, videos, or CDs

➤ Indoor golf putting sets

If you aren't sure what your teenage grandchild is into, suggest that he accompany you when you go to buy his present. If he wants something that costs more than you want to spend and he has some money of his own, offer to pay half or two-thirds of the cost.

> **Great Grandparenting**
>
> Hobbies are great for developing interests and skills, and doing them together will enhance your relationship with your grandchildren. You can buy equipment that helps them develop their own passions, or that invites them to join in your favorite pastimes. Are you or your grandchild a photographer? Gardener? Artisan? Stamp collector? Amateur magician? Bird watcher? Musician?

> **Great Grandparenting**
>
> Are you perplexed about what to buy for a grandchild with a disability? Toy store managers and major toy chains can advise you. For example, *Toy Guide for Differently Abled Kids,* available free from Toys 'Я Us, lists more than 90 toys, games, crafts, and types of sports equipment for children with disabilities.

Pricey Pastimes and Spoiling Kids

Gift giving is expensive, and giving toys to your grandkids is no exception. High-tech toys such as Nintendo and CD-ROM computer games are available for almost any age

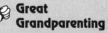

Great Grandparenting

When it's time to buy gifts for grandkids, consider buying from organizations that support worthy causes. The United Nations Children's Fund (UNICEF), for instance, offers art games, puzzles, and books for sale through its catalogue. You could explain to your grandchildren that the purchase of their gift will help a child somewhere in the world who is less fortunate than they are.

group, but they carry hefty price tags. Battery-operated jeeps and cars delight preschoolers—and toy salespeople working on commission. Add an accessory or two and an American Girl doll moves into the triple-figure category.

Marketers are delighted that baby boomers are starting to become grandparents; it means that many of them are also starting to become big consumers. "The grandparent market is just going to explode," recently remarked the president of an Atlanta-based marketing and sales company.

Marketers are excited at the thought of grandparents opening their wallets for their grandkids, but most grandparents operate within budgets and must think about how much they spend. You also need to take a good look at your grandkids and ask if it is healthy for them to be given expensive gifts on a regular basis. If kids are given whatever they ask for, they'll come to expect any whim as their due. This seriously undermines the spirit of giving and receiving gifts.

If your teenage grandchild tells you she'll just die if she doesn't get her own computer and it costs only $1,800, gently explain to her that a gift of that magnitude is not within your budget (unless that's not the case). Help her to understand that you, as most people do, have a limited amount of money to cover various expenses. Explain to her, without getting into specific numbers, how you must spend your money. Also point out how lucky your family is to have enough money to pay for all the necessary things such as utilities, food, and clothing (assuming that is the case). Broaden her perspective by telling her about people who don't have enough to cover even the necessities.

Perhaps you could offer to pay for a portion of the cost, or supply some new software if she gets the computer. Never spend more on your grandchildren than you can afford, no matter how much you like buying for them. It is unwise and not in your best interest— nor in theirs.

Keep It Equal

Of course, the cost of toys varies depending on the children's ages, but try to keep all gifts to grandchildren within a particular age group at about the same cost. When you commemorate a special event, such as a graduation or birthday, you cannot really hand out rewards all around without losing the very meaning of the acknowledgment. But you can remind non-receivers that they, too, will be given a prize or gift when their turns come.

Happy Birthday to You!

If you are able, and want to host birthday parties for your grandkids, the parents will probably be happy to share some of the planning responsibility. Here are some tips to help you when planning a birthday bash:

➤ Include the birthday boy or girl in the party decisions, since children always respond better when they are part of the action and know what to expect.

➤ Make it clear when the party will start and end. Parties should last no longer than an hour and a half for children five and under, and they can last around two hours for those six and up.

➤ Plan one central event or contest, with others around it. If the games they're playing don't seem to be drawing their attention, be flexible enough that you can switch to alternate activities.

According to Caryl Waller Krueger, a lecturer on grandparenting and author of *Ten Commandments for Grandparents,* "Youngsters are becoming bored with having to sit and watch hired clowns or attend parties at kid-oriented restaurants. Birthdays where kids play games and win prizes are regaining popularity. While these active parties are more work for the giver, they can also be more fun." She advises you to avoid the following pitfalls, among others:

➤ Being around for the beginning and end of the party, but not during the actual event (you may be well meaning and trying to be low-key, but it might be perceived as lack of interest)

➤ Running the party in a heavy-handed manner rather than letting the guests enjoy themselves without excessive adult formality

➤ Being overly concerned about neatness or manners

➤ Attempting to be the life of the party

➤ Engineering the games so certain kids win

➤ Rushing the guests from event to event

She also advises that you not comment on the gifts given, but view all with equal enthusiasm. Be sure to encourage your grandchildren to write thank-you notes for all gifts they receive.

Birthday Gifts

Memorable birthday gifts don't necessarily have to be material items wrapped in colorful paper and tied with ribbons. If you're like many grandparents, you can get really confused by the choices of toys. Go to the store to buy a doll, for example, and you'll see a dozen different sizes and models in a hundred different get-ups.

Here are some alternatives to gift-wrapped presents that are likely to make a big hit:

➤ A day's outing to a recreational area or park

➤ Tickets to a play, circus, musical, or sports event

➤ A series of lessons in music, ballet, or art

➤ A course in a hobby or craft that is of interest to your grandchild

➤ A gift certificate for the child and a friend to a restaurant they both would like

Gifts such as these are personal. They let your grandchild know that you are aware of his interests and care enough to encourage him in them. The announcement of such gifts can be presented with suitable enclosures in a colorful envelope.

Hartt to Hartt

We have a tradition that everyone enjoys: At each birthday celebration, while the birthday child gets great gifts and attention, everyone else present—children and adults alike—gets an "un-birthday" present. In our household, we carefully wrap and hand out such items as stationery, a new pair of socks, a hairbrush, and the like, all about the same in price and value.

Sharing with the Other Grandparents

Families, being what they are, are bound to hit snags from time to time. And snags tend to be more pronounced around holidays, when everyone is excited and busy. Family matters are not always easy. Young couples with children often have to choose to spend a holiday with one set of parents and not the other. Other young families end up feeling completely stuffed and half sick on Thanksgiving after eating two huge meals, one with each family, for the sake of family harmony.

To further complicate things, many families have to factor in step-brothers and step-sisters, step-moms and step-dads, step-grandmas and step-grandpas. Trying to work out equitable holiday arrangements can be a real challenge!

If you hear yourself from time to time saying anything like one of the statements below, it's time to come up with a better arrangement for holiday visiting:

"We wish our son would bring our grandchildren to see us on Christmas, but they have to spend the whole day with our daughter-in-law's parents."

"Our grandchildren always spend Thanksgiving and Hanukkah with us because we have a larger house and there's more for them to do here than at their other grandparents' house. Sometimes we feel guilty about the extra amount of time we get to spend with them."

It would be wonderful if there could always be an even balance of time allotted for both sets of grandparents and other family members. But the situation often isn't that equitable. And it can become quite lopsided in cases where there have been divorces and are six or more grandparents and step-grandparents competing for the attention of grandkids.

If dividing holiday time is a problem in your family, it's in the best interests of everyone to figure out something that's agreeable to all. Perhaps the "other" grandparents simply don't realize that you haven't spent Christmas with your grandchildren for the past three years, and they'd be willing to change their schedule. If feasible, suggest that both sets of grandparents get together with your daughter's family. Offer to host the event if everyone lives reasonably close. If that is not possible, consider arranging a schedule where you'll alternate holiday visits with your grandchildren from year to year. Maybe you'll have Thanksgiving and Easter one year, and Christmas the following year. That way, the other relatives will have opportunities to share some holidays with the grandkids too.

> **Great Grandparenting**
> No matter how lopsided or partial you think your limited time with the grandkids may be, don't let them hear you complain. If you have gripes, iron them out with *adults*—either the parents or the other grandparents—and always with the welfare of the children in mind. Grandparenting must be a source of joyous companionship and healthy personal development, not of criticism and friction.

Ultimately, it's up to the parents to decide where their children will spend holidays. If you don't get to see your grandchildren on an important holiday, it is understandable that you'll be upset. Explain this to your daughter. Perhaps something could be worked out. You'll have to be flexible, though. If she offers to have you visit at their house before she and her family leave for her in-laws, go ahead. Even a couple of hours is better than nothing.

The Least You Need to Know

➤ Try not to have overly high expectations about holidays, and don't try to have everything too perfect.

➤ Be flexible on the matter of observing traditions.

➤ Do some research and advance planning before deciding what kinds of toys—and how many—to buy for your grandkids as presents, and be mindful about spoiling them.

➤ When planning a birthday party for a grandchild, try to look at it through the eyes of the child being honored, not from the adult point of view.

➤ Plan holiday visits and celebrations so that all grandparents and close relatives have equal opportunities to spend time with the grandkids.

Part 4
Growing Bonds with Your Grandkids

One of the major reasons you visit with your grandkids is to establish strong and long-lasting relationships.

Sure, you want to have fun. Maybe you're even looking to get involved in some activities that will help you relive your own childhood a little. But you probably have a real desire to form a bond with each grandchild, one that develops early and grows stronger and stronger over time.

This part offers guidance on how you and your grandchildren can enjoy each other when you're together, no matter how limited the time. It also will show you how to continue the bonding process when you're apart.

Chapter 16

"When I Was Your Age"... Talking to Your Grandkids

In This Chapter

➤ Dialogue: then and now

➤ Memoirs and remembrances

➤ Yarns and oddballs

➤ Narratives with a purpose

➤ In recognition of parents

"When I was your age…"

Open a conversation with this line and you might as well tell your grandkids to tune you out. Openings such as "back when I was in school," or "I remember when I was a kid" tend to have the same effect. When your grandkids hear lines such as these, it makes them nervous. They think you're going to tell them about something they do that you did better ("You know, the way you kids study these days is okay, but when I was your age we had a specific time set aside every day for studying. That's how you really learn."). Or how life in general was better 50 years ago ("I don't know. We never had problems like that back when I was in school."). Or how you regularly endured hardships ("You know, I remember when I was a kid, we had to walk five miles to school each morning and five miles home.").

They don't know exactly what you're going to say, but if you start a conversation with one of those openers, your grandkids will have a pretty clear idea of the direction in which the conversation is headed. You can't blame your grandchildren for turning you off like a radio if they feel you're going to put them down in some way. Imagine if your boss came up to you every day to tell you that what you did that day was okay, but not as good as what he did when he was in your position. You'd be tempted to tune him out, right?

And yet, these very lines can be the start of some meaningful conversations between you and your grandchildren. Hearing you reminisce about your childhood can teach your grandkids a lot about history, culture, and you! Grandparents perform a great service for their grandchildren by providing them with oral family histories. You can make all those ancestors the grandkids hear about seem real with a funny story or two. "Remember the time Great-Uncle George and Great-Aunt Sally decided to take the pig to school with them so their father wouldn't be able to send it off to be butchered?" Anecdotes can bring the past to life and make your grandkids aware of their heritage and family history. This chapter will show you five ways to bring family lore to life.

Hartt to Hartt

When one of our sons complained that his preschoolers had developed a bad trait of conniving in order to get special treats, Marilyn admitted that she used to use cunning, too, when she was a child. Once, when seven, she had her eye on a bowl of hard candies on the hostess's coffee table. Knowing it was impolite to ask for one, Marilyn commented on how *pretty* the candies were, and of course the hostess asked if she would like some. "I remember how calculatingly I set about to get some candy," she told our son. He was relieved to discover that our grandchildren weren't the first in the family to use such tactics!

Roots: Family History

One of the most dramatic ways to bring family history alive is to take the grandchildren back to the place where you grew up, if possible. You might drive past the house where you lived as a child. Show your grandkids the fields where you played (if they haven't been paved over for parking lots or shopping malls), the schools you attended, and even your old fishing hole. They'll get a kick out of imagining you as a child their own age doing the same things they like to do.

If it is impractical or impossible for you to physically take grandkids back to your childhood home, try to think of other ways to do it. Do you have any snapshots of your house? Your friends? Any school pictures? If you moved to where you live now from another part of the country, or even a different country, you might be able to get a book or a video from the library that can give your grandkids a better idea of what your hometown was like. Be sure to tell them how it is that you came to live where you do now. Did you move because your father got a new job? To be closer to other relatives?

Once they know where you lived, show them who you lived with. A family tree will help your grandkids understand how and where all those ancestors fit into the family ("Oh! I never realized that Millie was Great-Grandpa's sister!). Let the children help make the "tree" on poster board so you can hang it in the kitchen or den for all to see. Show the young grandchildren where the names (or leaves) belong on the tree, and let the children paste them on. If you have an older grandchild with an artistic streak, she might make your tree a thing of beauty for the whole family to see. Encourage the grandkids to be creative when making the tree. It might become a family heirloom.

When you start putting names on the tree, start at the bottom, with the names of the grandchildren. Add cousins and other young peers, then the parents, and then the grandparents. Next, you can branch out to include the names of uncles, aunts, and cousins, some of whom may be familiar, some of whom may not.

The fun will come when you start on your ancestors, if your knowledge of family lore extends that far back. You can get a map of the United States, and perhaps the world, to show how far away some of your predecessors lived. Discuss under what circumstances they came to your town or to this country. Was it for economic reasons? Religious? Family? If you know, tell your grandkids how these ancestors traveled. Horses and wagons? Train? Ship?

Nearly every public library has books on genealogy that can help you get started with your family tree project. Many libraries have books containing records of marriages, taxpayers, births, and deaths that might help you garner some information about your ancestors. If your community has a historical society, you might check there for additional help. There's also computer software that can assist you with tracking and recording your family history. If your grandkids become interested in the family tree, think how fortunate you are. You'll share a special, ongoing project that will benefit the whole family when you finish.

Hartt to Hartt

Some 20 years ago we took our sons and Walter's father and mother back to his father's hometown. We found his boyhood home and it was in excellent repair. Excited by the beautiful place, we went to a nearby restaurant for lunch. There the elder Hartt spoke about his life in that house and about the town trolley, whose old tracks we had observed along one street. A large map on the restaurant wall showed the town landowners at the turn of the century, and there we saw the name, "Hartt, Ship Captain." We were delighted with this discovery, and the trip became a treasured family memory.

True Tales and Past Personalities

Every now and then, when your grandkids are in a listening mood, tell them some stories about their relatives and ancestors. No, not the one about Aunt Fanny and the band at her sister's wedding, but some meaningful tales that give them some perspective on who these people were and what they did. Children love true stories, especially those that relate in some way to their own family. The older children will even brag to their peers about notable events that involved relatives. When you tell family stories, try to focus on those that are humorous, adventurous, or inspirational. Some good examples:

➤ *Showing bravery in battle.* If Great-Great-Uncle Tom fought in the Battle of Gettysburg, not only tell the story, but read accounts of the battle and even visit the battle field, if feasible.

➤ *Rescuing a person in distress.* Tell them about the time you and your brother were at the lake with Grandmom and your brother fell off the dock and started to go under the water. Be proud when you tell them how grandmom jumped into that water, long skirt and all, to rescue your brother.

➤ *Trouncing the school bully.* Yep. The grandkids will love to hear about the time Uncle Will made up his mind he wasn't going to listen to one more joke about his glasses. The next time that big bully called him "four eyes," Uncle Will removed his spectacles and let the kid have it but good.

➤ *Getting an award as an underdog for an athletic feat.* Your dad didn't participate much in organized sports because he was too busy helping out on the family farm. He sure could run, though. Everyone found out just how fast he was the day the hardware store caught on fire. The owner of the store panicked and didn't know what to do, so your dad simply ran as fast as he could to the fire house, pulled the alarm, and alerted the firefighters. Tell your grandkids how their great-grandfather was later honored for his speed and service.

➤ *Founding an organization or club.* If your grandkids' great-grandmother was an original member of the local hospital's auxiliary, find out if there's a plaque somewhere in the hospital recognizing her efforts. If there is, take your grandkids to see it.

The stories you tell are best when they help to characterize a family personality. Almost every family tree contains people who have held positions of importance. They may, for example, have been military officers during a war, missionaries, women who were successful in professions usually associated with men, business leaders, teachers, authors, or inventors. Your grandkids also will enjoy hearing stories about their great-great aunt who was considered to be a little eccentric because she never had fewer than a dozen dogs living with her, or the uncle who was reunited with his childhood sweetheart after 50 years of waiting and wondering what had happened to her.

As you acquire information about your ancestors, or remember things you had already heard, think about short biographies for those relatives you want your grandchildren to know about. These could be written and used as captions for photos or portraits, or recorded onto a cassette. If you've located some photographs of ancestors who you can identify, you can make a great guessing game for your grandkids.

➤ Guess what this man with the beard did for a living?

➤ What kind of game do you think these little girls are playing?

➤ What kinds of animals do you think Great-Grandpa raised on this farm?

➤ At what time of year do you think this picture was taken?

Every family has its personalities—outlandish aunts or eccentric uncles or cousins with bizarre hobbies. The odder they were, the more interesting they'll seem to your grandkids. They'll be fascinated by stories about their Great-Uncle Bill, who enjoyed stints as a circus performer, skydiver, and airplane pilot before finally settling down to become a noted photographer. A pirate, stagecoach driver, wandering minstrel, or gypsy in the family will be just as interesting. The least you can expect is that your stories about these family characters will stimulate conversations. Your grandchildren may be drawn to the relatives you would least likely have them emulate—just as you probably were as a child.

Hartt to Hartt

In Walter's family, the person he found most interesting was called "Aunt Rollie," though she wasn't a blood relative. Aunt Rollie had raised Walter's mother for a time, and she was considered to be a member of the family. She was a prophetess, a writer on the subject of "End Times," who drew, in green ink, mind-boggling charts of the end of the world. She hired theaters in New York City's Times Square and gave lectures about the Judgment Day.

Anecdotes as Antidotes

Sharing memories, stories, and information about relatives can be great fun for you and your grandchildren. But these tales are perhaps most meaningful when they are therapeutic as well as amusing.

You can use stories to help your grandchildren deal with trying times and difficult problems in their lives. But first you need to identify the predicaments your grandchildren are facing. From the experiences of your long life, you're bound to have personal anecdotes that will meet your grandkids' needs for understanding and identify with their worries. Empathy with their fears and anxieties, coupled with stories about similar hard

Danger Zone
If your grandkids have serious problems, such as drug abuse, illness, or emotional disorders, stories about others with similar difficulties won't be instant "cures," so don't expect too much. Your frank talks, however, can accomplish two important objectives. First, they'll show the child that there are others in the same situation. Second, they'll open the door to alternatives and solutions that can eventually overcome the problem.

times that you encountered and overcame, will be comforting to your grandchild. It will also bring the two of you closer together.

Chances are that many of your grandchildren's worries can be soothed—or solved—with a good story. The following are not necessarily the most common or significant problems your grandchildren may face, but they do demonstrate how stories can be beneficial.

A 14-year-old boy is despondent because he's failing two courses in junior high and has been put on probation. You help him by telling a story about an aunt in her thirties who is now a successful business executive. In high school, you relate, she too was in danger of failing because she just couldn't seem to make it through algebra. She rebounded by taking algebra in summer school, and getting a tutor to help her with her math course the following school year.

A youngster with a slight leg deformity refuses to take swimming lessons because he's afraid he will always come in last when the class races. He changes his mind when you tell him that the disorder is common on his mother's side of the family and was successfully overcome by two of his uncles, who were top athletes in college.

A 16-year-old girl is taken to juvenile court after being at a party where police raided and found marijuana. You tell her about Jackie, one of her distant cousins who had a problem with drugs but overcame it and is now a happily married, working mother of two.

An eight-year-old boy says he hates everybody because none of the other kids will play with him after school. You tell him several stories about how you were just as unpopular in school—or thought you were—and how you reversed the trend by inviting kids to your house after school to play with your pet rabbit.

Telling Stories

The following tips come from one grandparent who is a lively storyteller:

➤ Make your account short, lively, and to the point. Long monologues will only bore your grandkids.

➤ Avoid what you think is "hip" language. You're probably 10 years behind the times anyway.

➤ Be yourself and don't talk down to your listeners.

➤ Go easy on tired old clichés: "Life is not a rose garden." "There's no free lunch." "People in glass houses shouldn't throw stones."

➤ Avoid critiques of youth culture or "today's young people."

➤ Don't criticize your grandkids' friends. They'll jump to their friends' defense and stop listening to whatever it is you were saying.

➤ Avoid negative comments about either of your grandkids' parents, whether justified or not. There are many things you can talk about in a positive way that will fascinate your grandkids. It makes no sense to spend the time you have with them being critical.

Putting Parents on Pedestals

Kids and their parents are bound to butt heads every now and again. It's as natural as sibling squabbling. While all kids and their parents disagree about some things (curfews, car privileges, homework, and bedtimes), other situations are more serious (drug or alcohol abuse on the part of the child or the parent, parental marital difficulties).

Understandably, you'll be very concerned if serious problems crop up between your child and grandchild, and you'll naturally want to help. But be careful. You stand to alienate both parties by becoming too involved. Be very careful about what you say to your grandkids about their parents. Also, be careful that they don't overhear you talking unfavorably about their parents. If your grandkids are disillusioned with their parents, they might adopt your opinions, even if it turns out you were incorrect. If they're defensive about their parents, your criticisms will make them only more so. You don't want to say anything to your grandchildren during a weak moment that might come back to haunt you later on:

> "Granny said Dad is a deadbeat and never pays his bills on time."

> "Grandpa thinks Mom works too hard and doesn't spend enough time at home."

> "My grandparents say my mother and father drink too much. They hope I won't grow up that way."

Use your memories to pass along good things to your grandchildren about their parents. Think of the incidents and events that show the parents to be humorous, loving, or generous. Forgo telling any negative stories and try to bolster the child-grandchild relationship.

Exceptions are cases in which you might talk confidentially with your grandkids to explain why a parent has a problem and needs their understanding or help. Some examples:

➤ A father has lost his job, and everyone must help to keep expenses as low as possible.

➤ The parents are planning to move to another neighborhood, which has made the children sad and angry. They need to know the reasons for the move and why Mom and Dad aren't to blame.

Great Grandparenting

When you sense that children harbor resentments against a parent, or that they're having difficulties with a relationship, convey your impressions to the parents. Tell the parents that you are doing your best to improve their relationship with their child by offering stories that portray them favorably.

➤ A mother has a heart problem, and the children must realize that she cannot join them in vigorous games.

➤ The parents are going on a short trip by themselves for R&R, and the grandchildren have to be reassured that they are still loved and will be cared for.

It is well and good to share personal information about family members with grandkids, as long as the information is upbeat and positive. Grandchildren do not need to hear about all of the family's problems unless they are directly involved. Answer their questions honestly, but don't offer more information than necessary. Be encouraging and supportive of your grandchildren's parents.

The Least You Need to Know

➤ Strengthen your grandchildren's sense of family history by describing their ancestors and family members.

➤ Research your family history and have grandchildren help you make a family tree.

➤ Use your story-telling skills to narrate events in your family's history.

➤ When your grandkids have personal difficulties that seem overwhelming to them, tell them stories about family members who had, and solved, similar problems.

➤ Make sure your grandkids understand that their parents love and value them.

Chapter 17

"Can We Talk?" Listening to Your Grandkids

In This Chapter

➤ Using your tongue for better bonding

➤ Sharing confidences with your grandkids

➤ Dealing with sex and other sensitive subjects

➤ Dialogues between the generations

➤ Learning from the young

They're an interesting mix, these grandkids.

Jimmy and Rachel, the little ones, love to talk. They'll talk about any topic at all in their peculiar, little-kid language. They love repeating what the other one has said, or saying over and over something that has caught their fancy. And, questions! They're always asking questions. They ask each other, their older brothers and sisters, their parents, and you. Of course, they rarely give you time to answer before they're chatting away again.

Teddy, the 14-year-old, on the other hand, hasn't said more than two or three words at a time to you for months now. You worry about him, but other grandparents tell you they have teenage grandkids going through the same thing. His parents complain that he spends too much time alone in his room, listening to music. You just wish he would open up and talk to you sometime so you could know if something is bothering him. You miss him.

Then there's Sara. Sara's only 11, but she's always been extremely vocal. She loves to talk about ideas, current events, and everything going on in her life. She'll tell you more than you really care to hear about each of her friends, her teachers, and all the people in her neighborhood. Sara is full of dreams and aspirations, and she wants to share every one of them.

They have different ways of doing it, but all these grandkids are communicating. Even Teddy tells you things, although you have to try a little harder to know what he's saying since his communication is done in ways other than speaking.

Successful communication with your grandchildren—especially the older ones—begins with an attitude. You have to be genuinely interested in listening to *their* opinions and ideas, not just in transmitting your own. It also requires you to be alert to events and situations from which a conversation can flow when you're together.

This chapter will show you which kinds of conversations are successful—and which are not—when trying to communicate with your grandchildren.

Comfortable Communication

You can communicate more comfortably and successfully with your grandkids if you follow this advice from an expert on child/adult dialogues:

➤ Become more familiar with subjects of interest to your grandchildren, such as their schools and classroom assignments, friends, sports, music groups, celebrities, and fashions. Reading popular magazines and watching hit TV shows will keep you clued in. Don't, however, assume that because you've perused a few magazines or watched a little MTV that you are "with it," and should be treated as a peer rather than a grandparent.

➤ Be alert to situations that suggest topics for discussion, such as birds outside on a feeder or foods being prepared.

➤ Begin a dialogue at a time when you won't be interrupted, and when your grandkid is not concentrating on homework, a television show, or a laptop computer.

➤ Listen as much as you speak, and if there are more than two of you, help keep the topics interesting to everyone so that no one monopolizes the conversation.

➤ Ask intelligent questions if a subject comes up that you are not knowledgeable about, such as your grandson's biology assignment or your granddaughter's new-found passion for playing the guitar.

➤ Promote a lively give-and-take whenever a subject is controversial, but do what you can to prevent hurt feelings, arguments, or quarrels. Make sure that everyone's opinion is respected.

➤ Avoid being critical or judgmental. Don't imply that because you are older and wiser, young people should heed what you have to say.

➤ Ignore grammatical errors. If you feel corrections are necessary, point them out later in a separate conversation. Correcting grandkids while they're talking sends a clear message that you're not listening to what they're saying, just the way they're saying it.

➤ Never pick on things that have nothing to do with the conversation, such as a child's odd haircut, mismatched clothing, or dirty feet.

➤ Never belittle something important to your grandkids, such as the best kind of softball or type of music—it may be inconsequential to you but not to them.

➤ Be slow to take offense if children make remarks that seem critical or thoughtless, such as comments about the feebleness of older people. In fact, take it as a compliment. If they considered *you* old and feeble, they probably would have thought twice about making the comment.

The art of conversation is just that—an art. It is listening as well as speaking, and listening well. If you're distracted by what the newscaster is saying in the next room, you're not doing a good job of listening to what your grandchild is saying. Some kids will tell you almost everything, while others will tell you next to nothing. Remember though, when your grandchild talks to you he's sharing a part of himself. Consider his conversation a gift, and make the most of it. If you have a grandchild such as Teddy, who does not find it easy to discuss anything, much less something that is important, be especially sure to listen closely to whatever he says. If he tries to talk to you and you don't hear him because you're thinking about something else or are otherwise distracted, he may think you don't care and then withdraw further.

> **Great Grandparenting**
> A good way for you to promote conversation is to model frank speech in front of your grandchildren. When the adults around your grandkids openly discuss a wide range of subjects and are able to courteously disagree with each other, the message is clear: There are no forbidden topics, and people can love and respect each other, even if their viewpoints are not the same.

Building Confidences

As a grandparent, you're in an enviable position. Your grandchildren may choose to confide in you about confidential matters they feel they can't discuss with their parents. This is particularly true with teenage grandchildren, who are constantly questioning their role in the world, their future, and most everything else. If your teenage grandchild trusts you to be open and non-judgmental, she may tell you her deepest feelings and dreams.

She may also tell you some things that are extremely difficult for you to hear. Let's face it. Life isn't easy for teenagers. They're faced with hard decisions, and they don't always make the right choices. Be aware that, if you cultivate a trusting relationship with your grandchildren, you might become privy to some disturbing information that will force you to make some tough decisions yourself.

It goes without saying that if your grandchild shares confidential information with you she expects it to remain confidential. This can be a gift to you, but it also can be a great burden. Experts in the area of family relationships say that you sometimes will be obligated to break a confidence if your grandchild is at risk.

Just as grandparents are obligated to step in if they believe that the behavior of their adult children is jeopardizing the well-being of their grandchildren (such as in the case of abuse or neglect), they are obligated to tell parents if the grandchild is participating in behavior that is harmful.

If your granddaughter tells you she is using drugs or alcohol regularly, having sex with different boys, is in an abusive relationship, or participating in any illegal behavior, you should tell her parents, experts say. The risk she runs while engaging in any of these behaviors is too great to ignore for the sake of a confidence.

Don't expect your granddaughter to like you for breaking a confidence, and don't expect her to confide in you again, at least not for a very, very long time. However, if you do not divulge this sort of information to her parents, you would bear responsibility should harm result from her behavior. If you do become aware of this sort of information and are going to tell the parents, inform your granddaughter first of your decision, and tell her you are doing it only because you love her and fear for her well-being. She may not believe you at the time, but some day she may understand that you acted in her best interests.

It is possible that if your granddaughter tells you information of this sort, it is because she knows she's in over her head, and is looking for help. She may know on some level that you will do what you need to do to help her, even if it means telling her parents.

There will be times when your grandkids will tell you something in confidence that upsets you, but you won't feel it is necessary to pass the information along to parents. Perhaps, for instance, your 16-year-old grandson tells you he skipped school with some friends one day last week and hung out at the mall. Explain to him calmly that such behavior is not acceptable, and why. Point out that the mall is a popular place and someone who knows he should have been in school could have seen him there. Try to let him see that skipping school is not a good idea, and then keep an eye on him. If you hear, or observe, that he's having trouble in school or might be skipping regularly, you may need to talk to his parents.

Confidences will emerge only when you have consistently displayed a non-judgmental attitude, established a climate that encourages open conversation, and shown yourself to be a sympathetic listener. They normally don't occur in response to your urging, "Is there anything you'd like to tell me?"

Do you remember knowing someone who could always make you feel better about yourself? Someone who didn't complain about your hair, look despairingly at your latest crop of pimples, or cluck about how sloppily you were dressed? If so, that person probably was a great boost to your self-esteem.

Improving your grandchildren's self-esteem is a real gift you can give to them, but good communication will be necessary to make it happen. If your grandkids reveal their fears and anxieties to you, they are telling you they trust you to be empathetic, understanding, and encouraging. Tell them the things you appreciate about them, and make them realize that nearly all young people have similar fears and concerns. Perhaps relate a story about when a child of yours was the age of your grandchild and going through a similar situation. Let them know through your listening and your answers that you really care.

Hartt to Hartt

When Marilyn was director of a child care center, she followed a rule with the children in her care that she now applies to her grandsons. Always give children tasks they can do, especially when they are very young. When they've completed the task, praise them for their accomplishments. This creates an "I can do" attitude toward life. In Marilyn's present position, she deals with many adults in the workplace and in training situations. She has found that people who are given jobs beyond their capacity or training, first feel overwhelmed, then discouraged, then angry, and finally they just give up. If you set somebody up to fail, don't be surprised when he does.

When you discuss confidential topics with your grandkids, there is a basic need for mutual trust and honesty. This doesn't mean you have to like or approve of everything your grandchild does and tells you about. Acceptance means that, although you reject certain actions or viewpoints, you don't reject the individual.

While you are respectful of your grandchild's opinions and feelings, he should be respectful of yours. Openness should be two-sided.

Sensitive Subjects

If the thought of a grandchild sitting down to tell you the details of his sex life is enough to make you run out the door, don't worry. He no doubt senses that this is not a discussion area with which you'd be comfortable and probably would be just as uncomfortable as

Danger Zone CAUTION
Being sympathetic, open-minded, and willing to talk to your grandchildren about anything doesn't immediately qualify you for the grandparents-of-the-year award. Even more important than knowing how to speak effectively is another skill: the art of listening. Although empathy, trust, and sympathy are components of a beneficial adult/child relationship, listening is the medium through which these elements can flow.

you. On the other hand, he may introduce the subject just to see your reaction. Sensitive concerns such as sex and morality will surface only when your grandchild feels relaxed in everyday conversations with you. If you feel incapable of talking about these issues, it's best to tell your grandchild straight out. If you feel he has a real need to talk to someone about these matters, perhaps you could arrange for him to meet with a counselor or a youth leader at a church, synagogue, or community group. Explain to the parents why you feel such a meeting is desirable and ask for their approval.

For generations, parents who are uncomfortable discussing sex with their kids steer them toward a book to pick up the slack. If your grandchild seems to be lacking information about sex and it is not forthcoming from parents, you might recommend *The Rules*, by Ellen Fein and Sherrie Schneider. This book offers discussions on dating, social customs, psychology, and mate selection. Perhaps you could read it along with your grandchild and discuss it afterwards. It sometimes is easier to talk about something someone else has said rather than your personal feelings. Other books dealing with sex and related topics include:

➤ *Questions Children Ask and How to Answer Them*, by Dr. Miriam Stoppard. This book contains four levels of answers for children from toddlers to 11 years old.

➤ *What's Happening to My Body? A Growing Up Guide for Parents and Daughters,* and *What's Happening to My Body? A Growing Up Guide for Parents and Sons*, both by Lynda Madaras. These books include detailed explanations and diagrams of the physical and emotional changes of puberty, with anecdotes describing the feelings of both boys and girls. Both books also discuss birth control methods.

➤ *The Wonder of Me—Fertility Appreciation for Adolescents and Parents*, by Ruth S. Taylor and Ann Nerbun. This book does not include information on birth control.

You may be perfectly comfortable discussing sex and other such topics with your grandkids. After all, many grandparents today are Baby Boomers who well remember the sexual revolution of the '60s and '70s. Times have changed, however. You'll need to talk not only about things such as teen pregnancy and abstinence, but also about topics such as AIDS and other sexually transmitted diseases, and about condoms and other forms of birth control as well. Keep in mind that current surveys indicate that a majority of teens—56 percent of girls and 73 percent of boys—have had intercourse by the time they're 18.

Sex is only one of many moral and ethical issues that might come up in conversation with your grandkids. Here's how you can prepare for the discussion of delicate or sensitive issues:

➤ Create an environment that nurtures and encourages open communication. Under such circumstances, both generations will feel comfortable talking to each other when the time comes.

➤ Discuss a sensitive subject as soon as the matter comes to light. The longer you postpone the conversation, the tougher it is to raise the issue.

➤ Discuss virtues, such as sincerity, honesty, and honor, as openly and frankly as you would school assignments and grades. You don't have to be a paragon of virtue yourself to be effective. In fact, you will be a more understandable person if you admit that you have slipped occasionally in the honesty department.

➤ Long before any situation arises, make it clear (in a non-preaching way) that you have always felt that admissions of wrongdoing are not a weakness. Then, when an incident occurs, explain that people are stronger when they acknowledge mistakes and, when necessary, apologize to anyone they have harmed.

➤ Establish the mental image of grandparents as anchors for young people who feel they are drifting away from their goals or social needs, and to whom young people can turn for security and confidence. Do this with statements such as, "You know I'm always here for you" or "You can talk to me about anything you want."

➤ Practice patience so that when you have to face a delicate discussion or situation with your grandchild, you can maintain your composure and objectivity.

➤ Be honest and forthright, show your love and concern, and explain how you are troubled and why.

➤ Make it clear that what your grandchild says is very important to you, and that you are speaking as one adult to another, not adult to child (assuming the grandchild is old enough to understand and appreciate this tactic).

➤ Avoid sounding critical of something your grandchild said or did, or passing judgment on what is being said now.

➤ Listen as much as you talk, and don't try to direct the course of the discussion.

➤ If you don't understand something, admit it.

➤ Be patient, and try to be relaxed. Children don't like to be pressured any more than you do.

➤ If you sense that a situation is getting out of hand and you aren't getting anywhere, urge your grandchild to discuss problems with another adult who is close—perhaps a favorite teacher, another grandparent, a member of the clergy, or a professional counselor.

> ♥ **Hartt to Hartt**
>
> Years ago, when Walter was starting out as an assistant priest, he arranged for a specialist to speak to the parish's youth group on the subject of sex. The speaker was a parishioner and a psychiatrist. He began his talk by acknowledging that he felt uncomfortable addressing them on this sensitive topic and asked for their understanding as he tried to tackle an assignment that was difficult for him. His candor enabled his youthful audience to talk freely to one another, as well as with him. As a result, a responsive and beneficial discussion followed.

The Grandchild as a Teacher—Wow!

As we get older, it's easy to forget many of our earlier life experiences. Caught up in day-to-day routines and problems, we might start to lose some of our capacity for wonder, or stop feeling that new and wonderful things lie in our futures.

Fortunately, however, none of this is true for the young. Being with your grandkids can actually rekindle your optimism and open your eyes again to see the world around you. Think how the following scenarios would light up your day and bring a bit of wonder back to your tired spirit:

> Your grandchildren run excitedly to see sandpipers scooting along the beach.
>
> Your teenage granddaughter tells you about the cute new boy in her class.
>
> Your 17-year-old grandson describes the super campus tour he has just had at one of the colleges he's applying to.

In such instances, your own senses are heightened, memories flood back, and you feel more alive and ready to share in whatever experiences lie ahead for your grandkids. Let your grandchildren be your "teachers" and you'll get a look at a whole new view of life. Here are some examples:

➤ If you're not yet familiar with the Internet or the World Wide Web, grandkids make the best teachers for showing Granny or Grandpa how a computer works.

➤ As you may recall from your own childhood, kids love to observe nature's many incredible beings in their natural habitat. If you've forgotten all about such wonders as ant farms and the way eggs hatch, stick with the kids for some interesting revelations.

➤ How long has it been since you read the funny papers (or comic strips, if you're not quite that ancient)? You can have a ball reading "Cathy" or "Dilbert"—or having them read to you by a grandkid who has recently learned how to read.

➤ You may not want to be reminded of how dumb you are. But if you want a challenge, try helping a 12-year-old with homework. You may learn a thing or two.

Once you've opened your mind to letting your grandkids teach you, tell them how much you're enjoying your "lessons." Grandkids of any age are sure to get a kick out of thinking that you're learning from them.

The Least You Need to Know

➤ Improve your relationships with your grandchildren by learning how to communicate with them more successfully.

> **Great Grandparenting**
> Both generations can profit from learning together. If your grandchild is having difficulties in a subject you know well, such as math, English, or a foreign language, see if you can help. Perhaps you can make the learning process creative, or something you can do together. If he's having trouble with French, for instance, give your grandchild some practical knowledge of the country, culture, and language. Reward his improved work with a visit to a French restaurant.

➤ Enjoy the confidences of your grandchildren as a means of filling communications gaps they may have with their parents. Be aware, however, that hearing your grandchildren's confidences can sometimes put you in a very uncomfortable position.

➤ Discuss delicate subjects such as sex, ethics, and morality in an open manner.

➤ Be open-minded and take advantage of all the things you can learn from your grandchildren.

NICE HAIRCUT.

THANKS GRANDPA.

Chapter 18

Understanding the Teenage Grandkid

In This Chapter

➤ The teens are coming

➤ Hats off to the seniors

➤ Etiquette simplified

➤ Appalling apparel

➤ Conduct becoming and unbecoming

You just can't understand how it happened so fast. It seems as though no-time-at-all ago your daughter sat in your kitchen and told you she and her husband were expecting a baby. You went through the pregnancy with them, eagerly anticipating the birth of your first grandchild. You watched the little guy emerge from a helpless baby into a rollicking toddler. You agonized along with his parents when he cried every morning for three months because he had to go to preschool. You bought him cute little sweaters and sat through all his beginner's soccer games. You congratulated him on his elementary school report cards and helped him with science fairs. You dropped him off at Cub Scouts and saw him advance to Boy Scouts. You even helped him pick out a new pair of jeans for his first junior high dance.

But now! Now he's a teenager and you don't know what to make of it! He gets into sullen, sulky moods when you can't get a word out of him. He wears really strange clothes and has an earring in one ear. You seldom see him without a baseball cap, turned backwards, which he rarely thinks to take it off when he's inside. You're worried sick because he's hanging out with that Johnny Jones and everybody knows what kind of kid he is. When he does talk, it's usually about subjects that are completely inappropriate such as sex or those beer parties that some kids have. You're just not sure you're going to be able to get through these next few years. And he's only the first grandchild. Could it be that the rest of them are heading for the same thing?

Relax. The teen years, though often trying, can be splendid times for grandkids and grandparents. At this point, your grandchildren are physically, emotionally, and mentally more mature and better able to relate to you.

The Teenagers in Your Life

Teens are busy people with their own, busy lives. If you want to see them, you'd better make an appointment. One good way to keep in touch with your teenage grandchildren is to extend specific invitations for them to visit.

Chapter 10 explained how to arrange a wonderful visit with grandkids of any age. But getting teenagers to visit can present a special challenge. Here are some tips:

➤ *Select a range of times when you know they're likely to be available.* You'll have a lot of competition for their time: School projects, sports and other extra-curricular activities, dates, socializing, driving lessons, and perhaps after-school and summer jobs keep them extremely busy.

Great Grandparenting
Don't discourage teens who want to bring along their laptop computers. They may need them to do homework, conduct research, and communicate with others. (If you're interested in obtaining a computer yourself, a grandchild might well make suggestions on what to buy and be a competent tutor when you get one.)

➤ *Suggest they come with a friend, if you're comfortable with the idea.* No matter how solid a bond your teenage grandchildren have with you, they still need the excitement of hanging out with a peer.

➤ *Line up sports they can participate in,* such as tennis, skiing, swimming, and sailing. Also, plan to introduce them to young people their age in your town who could be partners or opponents in games.

➤ *Make eating out a big drawing card,* describing restaurants they'd like to go to and foods they might try.

Just because you have to work a little harder at getting your teen grandkids to visit doesn't mean that they love you any less than they did when they were little. It simply means they have busy, active lives—exactly what you want for them.

Bonding with Teens

Bonding is a word you hear a lot these days. It's become a sort of buzzword for forming or strengthening any sort of relationship. You'd think the way that everyone seems to be bonding with everyone else, this world would be a really happy place. Parents and grandparents have always undergone true bonding with their children and grandchildren; it's only natural. With some it might take a bit more work, and you might feel sometimes (especially with teens) that your bonds are weakening. But don't despair. Familial bonds can be repaired and restrengthened with a little work.

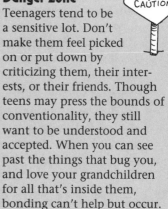

Danger Zone
Teenagers tend to be a sensitive lot. Don't make them feel picked on or put down by criticizing them, their interests, or their friends. Though teens may press the bounds of conventionality, they still want to be understood and accepted. When you can see past the things that bug you, and love your grandchildren for all that's inside them, bonding can't help but occur.

Consider the case of the Parkers. Melville and Sue Parker adopted their 15-year-old granddaughter, Melanie, when she was eight. They made the decision to adopt her so that she would have a secure family life, apart from her natural parents who had abused her.

The Parkers did not regret their decision when they saw that Melanie was regaining confidence in herself and seemed to be happy and much more outgoing than the cringing and reticent little girl she had been. But they were constantly concerned about how to bring up a teenager and how to talk to her about sensitive matters such as drug abuse, sex, and problems at school. Sometimes they had the feeling that she wasn't telling the truth when they asked if anything was wrong.

You may not find yourself in a situation as extreme as that of the Parkers. But if you find yourself in, or feel the need to initiate, a sensitive discussion with teenage grandchildren, here are some more guidelines:

➤ *Don't be shocked* (or at least don't appear to be shocked) by what they tell you.

➤ *Actively pursue communication* because many teens aren't likely to do so on their own.

➤ *Express love and caring without conditions,* regardless of what your grandchildren might be saying.

➤ *Don't compare times past with time present.* Your grandchildren are growing up and can't be expected to act the same or have the same ideas as people did several years ago.

➤ *Don't take it personally if your grandchildren seem distant toward you.* Teenagers often have trouble expressing important thoughts and feelings and may remain silent.

A high school teacher with two teen sons and two teen daughters (yikes!) reports that, in her view, the major obstacle to communicating with teens and adolescents is that they don't listen. Her experience as a teacher—and mother—is that teens listen for a very short time, and then you lose them. Their eyes glaze over and you know they're miles away. To combat this syndrome, she tries to be as interesting as a TV talk show when she's teaching. She moves constantly around the classroom, using many gestures and changes in expression. When that fails, she'll suddenly lower her voice, almost to a whisper, to regain their attention.

She has learned with her own children that the best time for weighty conversations is in the car. She believes her children respond to her in the car because there are few distractions, and they don't have to look her in the eye while they talk. She advises all parents—and grandparents—to take advantage of car time.

Respect for the Old Folks

You've heard it time and time again. "If you want to have others respect you, you've got to respect yourself." Your children and grandchildren will respect you, but you've got to show yourself to be worthy of it. A miserable, bigoted, mean older person will not be respected simply because he's older. But an open-minded, understanding, kind, and knowledgeable older person will be respected for her character and experience.

Great Grandparenting

One way for you and your teenage grandchild to increase mutual respect is to get away from your normal routines. You will then have the mutual opportunity to share first impressions of new people and places, and express wonder and delight at strange sights and unfamiliar circumstances.

Embarrassment works both ways, you know. If you are appalled at some of the outfits your grandchild comes up with, consider what she might think about some of yours. Some grandparents inadvertently lose respect because they become careless as they age and don't keep themselves or their homes as neat or clean as they should. Teenagers certainly aren't the neatest or most orderly human beings, but they are observant. Here are examples of some things that young people cite as reasons for lessened respect of older people:

"Grandpa is fun to be with, but I wish he wouldn't go into town with us in those baggy pants and the wrinkled shirt that don't match."

"Granny asks us to keep our room tidy, but then she leaves papers and slippers and toilet articles lying around all over the house."

"Old men don't have much hair left. But they'd look years younger if they wouldn't let it get scraggly and uncombed looking."

"We have to get Gramma a new robe. I think she's had that one since I was two years old."

"Why do they have to leave their false teeth right out in the bathroom where everyone can see them?"

"Boy is their car a mess! Whenever we go for a ride, we have to move raincoats or umbrellas, library books and cartons, and paper wrappings before we can even get started."

"You know, Granddad has a hearing aid, but he never wears it. He never hears what we're saying and he talks so loud that it's embarrassing!"

You may want to make a checklist of things to be more careful about when older grandchildren are coming for a visit.

> **Great Grandparenting**
> Attention to your grooming, speech, and manner of doing things is one of the best ways you can improve yourself in the eyes of your grandchildren. So, before they come, pay a little attention to your hair and clothes, stand up a bit straighter, and speak a little more dynamically. Give the house a good once-over. And for heaven's sake—get your false teeth off the counter!

Minding Their Manners

Teenagers and children are exposed regularly to public displays of bad behavior by people who somehow feel they are worthy of respect. Unfortunately, some young people who see this behavior go unsanctioned get to thinking that it's smart to be gross and vulgar. Take a look at TV. Characters are increasingly portrayed as rude and arrogant. Sitcoms emphasize vulgar antics. A popular radio host goes out of his way to be as profane and shocking as possible. A professional boxer bites off a piece of his opponent's ear in front of millions of viewers. There are more and more reports of college and professional athletes charged with crimes such as sexual assault or rape. Political campaigns thrive on mud slinging, and the actions of some candidates provide plenty of mud for their opponents to sling.

Courtesy, according to the wisdom of Confucius, is a way to mold character. It is a symbol of freedom, not restriction because it gives us the tools we need to operate successfully in society. Manners aren't just superficial acts, but deep characteristics of the acceptable ways to respond to and behave toward others. A code of conduct often brings order to situations that otherwise would be chaotic.

We all need to brush up on our manners from time to time. It's easy to become lax regarding courtesy and etiquette, but you can easily be a role model to your grandchildren of all ages by practicing good manners.

> ➤ Moderate any tendency you have to be testy with children who are slow to respond to your requests, who don't seem to grasp what you're saying, or who appear to be indifferent. Impatience simply breeds impatience.

> ➤ Don't use words such as "thank you" or "you're welcome" in a derisive way to show that you're irritated by a lack of courtesy.

➤ Avoid those petty negative traits that kids often associate with older people: crotchety, crabby, and touchy. Cheer up. Smile. Say something pleasant, and go on to other matters.

When you hear one grandchild insult another, say on the spot that an apology is in order. If you hear the old familiar refrain, "It isn't my fault...," explain in a calm, but firm way that you expect your grandchildren to abide by your rules of courtesy.

Good manners will be easier for your grandchildren to practice when you've established specific house rules as guidelines. If you consider it good manners that no one leaves the dinner table until everyone else is finished eating, then insist that everyone observe that rule. If you consider it bad manners to reach across the table for salt and pepper instead of asking that they be passed, make that a rule to be observed also.

You don't want to suspend the "good manners" rules that are part of your grandchild's life at home, or reverse any rules their parents have put into effect. Make sure your grandkids understand they are expected to follow the rules that apply at their own home as well as the rules of your home.

Don't be afraid to define good manners, in your own words, to your grandchildren at whatever time seems most appropriate. One definition understandable to all ages is that good manners means behaving in such a way that you make others feel comfortable, that you bear your share of common duties, and that in turn you are better regarded by those you are with.

Hartt to Hartt

Many years ago, we were invited with our six-year-old son to a parishioner's elegant home on Lake Michigan. We knew our hosts had live-in help, so we imagined that this would be a carefree visit for us as guests. Wrong! The house rules were announced to us upon arrival. Since the cook and housemaid were elderly, guests were expected to clean up after themselves and make their own beds. When two other guests failed to make their beds the next morning, they were taken to task. A bit unnerved, one replied, "We like to let them air out." Although we all laughed nervously at this rejoinder, our hosts' reactions made it clear that they were serious about their rules and that we, as guests, were obliged to follow those rules.

Dressing for Success

Generational conflicts regarding clothing are as old as...well, they go back a long, long way. This "clothes thing" is probably nowhere more pronounced than it is between teenagers and their parents or grandparents. Kids these days are wearing baggy pants that hang off their hips and drag on the ground, skirts so short you don't even want to look when they sit down , stretch tops that bare the midriff (and they're not intended for the beach, either!), and these all-black outfits that some kids never seem to get out of.

What to do? Do you make a big deal about their latest outfit, hoping they'll see the errors of their fashion senses and rush out to buy a wardrobe of tailored suits, wing-tips, and sensible pumps? Or, do you tell them how great they look in those baggy pants and untied sneakers? Probably neither.

You need to choose your battles wisely when dealing with teenage grandchildren. As offensive and unsuitable as their clothing might seem, you need to remember that dress constitutes a big part of teenage identity and divides the "ins" from the "outs" in their eyes. The other thing to remember is, whatever they're wearing is merely clothing. It is *what they wear,* not *who they are.*

If their clothes are buggin' you, you probably need to concede the battle and look the other way. Just ignore it. Not them, just their clothing. Nothing turns teenagers off like hearing a broken record: "Must you wear that shirt?" "Why do your clothes have to look so baggy?" "That sweater must be two sizes too big for you!"

Try to think about when you were a teenager. You probably had some rebellious ideas about dress codes, yourself. Remembering that, you can understand how it is with kids today. Or can you?

As much as you know that you should keep your mouth shut, because it's likely that whatever you say will only alienate your grandkids, you just may not feel comfortable with a teenager who wears saggy pants, a grimy sweatshirt, hair scrunchies, flashy bandannas, T-shirts with sleazy sayings, or skirts that are almost as revealing as bikinis. So, what are you going to do?

If you do remain silent, you won't run the risk of making your grandkid mad at you. But, not only will you have to endure the unruly sight of him, you know that sooner or later you're going to run into Barbara or Joan at the shopping center when he's with you.

So what's the answer? If you find it impossible to ignore the "clothes thing," there are some steps you can take to alleviate, if not obliterate, the problem:

➤ When you invite grandchildren to your home, ask their parents to oversee their packing and eliminate items they know you'd rather have left at home.

➤ Specify any articles of clothing (skirt, suit and tie, athletic gear) that your grandkids must bring along to accompany you to church, a favorite restaurant, your club, the tennis courts or golf course, the ski slopes, the beach, or a scheduled party.

➤ Part of your strategy can be to take your grandkids on a clothing shopping spree for their birthday or holiday present. Then you can select the shopping centers to go to and (to some degree) monitor their purchases. We call this the "planned giving" technique.

Great Grandparenting

According to *USA Weekend*, four in 10 U.S. schools have dress codes, but 79 percent of teens surveyed said they didn't want school officials to tell them what to wear. You have to tread lightly when imposing any rules that unfairly obstruct the natural rights of young people.

Remember, though, that clothing is only skin deep and not worth the hard feelings that a major confrontation over it could cause. Keep your comments (if you must make them) light and don't take it too seriously. This, too, will pass.

What do you do if you're going to visit *them?* You're pretty much locked into the situation. Again, you can employ the "planned giving" technique. Take them shopping, monitor their choices, and hope they'll wear the "approved" clothing for the duration of your visit. Or you could beg the parents to intercede with their clothing choices. If you're that hung up on it, you can enjoy your grandkids at home and seldom be seen with them in public. Note, however, that you're far more sensitive to the "clothes thing" than almost anyone else who will see your grandchildren. Try to remember their good qualities and don't pay too much attention to their duds.

Bad Behavior

Judging behavior is not easy. It's as chancy and subjective as trying to select a melon at the perfect point of ripeness. You almost never come out exactly right.

As a grandparent, you have something of an advantage over parents in trying to determine whether a child who has started off "bad" is really developing in the wrong direction. If you don't see somebody every day, it's easier to spot changes in their behavior than it is when you're with them day in and day out. You have a better idea of which problems are likely to lead to long-term damage and which will blow over. What's more, looking at the situation from long range, and a generation once removed, you may be able to see whether certain traits, such as rebelliousness or the tendency to be withdrawn, run in your own family.

Interpreting the Signs

Adolescents often exhibit certain behaviors that you might interpret as signs that they are troubled or mentally unbalanced, but which are quite normal for their age: shutting themselves in their room, hanging a **KEEP OUT** sign on their bedroom door, reacting violently to mild criticism, shutting you out abruptly when you praise them for a good deed, or making rebellious statements, and sometimes using foul language.

Unless you feel there are too many recurrences of such actions, or the teenager's behavior is destructive or a threat to others, accept it all valiantly as part of growing up.

While you don't want to interfere with parental child-rearing strategies, you should intercede if you detect any regressions in behavior you think the parents might not have noticed. Some could be slight abnormalities in development, but others could be the result of alcohol or drug abuse (see Chapter 25).

A friend of ours had a teenage son, Mike, who was not able to hold onto a number of weekend jobs he took. This was the first clue there might be some kind of problem. Then, they noticed their son had dark circles under his eyes, as though he was not sleeping well. Next, came a constantly runny nose, loss of appetite, and an overall sense that he was not well. Mike's parents expressed concern and kept a close watch on him, but didn't nag. Just as they were about to seek out a professional to see how they could help their son, he came to them, admitting drug use and asking for help. His parents responded immediately by getting him into a rehabilitation program. They found out later that Mike's grandmother also had noticed the changes in her grandson, and had been about to intervene when Mike came forward on his own. She had decided to give the situation only a short time more before getting involved for the sake of her grandson and his future. The parents and Mike were reassured to know they had this extra support and love to count on.

In Mike's case, it was pretty easy to detect a problem, even though his parents and grandmother didn't know exactly what the problem was. In some cases, however, it might be more difficult. Sometimes the signs of drug use or other serious problems are much more subtle. For instance, a teenager may be extremely quiet and withdrawn for long periods of time, showing no interest in others. He may cease contact with childhood friends and refuse to do things he always enjoyed, such as sports or hobbies. He might act impatient or hostile every time you speak to him, showing no courtesy of any kind.

If you see these kinds of signs, be concerned. Your grandchild could be suffering from depression or another illness. Talk to his parents and express your concern. It could be that they, too, are distressed by his behavior and your input is the confirmation they needed to seek help. Perhaps you could get the names of some good counselors or psychologists in your grandson's area.

> **Great Grandparenting**
>
> A common problem grandparents are likely to have with a teenager is arguing. The solution's simple: Don't allow yourself to get pulled into an argument. Let your teenager know what you want done—or not done—and don't repeat yourself. If you issue a warning, be calm and unemotional, and give it just once. And don't issue a warning or a threat that you can't enforce.

Drug and Alcohol Abuse

Of all the issues facing parents and grandparents of teens in the '90s, perhaps none is more frightening than that of drug and alcohol abuse. A national household survey conducted in late 1996 by the National Narcotics Intelligence Consumers Committee showed that drug use in children between 12 and 17 had more than doubled since 1992. Drug abuse is epidemic in our society, and our young people are at risk not only from the actual use of drugs, but from the violence spawned by drug use.

Great Grandparenting

One of your proudest, but most difficult hours as a grandparent may be the time you are called upon to confirm your love and support of a grandchild who is struggling with drug addiction. If you have a grandchild in this position, you must realize that you need to intervene and help, not ignore or keep the problem a secret.

Alcohol is thought of as a secondary problem, but its use is so widespread among teens as to be of crisis proportions. Figures from the office of the U.S. Surgeon General indicate that 500,000 teens—that's half a million—between the ages of 13 and 19 binge-drink at least weekly. The figures show that 95 percent of all high school seniors in this country drink, perhaps not weekly, but enough to have been drunk at least once. More than 10,000 teenagers die each year as a result of drinking, mostly in traffic accidents. If these numbers don't scare you, they should. Half a million kids getting drunk once a week or more is a deadly serious matter.

If you're the grandparent of a teenager and you suspect or discover that he or she is abusing drugs, you should not hesitate to intervene. Even if a grandchild tells you in confidence about drug use, you must warn him that you cannot hide such information from his parents. Tell him that recognizing his problem is a very important step toward solving it. Offer to be with him when he talks with his mother and father, and tell him you will stand by him while he works through his addiction.

If you think you're lucky that your grandchild is "only" smoking cigarettes, drinking beer, or using marijuana instead of "hard" drugs, you need to get back to reality. Not only are these habits addictive and harmful on their own, they also lead to increased drug use and addiction. Most authorities in the field point out that efforts aimed at the prevention of addiction must begin before adolescence. Most schools have implemented drug and alcohol awareness programs in the elementary grades. These programs, however, can't take the place of at-home education. Talk about drug and alcohol abuse with your grandkids and get a handle on how they feel about these things. Remember, in addition to being extremely risky, the use of all controlled substances and alcohol is completely illegal for anyone under the age of 21.

The Least You Need to Know

➤ Don't expect teenage grandchildren to be available for a visit with no advance notice. Make your plans with them well in advance.

➤ If you want respect from your grandchildren, make sure you carry yourself with dignity, grace, and good humor.

➤ When establishing rules to encourage good manners, be certain they are clear and workable.

➤ Before you get upset about what your grandkids are wearing, remember that the "clothes thing" is a temporary problem, and try to look the other way.

➤ Before you decide that a grandchild's behavior is "bad" or deteriorating, try to find out what the basic causes are.

➤ Be aware of the seriousness of drug and alcohol abuse among teens in this country and be prepared to intervene if you suspect or know your grandchild is using drugs or alcohol.

Chapter 19

Keep the Faith

In This Chapter

➤ What religion really is

➤ Sharing the faith

➤ Sorting out the faiths

➤ Guiding your grandkids in understanding and prayer

➤ Dealing with scary practices in the name of religion

➤ Accommodating different religions

➤ Exemplifying your faith to your grandkids

It would be so nice if it all proceeded smoothly. Your daughter would marry someone of the same faith, and they'd exchange vows at the church they've both attended since birth. Their children would be baptized, sing in the choir, be confirmed and married in the same church, with you in beaming attendance. You'd attend special services, church picnics, and other events as one big, extended family. Your places, and theirs, would be secure in the church graveyard and you'd know that you'll all rest together at the end of life.

Chances are, that won't happen. Your daughter might marry a person of a completely different faith, or she may just give up going to church. Maybe you've given up on church, too, or never went at all. She and her husband just might decide it's too much hassle to get the kids enrolled in Sunday school, and besides, Sunday is the only day they all have to sleep in.

There's no guarantee that your children's and grandchildren's religious beliefs and practices will mirror yours, or even come close. If your religion is very important to you, this might be very difficult for you to accept. On the other side of the coin, you might not be particularly religious, while your children and grandchildren are. This chapter will explore the religious implications of grandparenting—how to enhance your grandchild's religious experience, and how to resolve any religion-related conflicts that may arise. But before we do that, it will help to pause for a moment and consider what religion really is.

What is Religion?

You may be somewhat familiar with the traditional religions, such as Christianity, Judaism, Islam, and Hinduism. Perhaps you even belong to one. But being religious does not always mean being a member of an organized religion. There are ways of being religious that do not fit any one religious tradition. You can even be religious and not know it. Think about people who are passionate about a hobby—golf, for example. They might say, "Golf is my religion."

It may seem silly to call golf a religion, but isn't religion what is most important to us? Jesus once told a parable about a rich man who filled up his barns with treasures and said, "Eat, drink, and be merry, you have much goods laid up for many days." Jesus called the man a fool, for the man would die that very night. We might say that that man's church was his barns.

Some people live for fame, or success, or money, or for always feeling good. In fact, materialism and instant gratification might be called new and dangerous forms of American religion. The truth is that whatever takes over our lives and becomes all-consuming is our religion.

It is a mistake, then, to think that only some people are religious. Nearly everyone is religious in the sense of being driven by something that is all-important. This chapter is for readers who would like to help guide their grandchildren into a supportive and guiding faith.

Sharing Religious Traditions

It's only natural that when you're happy in your faith, you want to share it with those you love. You'd like to see your children and grandchildren in your place of worship, because it's made you happy and you want them to be happy. You'd like to share religious holidays, prayers, rituals, and beliefs. Be patient. You may have to wait. The practice of religion has a predictable pattern in this country. Studies show that anywhere from one-third to two-thirds of young people abandon the religion in which they were raised, mostly in their teens or late 20s. The same studies show that between 30 and 50 percent of the people who leave religion return, either to the same religion or another one.

The greatest inspiration for returning to religion, studies show, is having children. National studies, such as one by Dean Hoge, sociology chairman at Catholic University in Washington, D.C., have found that the birth of a child is the most important factor in a person's decision to return to religion. Sharing religious traditions is extremely important to most people, even among those who have denied their faith for a time—for whatever reasons.

Experts say that children force many "non-believers" to re-examine their beliefs and their mortality, particularly if kids begin asking about God. One couple whose son was attending a church-affiliated preschool was rudely awakened when their little boy insisted they pray before dinner. "We can't have him praying at school and not at home," the parents reasoned. They joined the church that sponsored the preschool soon after.

Most people who are raised within a particular faith keep some ties to that faith, or re-establish them later, if they leave. If you have grandchildren being raised in the same faith as yours, you can feel very fortunate. You'll be able to stand by and support them, giving them information about the established places of worship within the faith and what goes on within. You'll be able to celebrate your faith with your grandchildren, and share in all the joys and triumphs.

If your grandchildren do not share your faith, however, you'll need to make some provisions. If they are not affiliated with any religion, offer to take the grandkids to your place of worship, unless for some reason their parents do not want them to go. If the parents are intentionally raising your grandchildren with no religious study or consideration of any kind, you may want to talk to them, if it is important to you. If they agree to let you take your grandkids to your place of worship, make the experience as pleasant and positive as possible. Some suggestions are:

➤ Tell your grandchildren what to expect. Is it a special day within the religion? What will the topic of discussion be? Who will speak? Will there be any special music? Knowing what to expect will help them better appreciate the activities once they get there.

➤ Organize your schedule so nobody ends up rushing around at the last minute. Arrive early enough to give your grandkids a chance to look around and get settled before the service starts.

➤ Spend a little time after the service answering any questions your grandkids might have, or looking around the building and grounds if this is the first time they've visited with you. Explain the significance of items and symbols such as a baptismal bowl, cross, Torah, stained glass window, Sabbath lamp, and so on.

➤ Bring home a copy of the service program and encourage your grandkids to review it and remember and think about what was discussed.

It is right and perfectly understandable that you want to share your religious traditions with your grandchildren. Just be aware that if they're not receptive, pushing too hard will probably make them even more resistive.

Hartt to Hartt

When our child Peter was asked at bedtime to say his prayers with us, he refused because he said he didn't believe in God. This was hard to take from a three-year-old. We didn't press it, but continued to take Peter to church with us. We hoped that our prayers and the example of our lives would win him over. However, at 15, he asked to be excused from going to church since he felt uncomfortable pretending to accept something he did not believe. We accepted this, but it caused us much discomfort. Soon after college, Peter began to read the Bible on his own, and eventually came to believe it. This delighted us because it was Peter's own free choice and personal discovery.

Great Grandparenting

Even if a parent is outspoken in declaring a hands-off position when it comes to sharing religious traditions and practices, grandparents can still exert considerable influence in spiritual matters by their own example. The most effective method is to live your religion day by day and in this way serve as a role model. Remember that children have a keen eye for hypocrisy!

When Their Beliefs Are at Odds with Yours

As nice as the picture is of the extended family going together to mosque, synagogue, or church, it often does not happen. In fact, in some families, the subject of religion is taboo, right up there along with politics. Disagreements about religion are nothing new. Think of all the wars fought, and still being fought, in the name of religion. Then, consider how these conflicts contradict all that we normally associate with religion (kindness, love, commitment to a higher being).

If your daughter has taken up Judaism, your son-in-law is Catholic, your son has converted to Hinduism, and your granddaughter has discovered Jainism, try not to look upon the situation as only a problem. Religious difference is an opportunity for discussing and discovering values which are truly important. There are two rules for such discussion:

➤ First, you must be honest to your own religious convictions, even as you discuss those that are different from yours.

➤ Second, remember that religion must be a matter of each individual's free choice. No one should force his or her religious convictions on another person.

Some sensible approaches to the problem of mixed religious beliefs or affiliations within the family are:

➤ Learn as much as you can about all the religions represented within your family. Show a willingness to participate in services and special events of all of them.

➤ Assess the degree to which each family member is committed to his or her faith, and respect their commitments.

➤ Openly discuss the religious communities and creeds represented by family members, the extent of personal participation in services and practices, and how parents and other grandparents feel about the spiritual upbringing of the grandkids.

➤ Don't belittle those adults who are spiritually inactive or profess a lack of faith. Respect the decision *not to* practice religion just as you respect the decision *to* practice it.

➤ Never try to coerce a person to change his religion to yours, or to another.

If the religions being practiced within your family are nearly as numerous as the number of members, count your blessings that you are among thinking, caring people. Those who think about and search for meaning in religion are certainly at an advantage over those who attend services regularly without ever considering the content. So, if your granddaughter keeps up a running dialogue about Vardhamana Mahavira and asks you to accompany her to the Jain temple, go ahead. Show her that you respect her right to embrace whatever religion she finds meaning in, and encourage her to keep searching. You should be delighted that this young person is concerned enough about religion to make an individual choice.

You probably know many people who married partners of different faiths. Such marriages often work out with few problems. Perhaps the husband attends one house of worship and the wife another. Or, perhaps they simply stop observing their religions. The situation becomes more complicated when children are born and the decision has to be made whether to (a) join a middle-ground house of worship that combines some of the teachings of both religions; (b) let the children alternate between the two; or (c) forego participating in either religion until the children are older and can decide for themselves. This last alternative may not be the best solution. Children with no religious guidelines may still embark on individual journeys to truth, but will have to find their way without the guidance of a religious tradition.

And the Children They Shall Lead Us

Children are not only the number one reason that people return to organized religion, they often are the catalyst for parents and grandparents to begin deeper explorations of their faiths, look more closely at how they are living their lives, and consider their places among the world.

A new generation moves each existing generation one step up the ladder, reason enough for many to become contemplative about purposes, aspirations, and accomplishments. In addition, children are naturally curious about God, creation, and other big issues. "Grandmom, how did the trees get here?" or "Granddad, did God make the stars, too?" are common questions from children's mouths, but questions that deserve careful consideration and explanation. When children ask these and other weighty questions, it may cause us to re-examine our answers and come to deeper realizations of what we believe, and why.

Talking with your grandkids about creation and other religious issues may lead to, or accompany, praying before bed or at mealtime. It is fine to pass along prayers that you used as a child, but think about what the prayers say. Some may be frightening to young children, or have words too difficult for them to understand. Some guidelines to keep in mind when it comes to prayers are:

➤ Encourage your grandchildren to form their own prayers instead of repeating the ones they hear at their place of worship or at home. Tell them to think about the things for which they are grateful when thanking God, and to think about what is important when asking for help.

➤ Be patient when hearing your grandchildren's prayers; don't interrupt. One four-year-old we know stops after the first few words of his prayer and says, " I need to think about this," and then starts all over again.

➤ Do not judge the quality of your grandchildren's prayers.

➤ Share some of your prayers with your grandchildren and let them know why you pray for the things you do.

Explain to your grandchild what prayer means to you. Let them know that prayer works in both directions: we ask and God hears, and the answers come in many ways. A twentieth century theologian, Karl Barth, insists that the important thing about prayer is that since we are invited to prayer by God, a prayer never goes unanswered. So let your grandchildren know that prayer works in both directions: We ask and God hears and answers. Of course answers may not be what we expect or might prefer, but they are never simply absent.

> ### Hartt to Hartt
>
> When Marilyn was about seven, she was delighted to see a rabbit in the garden. For several days afterward, she looked for the rabbit again, but he wasn't there. Having been encouraged to pray since she was young, she went to the window, closed her eyes, and prayed out loud that God would make the rabbit come back. She opened her eyes but there was no rabbit. Disappointed, she went to find her father for an explanation. He told her God had answered her prayer with a "no."

When Religion Turns Ugly

You encourage your grandkids to pray, meditate, and think about religion. You try to put them on the right path by encouraging their parents to see that they get to church or synagogue or mosque. You've watched proudly as they've participated in religious classes and ceremonies. And, all of a sudden, your blood runs cold as you realize that one is involved in a mysterious and frightening type of religion—a cult.

Cults—with strange names such as Hare Krishnas, Moonies, Branch Davidians, and Heaven's Gate—are extremely scary to parents and grandparents because they fear losing any contact with a child or grandchild who might become involved. It also is normal to fear for the safety of a child or young adult who gets involved with a religious cult.

Experts say young people are often vulnerable to cults whose charismatic leaders can practice mind-control techniques. The young people who join cults often come from middle-class families and do not appear to be troubled or distraught in any way before becoming involved. In fact, psychologists said, testing on members of some extreme cults have shown them to be within the normal range of standard psychiatric tests. "Most people in cults are relatively normal, looking for meaning and intimacy," said Michael Langone, a psychologist and executive director of the American Family Foundation, which conducts research on cults.

> ### Danger Zone
> Patrick Ryan, involved in a cult for a decade, has spent the last 14 years helping people to break away from them. In describing his cult experience, he said, " Every minute of my day was controlled. It becomes an entire worldview. You are told how to brush your teeth, which way to sleep, which nostril to breathe out of first in the morning. When you internalize that worldview, it is difficult to come back into the world and make you own decisions."

Great Grandparenting

You select books for grandchildren on the three "R's" and other topics you think they should know about, from alphabets and birds to geography, science, technology, and zoology. Why not add the fourth "R" to their study—Religion?

If you suspect that your grandchild is involved with a cult or interested in cults to the point of getting involved with one, share your suspicions with the parents. Perhaps they will want to speak to a school counselor to see if other kids are also involved. This is a serious matter and must not be ignored. You may ask your grandchild to visit a religious leader at his or her place of worship, although that suggestion may be rejected if the young person is already involved with a cult. Advise parents to consult with a family counselor or a member of the clergy who can provide more information and tell them how to find help.

Extending Religion to Everyday Life

Connected with religious beliefs are the moral values by which we guide our lives. We all value something, but we have to accept the fact that the dominant values of the 1990s may be quite different from those values we knew as children. It is not your job to be judgmental, however, or to lecture your grandkids on the general state of morality as we near the end of the century. Rather, it's your job to convey to your grandchildren the importance of good values and how to incorporate them into their lives.

Your grandchildren can learn from you that good moral values spur a desire to help other people. Help your grandchildren understand that our deepest responsibilities are to those most in need. A perfect example of a human being who practiced this belief throughout her lifetime is Mother Theresa, who recently died. Perhaps you'd want to tell your grandchildren about Mother Theresa or get some information about her life to share with them.

One way to show by example a concern for others is to show others respect. Do you model respect for others as your grandchildren hear you speak on the phone or when you speak to a store clerk, restaurant waiter, or workman in your home? Do they hear you speak courteously with other members of the family? Do they see you reaching out with a helping hand to neighbors? Do your grandchildren see you active in civic and charitable institutions? Do you discuss the needs of society with them or within their hearing and suggest possible solutions for the common good? Grandparents should teach by example that they are concerned about those in need. Here are a few actions you can take to foster in your grandchildren a concern about good moral values:

➤ Talk about your responsibility for the world around you.

➤ Show a reverence for the mystery of life, human and animal.

➤ Show sensitivity to the rights of others. Treat everyone with respect.

➤ Be honest in your dealings. Don't brag about how you cheated on your taxes or how you got away with something.

➤ Show tolerance for those you meet who are different from yourself.

➤ Model civil behavior at all times. Mind your manners.

➤ Take responsibility for your own actions. Admit when you have made a mistake.

➤ Be willing to work for justice for others.

➤ Show daily habits of discipline and self-control.

While it may seem to be a very challenging job for a grandparent to tackle an assignment of such broad dimensions, you should recognize that by your words and actions you are already giving your grandchildren lessons in how to live their lives. Be alert to the many occasions that lend themselves to a discussion of morality; for example, the homeless person you encounter on the street, a news report of famine, or a natural catastrophe anywhere in the world. Tell your grandkids how they can help people in your own community who are poor, have no homes, or do not have enough food or clothing. There are also occasions begging for discussion when grandchildren ask for unreasonably costly gifts or few limits on entertainment or recreation.

Caring for Creation

There are less direct ways in which we teach moral values. Think about the way you treat the natural environment. Do you conserve water and energy instead of wasting them? Do you avoid the use of damaging pesticides? Every day and every moment present opportunities to demonstrate to your grandchildren your concern for the world and for everything and everyone in it.

Think of some activities at home and in your community where you can involve your grandchildren in taking responsibility for others. For example, take your grandchild with you when you go to visit a neighbor or friend and have the grandchild offer a gift of flowers she has picked from the garden, or a picture he has drawn. Others might include:

➤ Join a community project to clean up an area or otherwise improve it environmentally.

➤ Participate with your grandchildren in an event to raise money for an area charity, such as a walk or bowling marathon.

➤ Take your grandchildren to visit an elderly person in a nursing home.

➤ Ask your grandchildren to help you clean out an attic or basement, or sort through household items that you will be giving to benefit a local charity.

➤ Stop with your grandchild at locations where groups such as the Boy and Girl Scouts are washing cars or selling baked goods and give a donation.

➤ When you pass someone holding out a can for a charitable gift, either give or explain to your grandchildren later why you chose not to give at that time.

> ### Hartt to Hartt
>
> When we lived in Brooklyn, Marilyn and our 14-year-old son Peter were approached by a street person asking for money. Marilyn didn't give her any, and she felt it important to explain to Peter why. Peter thought that his mother should have given something and was eager to talk about it. Now, 16 years later, they both remember this woman and wonder if they did the right thing by passing her by.

"The healthy child environment, as well as the healthy adult environment, needs to provide more than just the survival needs of adequate food, clothing, and shelter" says Edward Fellhauer, a minister who works with young people. "These are things that will keep you alive, but they are not the things that will bring you into the fullness of life. This you will only get through the expressed love and affection of another person, someone who understands your true worth."

Teaching Values: What's Important, and What's Not

If it seems that your grandkids are on a quest to accumulate as many possessions as possible, or if they constantly want things that are more expensive or more complex, or want just—more—don't despair. This frenzy to acquire material things is garnering attention from all corners. It's been termed a nationwide epidemic and has even been given a name: affluenza.

The Public Broadcast System (PBS) recently aired a show of that name, examining the phenomena. The show pointed out that more Americans visit a mall each week than a house of worship. The average consumer spends six hours a week shopping, but only 40 minutes playing with his or her children. A million Americans declared bankruptcy last year, many as a result of obsessive buying. Remember our earlier discussion about what religion really is.

Despite the accumulation of more and more possessions, the sense of well-being among Americans is not as strong today as it was in the past. In fact, the PBS documentary pointed out, many people feel that the more they buy, the less they have. "Never has so much meant so little to so many," observed Scott Simon, the host of the show.

Try to help your grandkids rediscover—or discover, if they never have—the value of non-material things, such as family relationships or a sense of pride in a career or hobbies. Listed below are some ways to help them appreciate non-material possessions:

➤ Make their ancestors come alive with old family portraits and pictures that portray their relatives doing ordinary things such as having a family picnic or working at their trade.

➤ List some of the professions or occupations held by their forebears and explain what they were and how they contributed to society.

➤ Promote pride in the accomplishments of your grandchildren's ancestors and talk about what their daily lives might have been like.

➤ Motivate your grandchildren to think of themselves as contributing in the future by asking about the work they imagine themselves doing when they get older.

➤ Describe to older grandchildren the kinds of employment opportunities that you can see would match their current interests and capabilities.

➤ Discuss the wide range of career opportunities available today that not only pay a living wage, but provide the intangible reward of service to others.

If you are discouraged by the apparent affluenza epidemic in our society and how it might be affecting your grandkids, take heart. The television documentary indicated that a "cure" is beginning: There's a quiet revolution of people examining what is important to them and discovering it's not the accumulation of possessions.

The Least You Need to Know

➤ Share your faith and its traditions with your grandchildren, when possible.

➤ When your grandkids' beliefs differ from yours, learn all you can about what they believe and how they practice those beliefs.

➤ Teach your grandkids that prayers are answered, although not always in ways they might expect.

➤ Act quickly and firmly if a grandchild shows signs of getting involved with a religious cult.

➤ Instill in your grandchildren an appreciation for the diversity of religion.

➤ Be a living example for your grandkids by showing high moral character and good values.

Part 5
Uneven Roads of Grandparenting

Grandparenting is not always a smooth path. Things happen. Situations change—sometimes not for the better.

Whether the changes involve a move that separates you from your grandkids, or a problem that puts you in the position of having to raise your grandkids, this part of the book provides you with commonsense suggestions and sympathetic advice for dealing with the bumps in the road. It also covers the sensitive issues of talking with your grandkids about aging and death.

It reminds you that wherever there are uneven roads to navigate, there are also by-passes that sometimes reward travelers with fresh and unexpected vistas.

Chapter 20

Grandparenting on a Budget

In This Chapter

➤ What to do when you have more outflow than input

➤ Having fun without funds

➤ Tightening the purse strings

➤ Lowering your grandchildren's demands

➤ Helping your grandchildren operate within a budget

You love having your grandchildren visit you. You love taking them to restaurants, plays, zoos, and museums. They're still talking about what a great time you all had earlier this summer on your weekend trip to the beach. The only problem is, all these outings are getting to be more than your budget can bear. It seems that the older the grandkids get, the more expensive they become. Their clothes cost more, their toys cost more, the trips you take with them cost more. They no longer want to order off the kid's menu at the restaurant, and they've all seemed to develop an affinity for steaks and seafood. You don't want to seem cheap, but you're really getting worried about your ability to finance all their wants.

So…you want to have a great time with your grandkids, but not go broke in the process. Not a problem—you can do that!

All it takes is some imagination, a little research, and a willingness to try new things. Grandparenting on a budget may actually enhance your experiences with your grandkids. Let's face it. Many kids today have too much: too many toys, too many clothes, too many gadgets. Watch a kid at a birthday party sometime, opening presents. Half of the gifts get put aside with hardly a second glance because she's already got something like it at home. All the "things" have lost their allure because there are too many of them. It's a tendency of parents and grandparents to overdo. You find out your little granddaughter got a "Thomas the Tank Engine" video that she just loves. Next thing you know, between you, her parents, the other grandparents, aunts, and uncles, she has 12 "Thomas" movies and is sick of all of them. They don't mean anything to her anymore because she's oversaturated.

The same goes with outings. If kids eat at the place with the golden arches three times a week, it gets to be just another meal. But, once a month can be a real treat. If you go to see every movie that comes along, movie going gets to be an expected function, not a special, fun thing to do.

There are things you can do with your grandkids, however, that cost next-to-nothing, or nothing, and will be different and enjoyable for all. Kids are delighted with things that are spontaneous and out of the ordinary. For instance, the next time it rains, drag out your old ponchos and raincoats, and tell your grandkids to suit up. Take them for a rain walk and see what you see. You're liable to see certain critters, such as worms and salamanders, on a rainy day. You'll have a great time stomping and splashing in puddles. If you're really lucky, you might even see a rainbow.

You don't have to make a big deal to your grandkids about not spending money, but it doesn't hurt to clue them in on the economic realities of life. Teach them how important it is to save money, and give them an idea of the relationship between earning, saving, and spending. Your grandkids might love to get presents, but they're sure to remember rain walks and rainbows long after that Tickle Me Elmo doll has been forgotten. This chapter looks at ways in which grandparents can have great times with their grandkids without spending a lot of money, and also teach them some valuable lessons about money.

Hartt to Hartt

Our friend found that her grandchildren, 6 and 10, kept asking for more, and then complained that what they got wasn't as great as they had anticipated. She was greatly heartened, however, when driving with them one evening, they saw a huge, perfect rainbow was filling the sky. The children were completely awed by this vibrant rainbow, and more excited than she had seen them in months. The experience confirmed her suspicion that kids may indeed be desensitized to "things" because they have so many, but, fortunately, they still believe in the magic of rainbows.

Greeting the Grandkids with a Limp Purse

If you're on a fixed budget, you're not alone. Many people are trying to stretch their dollars to cover expenses, which seem to be constantly increasing. If you are seriously watching your spending, there's not going to be extra money when the grandkids come to visit. Some grandparents might feel bad if they can't offer their grandkids treats and presents, and actually avoid visits. Innovative grandparents, on the other hand, will find ways to show them good times without spending. If you're clever, your grandkids will be having such a good time they'll never notice that your wallet hasn't been out.

Fun Choices on a Budget

You probably know what your grandkids like to do and what their interests are, so you can plan accordingly. Most newspapers have an end-of-the-week section that lists activities for the upcoming weekend. Keep an eye open for opportunities to participate in fun and interesting events that don't cost much, if any, money. Some ideas of things to do and places to visit while staying on your budget are:

➤ Visit a park that has playgrounds, hiking trails, picnic areas, and other outdoor activities. Pack a picnic lunch and eat outside. If there are fireplaces or grills, take along some wood or charcoal and build a fire. Let your grandkids roast hot dogs and marshmallows on pointed sticks (green, please—dried sticks will burn).

➤ Attend church or community-sponsored cookouts and activities such as concerts.

➤ Participate in neighborhood events, such as block parties or yard sales, to which all participants contribute food or supplies.

➤ Borrow some bikes and take off. Pack some sandwiches in a backpack and make a day of it.

➤ Go to see school athletic events. Tickets for these don't cost much, and some of them are free.

➤ Buy tickets to amateur plays and performances by choral groups.

➤ Watch exhibition matches or group lessons by pros at local tennis, golf, swimming, and other sports centers.

➤ Take guided nature walks, and visit arboretums and botanical gardens.

➤ Visit historic sites, which usually have reduced rates for children and seniors. Look for special days when volunteers may dress in period costumes and re-enact activities or practice crafts of days gone by.

➤ Take an exercise, aerobics, or yoga class at a community center.

➤ View cultural, historical, and natural history exhibits at colleges, schools, and public museums.

➤ Take a bus tour, or get in your car and go see fall foliage or other attractions.

 **Great Grandparenting**

If you do a bit of scouting, you might be amazed at the number of free or low-priced recreational events and programs you can find in your town or county. Contact your local visitor's center, the chamber of commerce, senior centers, youth centers, public museums, schools, colleges, and even large companies. And don't forget to read the section of your daily paper that lists upcoming events.

➤ Take advantage of marine cruises sponsored by government or other public research associations.

➤ Sign up for arts and crafts lessons for children.

➤ Watch plays performed by summer and community playhouses.

➤ Take plant tours sponsored by companies whose manufacturing and production operations are interesting.

➤ Take safety and first aid courses, with demonstrations.

If you're lucky, you'll spot something in your local newspaper such as this notice that appeared in the *Hilton Head* (South Carolina) *News*:

"The Kid's Ten Cent Carnival will be held at the Plantation Fire Station May 17. The event, which attracts thousands of children each year, is sponsored by volunteer firefighters who staff numerous games, dunking booths, and food stations. Tours of fire trucks and ambulances will be available, as will be refreshments and easy-to-learn first-aid lessons for all kids."

Don't overlook simple things such as a visit to a neighbor or relative, a cookout at your house, a long walk at dusk, or a fishing trip at the local park. These are just a few of the many, many activities you can enjoy on a budget.

Coping with Iwanna and Igotta

It's not a pleasant thing to think about, but parents occasionally seem to take advantage of grandparents' good natures. It might be time to have a chat with your son or daughter if you hear sentences such as these coming from your grandkids:

"I wanna get some ski equipment and Mom said maybe you'd take me shopping as a birthday present."

"I'm coming to your house in July and Dad said maybe you'd take me on that river trip we talked about last year."

"I gotta have a new bike because mine is all rusty, and Dad said you could get one for a good price at the discount store near you."

"I didn't bring my dress-up suit because it's too small, and I gotta have a new one if you want me to go to church with you."

If you believe that parents may have delayed buying certain expensive items for your grandchildren and have instead suggested that perhaps gramma and grandpa could foot the bills, you have a couple of choices.

Go ahead, if you can afford it, and buy the item. But make it clear that it will be a birthday, Christmas, or other special gift, not an extra present. If you don't have the money for such an item, be candid with your son or daughter and propose that the parents pay for it. Or, offer to match funds, if feasible. Explain to your son that he's merely setting his own child up for a disappointment if he suggests you'll buy something that you're not able to.

Plans to Offset Unreasonable Expectations

If your grandkids fall into the "why have just one video when with a little fuss I can get twelve" category, they may think they're entitled to whatever they want, whenever they want it. Many kids seem to grow up these days thinking their families are obligated to supply all their wants and needs. If they don't get what they want, some of them can become downright cranky and discourteous. If you find yourself the recipient of an "I don't see why I can't have this now," attack, don't panic. There are steps you can take to improve the situation.

➤ Find out what your grandchildren really want or need, and make a priority list. Explain that they may have to wait a while for the more expensive items, but you'll start a kind of homemade "layaway" plan for the future.

➤ Make it clear that this is a two-way street and you expect them to earn some of the money toward these purchases that they simply "must have."

➤ Work out an earnings plan if your grandchildren are old enough to work or earn an allowance, and explain how they can earn money to expedite the purchase of whatever it is they want.

➤ After you've created an action plan, you may want to take them to your bank to open a small savings account. (Or you may contribute to a savings account their parents have opened for them.)

➤ Coordinate your plan with the parents, and commit them to matching contributions toward the overall goals, if they're in a position to do so.

Delaying gratification for grandkids might make them irritable, but it will be good for them in the long run.

Great Grandparenting
To make saving fun, you could purchase a World of Money Allowance Kit, available from bookstores and some toy stores. The kit is designed as a three-part system: Whenever children receive their allowance, they allocate one-third to spending or giving, one-third to saving, and one-third to investing. The kit includes an instruction book, a bank compartment, a money wheel, and stickers.

Be patient with them and their demands, for it is our society that has created those demands. Advertising on TV and in newspapers and magazines is very seductive to kids who are constantly bombarded by images of things they're told they want or should have. You'll do them a favor if you can make them understand that good things are worth waiting for.

The Haves and Have Nots

If your grandkids can't understand why you'll be cooking at home tonight instead of going to the neat restaurant where Daddy takes them every Friday, or why you won't buy those awesome sneakers for them like Mommy would, you need to sit down for a chat. Tricky problems can be triggered when the parents are affluent and the grandparents are not—or vice versa. If your grandkids have grown up in an affluent household, and don't understand that your financial situation is not the same as that of their parents, they won't understand why their lifestyle may be different when they're at your home. They could resent you or perceive that you don't care about them, if they measure affection with purchases.

Both the children's parents and you should, in simple terms, discuss the situation with your grandkids. Explain to them that some people have more money than others and are able to buy and do more. Try to make them understand that there are different ways of showing love, and giving gifts is just one of them. To keep things in perspective, tell them about people who are too poor to even afford food, housing, clothing, and medical care. Try to make them appreciative of all they have, and realize that the whole world does not live the way they do.

If, on the other hand, you are financially comfortable, you might choose to do something to give your grandchild an advantage for the future by setting up some sort of account in which you'll invest money for him to use for college or other purposes. These types of accounts can provide great peace of mind to anxious parents who aren't sure they'll be able to cover all these expenses. There are many avenues for putting aside money for your grandchildren, all with varying tax regulations and other restrictions. Be sure you do some research or check with a financial consultant before opening accounts.

Money Management for Kids

By the age of eight or nine, your grandchildren are old enough to understand where both generations of the family stand on financial matters. They can then understand what's affordable and what's not, and why one family may be able to afford more or less than another.

With your guidance, grandchildren can learn that living within their means will make them feel good about themselves. As they grow older, they will actually enjoy the challenge of seeing how much they can save and how, with a little forethought and ingenuity, they can trim their budgets.

Work with the children's parents to explain to grandchildren how they can manage their allowance, how they can earn money for special needs, and why they should set up priorities for things they want to buy.

You'll help your grandchildren understand that money isn't everything if you replace pennies, quarters, and dollars with special favors or treats to compensate them for an achievement or job well done. Keep some small "rewards" on hand, such as minibooks, award certificates, small toys, or gift certificates to their favorite fast-food restaurant.

Hartt to Hartt

We recall a story a teenager told us about going with three friends to their respective homes to ask their parents for money for an outing. The teen was impressed when one dad promptly handed his son a wad of bills, but was embarrassed when his own father questioned him about where he was going and when he'd be returning. He also didn't give him a very large sum of money.

But when the three were on their way, the boy who had received the large handout said he wished he had a dad like the one who asked questions before providing any cash. "Dad doesn't really care about me," he said. "He just wanted to get me off his back."

Pocket Money When $$$ Is Tight

By the time grandchildren are old enough to want to have a bit of money for themselves, they're old enough to earn it. You can help them find assignments that are enjoyable, productive, and that will make them more aware of the value of money.

Here are some entrepreneurial endeavors that are rewarding:

➤ Walking a neighbor's dog (when there is a safe area in which to do so).

➤ Opening a lemonade stand, the old standby for kids, but perhaps with the added sales appeal of goodies like gramma's cookies, popcorn, or roasted nuts.

Great Grandparenting

"Your grandchild needs to learn that getting everything he or she wants on demand isn't nearly as satisfying as yearning and working for it," says Susie Levin, a popular speaker on the subject of grandparenting. "Sometimes this message needs to be taught by giving kids practical financial guidelines both by word and example."

➤ Washing cars—always great fun because the kids can squirt hoses, douse each other, and have an excuse for getting wet.

➤ Washing driveways and walks—similar to washing cars, it's great fun.

➤ Helping out at a party for toddlers and preschoolers. Kids are creative enough to make funny signs, paint balloons, play music, or give puppet shows.

➤ Cleaning out the garage and holding a garage sale.

➤ Baby-sitting (for responsible teenagers who have parental approval to do so).

It's never too early to start teaching kids about money. Too many of them grow up with the idea that if your money runs out, you simply head to the ATM machine and get more. When your grandkids begin earning their own money, encourage them to be entrepreneurs. Help them write up a simple business plan and determine how they'll run the business and what they'll do with the money they earn.

The Least You Need to Know

➤ Teach your grandchildren to understand the value of money and the reasons why many families have tight budgets.

➤ Compile information on the multitudes of things that your grandchildren can see and do locally at very little expense.

➤ Learn how to deal with children and young people who have had no monetary guidelines and who make unsuitable demands on your budget.

➤ Be sensitive to family situations in which either the parents or grandparents are more financially well off than the others.

➤ Come up with ideas for how your grandchildren can earn and save money for special purposes.

Chapter 21

Grandparenting from a Distance

In This Chapter

- ➤ Visit or be visited?
- ➤ Remote reach-outs
- ➤ Perfect pen pals
- ➤ When a grandparent's marriage breaks up
- ➤ Grandparents galore

Grandparenting from a distance is not ideal, that's for sure. It just doesn't let you be as close as you'd like to be. Even if you visit frequently, you're bound to miss a lot of growing up. It's tough getting reports over the phone of how little Tommy took his first steps, moved out of his crib into a big-boy bed, cried on his first day of kindergarten, or lost his first tooth. It's fun to hear him babble away into the receiver, but it's not like holding him in your arms, kissing him goodnight, and drying his tears after a fall.

If you're long-distance grandparents, you can take some consolation in the fact that you're not alone. Most grandparents, actually, live too far from their grandchildren to visit easily and regularly. Being a grandmother in Pennsylvania with grandkids in California is a daunting problem for the older widow who is reluctant to travel alone, but is desperate to spend time with her grandchildren.

Visits can be expensive, tiring, or just not easy to fit into busy schedules. The Pennsylvania grandmom loves to visit (once she arrives), but lately it seems that her grandkids (ages 12 and 15) don't even notice she's there after the first couple of days. They're too busy with school, friends, after-school sports, and baby-sitting to spend much time with her. The 15-year-old has given up her summer visits to Pennsylvania—there's just too much to do at home. The 12-year-old still comes, but who knows for how much longer.

On the other side of the coin, there are lots of grandparents who are too busy to visit their grandchildren more than once or twice a year. Grandparents who are still working have only a limited amount of time off, with lots of activities to fill that time. Those who don't work, or work part time, have more leeway, but are likely to be booked up with clubs; volunteer work; courses; and late-blooming ventures into arts, hobbies, and other endeavors.

Keeping in touch long distance has been cited as one of the most challenging duties of grandparenting. Many a frustrated grandparent has thrown in the towel and given up trying to reach out. Don't! This chapter is designed to give you some workable ideas for dealing with long-distance situations.

Your Place or Ours?

If you're content with your present living arrangements and the amount of time you get to spend with your grandchildren, you're in good shape, and way above average.

If, as is more likely, you feel you don't get to spend as much time with your grandchildren as you would like, you need to ask yourself some questions:

➤ How often can you get one or more of your grandchildren to visit you each year?

➤ How often is it convenient, and enjoyable, for you to visit your grandchildren's home or homes?

➤ What are the pros and cons of visiting your grandkids?

➤ What times or seasons of the year are better or worse for you to visit?

➤ What attractions and inducements do you offer your grandchildren to visit you?

➤ Will these enticements diminish as your grandkids grow older? Or will they increase?

➤ What obstacles are there in the way of their visits at certain times of each month or year, such as school, religious commitments, membership on sports teams, or attendance at non-school courses and lessons?

➤ What seasons of the year are most appealing to them to visit at your home?

Once you have the answers, you will be in a better position to plan ways to make visits (both to and from) more convenient, as well as more fun. If you want to be really organized about this, you can make a calendar chart and color code it to show the best, worst, and so-so times for visits.

A Question of Space

Sometimes getting to your grandkids is not the problem—it's where you're going to stay once you're there. If your son's or daughter's house is filled to capacity with the grandkids, the pets, and all their "stuff," you may have to be creative. If you've moved to a smaller home or an apartment or condo, you might also be lacking in space. Let's face it, as much as you love your grandkids, five people in a small one-bathroom apartment is just not going to work! If the home environment (whether yours or theirs) doesn't allow for comfortable visits, consider these options:

➤ Ask a good friend or friendly neighbor to accommodate one or more of your family members, who do not require care or supervision, at his or her place for a few nights.

➤ Stay at a nearby inn or motel when you're visiting your kids and grandkids.

➤ Pitch a tent in the backyard if you love the great outdoors and are accustomed to camping out, or have your grandkids sleep in a tent in your yard.

➤ Have your grandkids bring sleeping bags, or borrow them from someone you know. Designate some floor space as a sleeping area to handle the overflow.

➤ Rent an RV (recreational vehicle) or camper to park in the driveway or rear of the house.

➤ Host only one or two grandchildren at a time.

➤ Alternate visits to the grandkids' house—grandpa or grandma going alone each time.

While none of these solutions is perfect, they might give you some ideas to minimize problems and allow you to spend more time with your grandkids. Kids often are intrigued by alternative sleeping arrangements and may welcome a week in a cozy floor bed. Remember, every problem has a solution!

Hartt to Hartt

Friends of ours have an interesting arrangement to compensate for the fact that two grandparents live in the same Connecticut city as their son, daughter-in-law, and three grandchildren, while the other two grandparents live about 900 miles away. The faraway grandparents, who live on an island in South Carolina, exchange homes twice a year with the Connecticut grandparents. This way, there's plenty of room for everyone. The South Carolina grandparents get to spend concentrated periods of time with their grandkids, while the Connecticut grandparents have some great vacations! And, neither set of grandparents has to worry about their homes while they're away.

Party Line: Keeping in Touch Long Distance

If you find it difficult to keep up regular communication with your grandkids, you may have to look at some less conventional methods than letter writing and telephone calls. Here are some other methods of getting through to your grandkids:

➤ Ask a grandchild to start a story, to which you will add the next episode. Sending the manuscript back and forth, with you and your grandchild contributing episodes in sequence, is great fun, and it will stimulate some entertaining exchanges of ideas.

> **Great Grandparenting**
>
> If you have a computer with a modem, and so do your grandchildren, get online and start e-mailing them. Ask someone who's in the know about computers how to go about doing this. Your grandkids will think it's "totally awesome" when you start asking for their e-mail addresses! There's a bonus, too. E-mailing is fast, convenient, and cheap.

> **Great Grandparenting**
>
> If you find your grandchild isn't in the mood to talk when you call and you're spending all your time on the line with a parent, suggest a conference call. Such calls are easy to arrange and may add just the extra dimension you need to stimulate a reluctant talker.

➤ Start a picture in pencil, pen, crayon, water color, or any other medium your grandchild will enjoy. Send the incomplete picture to your grandchild, and ask him or her to finish it and send you the results. Be sure the picture is hanging in a prominent spot the next time your grandchild visits your house! Or, ask your grandkids to send you some of their own original artwork for your "gallery." They'll be flattered that you asked.

➤ Plant twin gardens—one at the grandkids' home and one at your house. Every two weeks or so, take snapshots of the gardens at each end and mail them to compare growth. This is a better activity for the summer months, but it could be accomplished during the winter with an indoor planter.

➤ Give grandchildren disposable cameras from time to time so they can take snapshots to send to you in exchange for ones you send them. This is an especially good idea to do for a birthday, start of a new school, going to camp, Halloween, Thanksgiving, and other holidays.

➤ For children who are old enough to write well and who enjoy writing, give a diary as a small gift on an appropriate occasion. Explain that the grandchild should record the activities and events of her life, and that you'll read the entries together on your next visit. Be sure to tell her that you will respect her privacy and read only what she deems appropriate for your eyes!

➤ Ask your grandkids to send you simple recipes for cakes, cookies, and such, which you will then bake and send to them on special occasions.

There are dozens of creative methods of keeping in touch with grandkids; those mentioned previously barely scratch the surface. Whatever you decide to do, make sure it will be fun for both of you and won't be too difficult or take up too much of your grandkids' time.

The Write Stuff

The story goes that Andrew Carnegie, the famous industrialist/philanthropist, had a favorite grandson he liked to visit and write letters to. He became frustrated, however, when the boy went off to camp and stopped answering his postcards and letters. Carnegie finally wrote the boy a brief letter, ending with a postscript, "P.S. Enclosed is $10 for spending money. Buy whatever you want."

Carnegie, according to legend, did not enclose one red cent, but he practically guaranteed that he would hear from his grandson. Sure enough. Very soon he received a note from the boy, "Dear Grandpa…." You can guess the rest.

We're not advocating that you resort to trickery to get your grandkids to drop you a line, but sometimes you may have to use a little ingenuity. And, isn't it worth it when you see one of their hand-addressed envelopes in your mailbox, along with all the bills, catalogs, and announcements that you may have won $20,000 a month for life?

Letter writing is said to be the second most popular way of communicating, after telephoning. That statistic, however, probably doesn't take grandchildren into account. While there is no doubt that grandkids love to receive all kinds of mail, getting them to respond can be a problem. Try some of these ploys:

➤ Send them postcards, stamped and pre-addressed. The cards should all have different scenes of animals or birds or the changing seasons. Tell your correspondents-to-be that you'd like to hear from them at the end of each month, with a couple of sentences describing the most important thing that happened to them during that time. Promise that upon receipt of each card, you'll send them a prize.

➤ Provide grandchildren of suitable age with a small tape recorder, a package of cassettes, and mailing envelopes; say you'll send them two blank cassettes for each one they return to you with a message.

➤ At an appropriate holiday or occasion, send grandchildren personalized stationery with their names on the paper and envelopes. Put your address and stamps on a couple of the envelopes.

➤ Send older grandchildren magazine and newspaper clippings you know will interest them, and ask them in turn to send you clippings, perhaps from their school newspaper or a hobby or sports magazine they like to read.

➤ Start a pen pals club with grandchildren, nephews, nieces, aunts, uncles, and other family members. Or, you might also want to mail out an occasional family chain letter.

237

➤ Have snapshots of the grandkids made into postcards (any photo studio and many neighborhood print shops can make them), and send them to the parents, with instructions that you want at least one of them mailed back to you by the child in the photo.

Hartt to Hartt

A grandfather we know, who has a large family scattered all over the country and abroad, has a favorite hobby. He publishes a monthly newsletter, which he distributes to his children, grandkids, stepchildren, and other relatives. It contains family news, cartoons, jokes, puzzles, want ads, and so forth. It's so lively and readable that he's able to threaten recipients that if they don't send him news from their outposts from time to time, he'll take them off the mailing list. It works!

(Not) Home for the Holidays

The mail is also very useful in helping celebrate holidays or other special occasions that you won't be able to enjoy in person with your grandkids. When you can't be on the scene, do the next best thing—mail something of mutual interest. This could include:

➤ A small photo album with snapshots appropriate to the holiday or season

➤ A cassette with conversation, stories, or songs (such as "Happy Birthday to You")

➤ A videotape of a short trip you took or an activity you tried, which you hope the grandkids can experience in the future

➤ A family tree sketch, with small photos of relatives and close friends, to which the kids can add their own personal snapshots

➤ A book that is appropriate to the occasion, with a related inscription

There's no doubt about it. Keeping in touch is vitally important to maintaining a good relationship with your grandchildren. Writing letters and sending small gifts or items of common interest is a great way to let your grandkids know you are thinking of them, and to keep you in their thoughts as well.

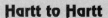

Hartt to Hartt

Among the most successful "calendar event" gifts we have sent to our grandchildren when we couldn't be with them have been costumes of their favorite characters. Children are used to seeing such costumes at Halloween time, but it's a real surprise to get them at other times of the year. What could be more exciting for a little girl than to receive a princess costume for a birthday in June or for a little boy to get a baseball costume at the beginning of the big league season in April?

The Divorced Grandparent

It seems that divorce—the D word—has touched nearly every family in America in some way. As you know, it is very prevalent—50 percent of all marriages will end in divorce. America has the highest divorce rate in the Western world—60 percent higher than in Sweden, Britain, or Canada, three times higher than in Germany or France, and 10 times higher than in Italy. There's no question that divorce is hard on everyone, and when grandparents divorce, it can be extremely upsetting to not only the divorcing couple, but to the couple's children and grandchildren as well. It complicates matters and challenges the image of grandparents as stable and dependable.

If grandparents are divorced and living in separate homes, whether singly, married, or with a companion, plans for visitations can become quite complicated. When the divorce has been anything but friendly, there often are frictions that affect everyone. Sometimes, grandparents with grudges against each other use their grandkids as sounding boards to bad-mouth their former mates.

Is it better, under such hostile circumstances, not to bring the youngest and oldest generations together at all, at least until things cool off?

Grandparents, regardless of what's going on in their lives, bear a responsibility to their grandchildren. While it may (or may not) be appropriate to discuss your divorce with an adult child, it is not appropriate to discuss your divorce with grandchildren. A simple, unemotional explanation as to why you and grandpa will no longer be living together is all that's necessary. Reassure your grandchildren that the divorce will not alter their relationship with either grandparent, and that both you and your former spouse will always love them and care for them. Each grandparent should talk to the grandkids and make sure to reinforce what the other grandparent has said, or will say. Never try to get your grandchildren to side you with against their other grandparent—it's unfair, and when grandchildren are old enough to realize what you did, it will come back to haunt you.

If you feel you cannot be with your grandkids without expressing bitterness or anger toward your former spouse or burdening them with your problems, perhaps a cooling-off period is in order. Remember, if the divorce is new, your grandchildren are likely to be upset and confused about it. Consult with the parents to see how they feel visits should be handled. If one of you has a new spouse or companion, it might take the grandkids, as well as your adult child (not to mention the new person), some time to get used to the idea. In this case, it's best for the grandparent to visit alone until the grandkids are ready to meet someone new.

The Divorced Parent

If the parents are the ones getting divorced, be prepared for a time of extreme upset and emotion. While divorce is difficult—often agonizing—for everyone, those most in need of support, encouragement, and love are the children. You'll need to ask your son or daughter what role they hope you'll play if a divorce or separation occurs. You should make it clear, however, that you will not participate in trying to turn a grandchild against the other parent. While you may find you want to side with your own child, you should try to appear neutral in front of your grandkids. If you don't, they might feel pressured to agree with you, thereby betraying one of their parents.

Psychologists tell us that when parents are at odds with each other, children often assume they are to blame. Grandparents can play an important role by assuring grandchildren that they are not the cause of the split and that they are still loved by both their mother and father.

You can go a step further by promising younger grandchildren that they will still see both of their parents and spend special times with them, as well as with you. If the custodial parent is extremely upset about the divorce and either neglecting parental duties or burdening the kids with his or her anguish, try to get the grandkids for a visit, or at least take them out for day trips. They no doubt will be very sad and upset about the changes in their lives, and will need reassurance and love. They also will need time to forget their problems and have fun. *Note:* Before you say anything to grandkids about spending time with both parents, be sure you know the visitation arrangements. Don't make any promises that can't be kept. Your grandkids are especially vulnerable at this point and must not be subjected to any more disappointments.

Grandparents as Victims

One lamentable result of divorce is that grandchildren are often moved far away or purposely withheld from contact with their grandparents. This might happen, for example, when a wife who has custody of the children is so bitter she puts her ex-husband's mother and father "off-limits." In extreme cases, this may even include forbidding grandparents from making phone calls to the children or sending birthday gifts. A vengeful parent might even confiscate mail from the grandparents.

If you ever find your grandparenting splintered by this kind of animosity, and you're completely cut off from communication, there are steps you can take to help heal the wounds:

➤ *Keep a diary* and write in it thoughts that you have of your grandchildren throughout your period of estrangement. Always make diary entries on their birthdays, graduation days, or other dates personally important to them.

➤ *Send cards and letters regularly,* even if you get no answers and suspect they're not being delivered.

➤ *Keep copies of your correspondence* in your journal or a separate scrapbook.

➤ *Start a savings account for each grandchild in absentia,* no matter how trifling, and make special contributions if you have been directed not to send gifts.

➤ *If you've been cut off from your grandchildren by a vengeful former son- or daughter-in-law, ask your own child to intervene.* Could you arrange to visit when the grandchildren are with your own child? Or, could your own child at least give your grandchildren messages? You want your grandkids to know that you love them, regardless of the situation.

➤ *If worse comes to worst, you may want to consult an attorney* to see if you have any legal recourse in this situation. Be prepared though, for some unpleasantness if you do this. Your former in-law will resent it, and, if you do get to see your grandchildren, it may take some time to rebuild your relationship, depending on how much influence the angry parent has had on them.

As difficult as these situations are, keep heart. Most periods of bitterness and anger end, or at least diminish, and you may be able to re-establish contacts and bonds with your grandchild if you're willing to wait it out. Or, one day, as young adults, the grandchildren may search you out. You'll be able to show them, through your journals and other gestures, that you loved them and were thinking about them all along.

Multiple Grandparents

When remarriage results in a small squad of grandparents, stepgrandparents, and sometimes adopted grandparents, you may find yourself unhappy with your status. This kind of situation results most often when one grandparent or pair of grandparents lives farther away than the others, or has only recently joined the family through marriage.

Great Grandparenting

If your son or daughter is getting a divorce and if you're on good terms with the other grandparents, contact them as soon as you hear about the impending split. This is the point at which all members of the first generation should come to an understanding of ways in which the grandchildren can be protected. Resolve that you all will do everything in your power to let the grandkids know you love them and want to keep them close to you, in spirit if not in actuality.

If you feel that you're on the outside looking in, you might want to take steps to improve your status. Offer to have the grandkids for visits, or to take them along when you go on a trip. Consider, though, that moving from an outsider to an insider may involve a lot of work. You could even turn out to be the object of slights, snubs, or even outright rejections. If you're elderly or not in the best of health, or content with the amount of time you get with your grandkids, you may want to focus your energies on something less frustrating. If you're determined to have a go at it, there are ways to overcome the limitations of distance or fading communications. Consider the following strategies:

➤ Plan "Grandparent's Day"—a gathering of all grandparents at the most convenient time and location for all. Get to know each other better, and discuss openly and frankly how to arrange visits to and by grandkids, so that everyone benefits and no one is slighted.

➤ Organize a family reunion. If your family already holds regular reunions, you're way ahead of the game. If not, you should know that planning one is a big challenge. Nevertheless, a family reunion is the best way to review your heritage, get acquainted or reacquainted with distant family members, and strengthen your family ties. It's the opportune time, too, for grandparents to find out what the grandkids are up to, where their interests lie, and how to make a visit to your house more irresistible when you issue your next invitation.

➤ Decide which grandparents you enjoy most and are most compatible with. *Suggest that they visit you,* along with older grandkids with whom you can all enjoy games, entertainment, outings, sports, and socializing.

Hartt to Hartt

We participated in a family reunion that was held over a weekend, when we met grand-nieces and nephews for the first time. What really stands out in our minds, however, was the evening that each family group did a version of "Show and Tell." Some did skits, others sang songs, while some younger family members simply introduced themselves. But, one family member had brought along home movies he had taken 30 years earlier, and showed us sometimes hilarious, sometimes tender scenes from the lives of some of the parents present who, in the movies, were then children. The laughter and tears brought us all together.

The Least You Need to Know

➤ Consider circumstances and busy schedules when determining whether it's practical to visit the grandkids or have them come to you.

➤ Use your ingenuity and creativity to avoid losing touch when you live a long distance away from your grandchildren.

➤ Liven up your letters and send creative packages to prompt more frequent responses from your grandchildren.

➤ Make communication and discussion your number one priority when divorce in either generation will affect visits.

➤ When the grandparent population in your family exceeds four, use your wits to share your grandkids with the rest of the family.

Chapter 22

Parenting All Over Again: When Your Kid Isn't Able

In This Chapter

➤ Circumstances and resources affecting grandparents who parent

➤ Drug and alcohol abuse that threaten grandchildren

➤ Your grandkids' parents and financial difficulties

➤ Talking with older grandkids when their family is disintegrating

➤ Eliminating labels that hurt kids

➤ Ideas for grandparents as surrogate parents

"Parenting has been called the toughest job in America. And for some, the job gets tougher the second time around."

This was the introductory sentence to a newspaper article, telling the story of two grandparents who rescued their grandson, John, from a foster care center after his parents were declared unfit. John was a one-year-old when he went to live with his grandparents.

Great Grandparenting
You can get help as a second-time-around parent. Contact the Grandparent Information Center, sponsored by the American Association of Retired Persons (AARP) at 601 E Street NW, Washington, D.C., 20049. The center, which also can be reached by phone at 202-434-2277, offers information of concern to this special set of grandparents, including legal, financial, medical, and emotional issues, as well as a free newsletter, *Parenting Grandchildren*.

Ten years later, John calls his grandparents the only real parents he has ever known. Although they love him and he loves them, the road has not always been smooth. It's sometimes hard for John to understand why his grandfather won't toss the football with him, or why his grandmom doesn't sit outside in the cold to watch all his soccer games like the other moms. The kids at school look at him funny when his grandparents show up on at Meet-the-Teacher night. And, his grandparents don't mingle and joke with the other parents. They always appear to be a little out of place and a bit uncomfortable.

John's situation is by no means unique. Grandparents head nearly four million households in the U.S., with about one and a half million of these homes consisting solely of grandchildren and grandparents. These numbers are likely to continue increasing in the future as the divorce rate climbs and as older people live longer and are able to care for children who need help.

When grandparents take on child-rearing obligations, they face emotional, financial, and social problems—sometimes legal obstacles as well. In this chapter, we won't advise grandparents to jump in and become parents all over again at the slightest provocation. But we will provide some insights into tough family situations and how to attempt to alleviate them, with the child's welfare and future always in mind.

Dealing with Alcohol or Drug Abuse

It is estimated that 85 to 90 percent of grandparents who are raising their children's children are doing so because their child is abusing drugs and/or alcohol to the point where the children are not properly cared for. Grandparents in this situation are faced with tough issues. One is the immediate problem of taking care of the grandchildren. Another is dealing with your adult child who is in a crisis situation. You may have tried to ignore your child's problem, or pretend it wasn't all that bad in order to keep the family situation intact. Now you've found out you can no longer do that, either because you've acknowledged your grandkids are at risk, or an outside source such as a social worker or child welfare representative has determined them to be at risk. You'll be grieving for your child's situation, but your immediate attention must be on your grandchildren. And, you're going to need some help.

> ### Hartt to Hartt
>
> Former neighbors of ours became surrogate parents of a 9-year-old grandson and an 11-year-old granddaughter after their daughter and son-in-law went on drug-related binges and were brought to court for temporary abandonment and endangering the lives of their children. Our neighbors expected the arrangement to be temporary; eventually the kids were to be placed in the care of an aunt and uncle. It didn't happen. Now, six years later, the grandmother (age 62) is more vigorous than ever, relishing the youth activities with which she's involved. But her husband, who's 66 and in poor health, struggles to keep up. Fortunately, the kids have become admirable young adults and are taking over more responsibility on their own.

Physical and Sexual Abuse

We said earlier that 85 to 90 percent of all grandparents raising grandchildren are doing so because their children are excessive users of drugs and/or alcohol. Nearly all of the other 10 to 15 percent are doing so because their grandchildren have been sexually and/or physically abused.

This situation can be equally, if not even more, devastating for grandparents than drug or alcohol abuse. Since there is a tendency for abuse to run in families, grandparents might feel they have contributed to the problem. You may experience rage at your adult child for abusing your grandchildren or allowing another to abuse them. You might also be gravely concerned with the mental state of your child, or worry that your child, as well as your grandchild, is or has been the target of abuse. And, you will feel fear for your grandchildren.

Again, as with drug and alcohol abuse, you may have tried to ignore a problem you've suspected. Perhaps the thought of abuse is revolting to you and you didn't want to deal with it or bring shame upon your family. How can you tell if a child has been abused? A child may be abused if he has more cuts, bruises, and skin blemishes than normal, and frequently offers stories about how he got them. The child may also become increasingly timid and easily startled by unexpected noises or normal scolding. If you ask a child if his mom or dad hit him, chances are he'll say no, but watch for avoidance of eye contact and other signs that he's lying.

If you suspect your grandchild is being abused, it is your responsibility to intervene. Try to keep the child with your for a few days while you contact someone who can offer help.

You may want to take a child to a doctor, who might be able to determine how the injuries occurred. If you confront your adult child about the suspected abuse and do not get a satisfactory answer, threaten to notify your local child welfare department and be prepared to do so, if necessary. Consider the following points as you plan what to do next.

➤ *This is clearly a crisis, and the rules about non-intervention don't apply.* You've tried over the years not to tell your children how to raise their kids but an abusive situation requires your action.

➤ *Almost any social service office can provide the names of local child-abuse organizations you can contact for information.* These organizations, including your local United Way, have counselors and social workers with whom you can discuss your suspicions and decide how to proceed.

➤ *You need to learn the reasons why the parents are behaving as they are.* Are they into drugs? Is there a history of abuse in the family? Your counselor or social worker can investigate to begin to uncover the truth.

➤ *If the parent agrees to let you take your grandchildren, go ahead and get them out of the abusive household.* If your child refuses to let you take them, and you think they are in danger, contact a local social service agency, such as children and youth service. Stress that it is an emergency situation.

If the situation is explosive and you fear for the immediate safety of your grandchild but cannot get a representative from a social service agency to the house very quickly, call the police. You cannot afford to have your grandchild remain at risk. If you want to remove the children from the parent's house and take them into your home, you will need to petition the court for a custody order.

Hartt to Hartt

Many years ago, we lived in a small, southern town. Our children became friendly with three siblings who were in foster care. Marilyn was substitute teaching at the time, and had one of these children in her class. She kept a close eye on him, based on comments our own son had made. Marilyn began to suspect the boy and his siblings were being abused in the foster home, and she called the local division on youth and foster care. A caseworker came to see Marilyn and admitted the agency already was aware that these foster children were being abused. However, they had no other homes that would accept three children, and felt it was a top priority to keep the siblings together. Agency officials pledged they would keep a watchful eye on the situation.

Poverty and Bankruptcy

Money problems may not seem so bad after you've read about all the other problems in this chapter. But financial problems can be devastating, and they can threaten the stability of a family. If your son or daughter and spouse are experiencing severe financial difficulties, you'll wonder whether or not you should intervene.

Psychologically, it's detrimental for grandparents with plenty of money to provide unsolicited cash or valuables to parents who just happen to be at a lower economic level. It can be very demeaning to parents who are hard-pressed for funds to see the grandparents lavishing expensive toys and designer clothing on their children.

However, if the parents are temporarily unable to maintain an acceptable standard of living due to job situations or other factors, your help is likely to be appreciated. If the situation is very bad, and both parents are working extra hours or more than one job to earn money, you may even offer to take your grandchildren into your home until the circumstances improve. Be diplomatic and considerate:

➤ Offer your help, but don't offer criticism or condemnation. Have a frank discussion with your son or daughter and spouse.

➤ Bear in mind that any censure and disapproval you voice are likely to filter down to your grandchildren, and in the long run they will suffer along with their parents.

➤ Never give the grandkids presents that are more expensive than what they would receive as gifts at home.

➤ Buy your grandchildren clothes (especially replacements for worn items) as needed, but don't go overboard. What they really need and what they want may be two entirely different things.

➤ Make a special effort to teach the grandkids about the value of money (see Chapter 20, where we discuss enjoying your grandchildren on a budget). Explain in a loving and non-critical fashion why the family is having monetary problems and why many other families are in the same boat.

➤ Help with mounting bills in inconspicuous ways; for example, pay a share of any services you have benefited from, such as telephone calls, transportation, or food.

When financial disaster has struck one generation of a family but not the other, it may be feasible to consolidate living arrangements so all three generations are living harmoniously under one roof. Children often thrive when living with more than two adults who are communicative and caring.

Of course, the transition from a nuclear family living together to an extended family living together is bound to take some getting used to by everyone. If you have a large home where everyone would be offered some degree of privacy, you probably have a good chance of a successful transition. If your living space is small and privacy will suffer, be sure to discuss the situation thoroughly and carefully before embarking on such a venture.

Simplifying the Facts

How do you tell a five-year-old boy that his widowed father has a criminal record and is not going to be allowed to care for him? Or a seven-year-old girl that her parents have been killed in a plane crash and her grandparents are the closest relatives? Or two preschoolers that their parents are divorcing and their grandparents will be taking them to their house for a while?

Your best approach is a frank one, making it clear what will happen, where the child will be living, and what situations will and will not change in their lives.

Young tots recover from these severe, and oftentimes abrupt, dislocations, and they adapt to new ways of living more readily than older children. Traumatic events, however, such as the loss of a parent, can result in behavioral changes or problems in children as they experience intense feelings that they don't know how to deal with. They will need continual reassurance and emotional support, experts advise. When talking to them about the changes that are going to occur in their lives, try to remain calm, show authority, and talk about the future in a positive manner.

Older children are more resistant to change than younger ones, and are likely to have a harder time dealing with major changes in their lives. Be as supportive and affirmative as possible, but don't suppose that you know exactly what the child is feeling. If your grandchild is coming to live with you, he may resent having to have to leave his own home, regardless of the situation there. This is a problem with which you probably need some help. Consult a psychologist, therapist, clergyman, or other professional on how to handle this problem. You will need some guidance for your initial conversation with your grandchild regarding impending changes, as well as help in planning for the future. Your grandchild also will benefit from talking with a counselor or psychologist.

Hartt to Hartt

A high school teacher's 16-year-old student, Amy, confided that her mother was abusive, pregnant again, and had told Amy she wanted her "out of her life." Amy was thinking about dropping out of school. The teacher got involved and asked Amy if she had a grandparent who lived nearby. Amy said yes, but that the grandmother was too old to help. The teacher phoned Amy's mother and said she was concerned that Amy was thinking about quitting school and she wondered if Amy could live with her grandmother. Perhaps Amy could help her around the house in exchange for room and board, the teacher suggested. Fortunately, the plan worked out. Amy moved in with her grandmother and graduated with her class.

Erasing the Curse from "Adopted," "Foster," and "Step-"

"You can't tell me what I have to eat. You're not my real grandfather!"

"The other kids tease me. They say I don't have any parents, only grandparents."

When you take a child or children whose parents are no longer alive (or who are unfit to care for them) into your home, you may have to overcome many obstacles to the new relationship.

One of the ways to ease the transition is to avoid using terms such as foster children, adopted baby, and stepparent. These terms make kids feel different or somehow inferior to a "regular" child who lives with his own mom, dad, and siblings. While you and your grandchild both know that your family is different from other families, you are still a family and should try to make it as "normal" as possible for the children.

This is not to say that the children should start calling their grandparents "Mom" and "Dad," or should not acknowledge that their situation is different from that of their friends and classmates. But, today's society has many kinds of families, from traditional to two parents of the same sex. Make your living situation as normal and stable as you can, and let your grandchildren know that you love them and will care for them.

Adults may not mind saying things such as, "I was adopted when I was an infant," or "She's my stepmother." But children can feel rejected if adults refer to them as having anything but a "normal" relationship with the key members of their family.

Why are these words so problematic? For one thing, the myth of the "wicked stepmother" in children's literature has never completely disappeared. Many children still suffer from the circumstances surrounding remarriage, particularly when a stepfather or stepmother favors his or her own children more than the ones who have newly come under the stepparent's care.

In general, though, many of these terms are problematic because they come into use as a result of a traumatic event or circumstance: the death of a parent, a divorce, and/or problems that make it impossible for parents to continue raising their children properly.

As a grandparent, you can help encourage a good "blend" when there is a hodgepodge of natural grandparents, stepgrandparents, adoptees, or foster children in your family. You are in the best overall position to harmonize built-in jealousies, rivalries, dislocations, and rejections, and to bring order out of chaos.

> **Danger Zone**
> Grandparents lose their credibility and do no one any good when they take sides in family disputes because they dislike an individual or disagree with a point of view. You don't have to agree with everyone, and you certainly can't like everyone equally. But you're old enough and experienced enough to be a moderator and to neutralize (to the best of your abilities) the actions and attitudes that threaten to split the family apart.

When Grandparents Become Surrogate Parents

Just at a time in your life when you expected to be retiring, traveling, socializing, and relaxing, you find yourselves involved with changing diapers, warming bottles, or chauffeuring grandchildren to Little League or Girl Scouts!

If this has happened to you, or you suspect it's going to, it's time to take parenting classes, read new child-rearing books, and learn what kinds of activities will enrich a child's life, in addition to school. You may have done all that once or more in decades past, but you'll need new information to keep up with today's world.

You'll also need a support system. Being placed into a different lifestyle than that of most of your friends is going to impact your social life and activities, and you'll have to work harder to maintain your friendships.

The concept of grandparents raising grandkids has gotten more attention in recent years as the numbers increase. To give you an example, the 1970 Census showed that about 957,000 children across the country were being raised by grandparents who were the primary caregivers. By 1997, that number had increased to about 1.5 million. New York City alone has at least 14,000 grandparents raising grandkids.

Some cities have addressed the issue. In Boston, ground recently was broken for Grandfamilies Homes, a $4-million, 26-apartment complex designed exclusively for grandparent/grandchildren families. The apartments have handicapped access and are toddlerproof. Programs offered for both generations by the YMCA will include computer classes and aerobics.

In Portland, Oregon, a program to assist grandparents raising grandkids was started in 1991 by the city's Urban League. Its membership has grown from five when the program began to 150 now.

If you're aware of other grandparents in your situation, try to get to know them better. You may become mutual sources of advice, or at least able to suggest sources of information that will be helpful to the other. Public and private schools; churches, synagogues, and other religious centers; pediatricians; child psychologists; and senior citizens clubs may also guide you to other places that can offer assistance.

If you find yourself parenting when you should be grandparenting, try not to become discouraged. While your situation may often be difficult, think about what you are doing for your grandchildren, and the opportunities you will have for a special relationship with them. While many ideas about parenting have changed since you were a parent, some of the basics are still the same:

➤ *Children need love.* You need to be just as loving as a grandparent as you would be as a parent. If children don't find enough love and caring at home, they will often turn to outsiders for affection—sometimes with disastrous results.

➤ *Children need structure.* Although grandparents who see their grandkids only infrequently can afford to be lenient and stretch some of the rules, you cannot, as a surrogate parent, hedge on the restraints and limitations that have to be imposed on your grandchildren.

➤ *Children are not alike.* Make your disciplinary guidelines appropriate for the age, capabilities, and personality of each child. What will work for one may not work for another.

➤ *Don't try to do everything yourself.* Children can handle responsibility. Let grandchildren undertake whatever tasks they are capable of doing, whether it's making sandwiches, raking the yard, vacuuming, feeding the goldfish, cleaning up their rooms, or running a computer.

> **Great Grandparenting**
> Despite the demands of child-rearing, you need to keep your friendships with your peers alive. In order to be a good surrogate parent, you should continue your hobbies and interests, and socialize with your friends and neighbors. The fuller your life, the better the lives of your grandchildren will be.

➤ *Don't emphasize money.* Encourage pursuits and pleasures that require little or no cost, such as sitting with you and reading books, gardening, taking nature walks, painting, doing crafts, and other creative ventures. Giving children money or buying them things doesn't take the place of good parenting. Trips to the movies, restaurants, shows, and amusement parks can't substitute for positive personal endeavors.

➤ *Stay open to new ideas.* Be willing to learn, thereby not only improving your parental capabilities, but also serving as a role model for your grandkids. Take the opportunity to enjoy seeing children gain new skills by honing some of yours—or learning new ones—together.

If you are the primary caregiver, you will need to immerse yourself in every aspect of your grandchildren's lives. If you've forgotten what a demanding job parenting is, you'll soon be reminded. Unless the parents have certain visitation rights, you won't have much respite. Remember that grandparents can ask for help. You can hire babysitters like parents do, or call upon friends to help in some way.

Calling in the Troops: Older Uncles and Aunts

If your family is large, you may have a number of older relatives who relish the idea of being asked to join your multi-generational segment of the family. Or you might find several friends whose own grandchildren live far away and would be delighted to play the role of "surrogate aunt or uncle," while you take on the role of parent.

Hartt to Hartt

Our co-author spent six years during the Depression, from the age of 10 to 16, in a large, 19th-century home with a multi-generational family. The family consisted of grandparents, parents, a brother, an unemployed uncle, an aunt, the family dog, and quite often a visiting cousin or uncle. It was a delightful arrangement, and, with plenty of bathrooms, bedrooms, and quaint little alcoves, there was lots of privacy, but never a lonely moment. Everyone had difficulty making ends meet in the early 1930s, but belt-tightening was accepted by all—if not cheerfully, at least with forbearance.

The Least You Need to Know

➤ If you are grandparents raising grandkids, know that you're not alone. There are 1.5 million of you in the U.S. and there are many resources available to help you.

➤ Be prepared to intervene if you have grandchildren who are being abused or neglected. It is better to alienate your son or daughter than to have your grandchild injured, or worse. Consult child abuse counselors if the situation is not an emergency.

➤ Explore different ways to help your children and grandchildren when financial difficulties hit.

➤ Seek help from professional counselors for yourself and your grandchildren if they move in with you due to tragic family circumstances such as death, incarceration, or divorce. Consult a counselor about the best way to explain the circumstances to older grandchildren.

➤ Eliminate from your vocabulary labels that downgrade kids whose lives have been disrupted, and make their family lives as normal as possible.

➤ Give your grandchildren as much love as you can and trust that you'll do just fine if you're called on to be a surrogate parent.

Chapter 23

Mind-Boggling Challenges

In This Chapter

➤ Explaining prejudice and bigotry to grandchildren

➤ Children of cross-cultural descent

➤ Out-of-wedlock dilemmas

➤ Helping troubled grandchildren or those with disabilities

➤ How to deal with sex in the youngest generation

By the time you get to grandparenting age, you've been through a lot. You've watched many events unfold in front of you and get resolved in one way or another. There aren't as many surprises in life as there once were. But, every now and then, something comes along that knocks you for a loop.

I mean, there you were, watching the Sunday afternoon football game, when your 16-year-old grandson asks if he could talk to you for a minute. "Sure," you say, wondering what's so important that it can't wait until half-time. You don't realize this is going to be momentous until you look at his face, and then you instinctively reach for the remote and turn off the TV. He's pale and it looks like he's been crying.

As much as you try to prepare yourself during the few seconds before he starts talking, it still feels as though somebody kicked you in the gut when your grandson tells you that his 15-year-old girlfriend is pregnant and they don't know what to do about it. All he knows is that his mom's gonna cry and his dad's gonna kill him. He can't even think about what his girlfriend's parents will do.

No family is immune to special situations and problems, regardless of its ethnicity, financial position, or geographical location. There are unmarried pregnancies, interracial marriages, homosexual relationships, emotional and physical problems, and many other stumbling blocks that occur during life. Things happen, and, when they do, we've got to deal with them.

When kids in trouble turn to their parents for understanding and rescue, it's generally a positive move. But, often parents are too close to a situation involving their own kids to be objective. Psychologists say it's extremely difficult for parents not to think of their kids as being part of themselves, so it's hard for parents to see their children as separate people. As a grandparent, you can offer a more balanced and less emotional perspective—and this chapter will show you how.

Facing Prejudice and Bigotry

During your lifetime, you've seen our society become more ethnically, culturally, and spiritually diverse. The boundaries have blurred. Unfortunately, many people's tolerance level is still at about zero when it comes to accepting people who are different.

It seems that young people, with their open minds and idealism, would not be eager to participate in bigotry and prejudice, but many are. Skinheads, neo-Nazis, and other hate groups are on the rise, with frightening consequences. Unspeakable acts have been committed by these groups—church burnings, cemetery vandalisms, and more. If your grandchildren are "different," as nearly every child is in some way, they likely will be the targets of some sort of bigotry at one time or another. Let's face it. Although we most often think of prejudice in terms of race, there are many other targets for it as well. People with disabilities have become targets recently, with terrifying frequency. Over-weight people, homosexuals, the elderly, and different religious groups are all subjects for bias and prejudice.

Prejudice simply means having negative feelings and attitudes toward a distinct group. Literally, it means pre-judging such people, and not liking them because they are differ-ent without knowing anything about them personally. Racism is believing that people from one distinct group are somehow superior to people in another distinct group. The two go hand-in-hand, and create a cycle of inequity that is difficult to break.

You should try to prepare your grandchildren who might be the targets of prejudice and bigotry by explaining to them that these attacks are not directed against them as a person, only as a member of a particular group. While prejudicial attacks seem very personal and threatening, they are launched only because the target has certain characteristics, such as dark skin, a disability, or obesity. It is a difficult concept for kids to grasp, but it is imperative not to allow them to feel that there is something wrong with them that triggers these attacks.

Explain to your grandchildren some of the root causes for prejudice:

➤ Insecurity about one's own place in the world, a job, or social status causes some people to try to make themselves feel important by putting other people down.

➤ Lack of positive exposure to people of many different backgrounds causes some people to regard those who are different from them with suspicion and mistrust.

➤ Lack of education and historical and cultural understanding about our world and its many different people causes some to be intolerant toward those they don't understand.

➤ Anger about life circumstances causes some people to look for someone to blame.

Being a target of prejudice or racism can be very difficult, demeaning, and scary. Comfort your grandchildren, but never display reverse prejudice or racism toward the group that has harassed them.

Multi-Cultural Unions

Golfer Tiger Woods, who at 21 became the 1997 Masters champion and led the PGA tour's money list, is the best friend that kids of biracial couples could have. Neither black, nor white, nor yellow, Woods proudly refers to himself as "Cablinasian," for he contains a bit of everything. He has shown mixed-race kids how to be proud of who they are with his frank discussions on race, his closeness to and respect for both his mother and father, and his million-dollar smile.

While Tiger has made great strides for people of mixed races, kids in that category will still have trouble—you can bet on it. But, if you have grandchildren who are the offspring of biracial couples and who are troubled by the fact that they "are not like other kids" or have been subject to torment, you're in a good position to offer help.

This assumes that you're fully accepting of their ethnicity and can be genuinely supportive. If you don't like their dad because he's black, your grandkids won't be able to help thinking you don't like them, either. After all, they're half black. If your son or daughter has married a person of another race, you will need to show your grandchildren that you respect and support the marriage and their family before you can help them with overcoming prejudice from others.

Many grandparents have missed out on getting to know their grandkids because they refused to accept their child's marriage. Not only do they deprive themselves of priceless family relationships by doing this, but they deprive their children and grandchildren of those relationships, as well. Grandparents in this category need to re-examine their priorities and really think about what is important in their lives.

To help your grandkids overcome the sting of prejudice, be positive, assertive, and forceful. Don't minimize the effect of the attacks on your grandchildren, but don't let them dwell on them and feel sorry for themselves. "Oh, for heavens sake, we're not going to let that sad, angry boy ruin our day, are we?" you might say. Discourage them from thinking of themselves as victims. Then divert their attention by helping them with their homework, playing a game, taking them shopping with you, or whatever.

You can help your grandchildren lose their fears and anger by teaching them tolerance and explaining why the world is a better place because of the many different kinds of people who populate it. If you're talking to young children, point out the hundreds of variations that make nature so lively and exciting. For example:

"Wouldn't it be dull if all the birds were the same size and color?"

"It wouldn't be much fun to go to the zoo if all the animals looked alike and made the same noises."

"How would you like to grow a garden where all the flowers were pink and six inches tall?"

Watch a couple of episodes of *Sesame Street* with young children and point out all the different kinds of creatures that make up that wonderful neighborhood. Through the years we have seen people with disabilities, people of different ethnicities, interracial couples, the odd phenomenon of Bert and Ernie who live together with no adults, elderly neighbors, and monsters all living harmoniously together.

Older children will respond well to a short course in overcoming bias and celebrating racial and cultural differences. You can allay their fears and strengthen their self-confidence by talking about prejudices and the value of their own heritage, as well as by reading to them or giving them books on the subject that are suitable to their ages and reading abilities.

The National Association for the Education of Young Children has a good booklet that you can send for. It's called "Teaching Your Children to Resist Bias," and it's available for free by sending a stamped, self-addressed #10 envelope to 1509 16th Street, NW, Washington, D.C., 20036-1426. Ask for publication #565.

There also are many good books dealing with prejudice and discrimination in your local library. Two books that deal with the effects of prejudice in a very effective way are: *Black Like Me*, by John Howard Griffin and *My Sweet Charlie*, by David Westheimer. Check these books first to make sure they're age-appropriate. They are not for younger children.

Some key points to cover with your grandchildren:

➤ Build their self-esteem by describing the origins and merits of the backgrounds from which they've sprung.

➤ Coach them in ways they can respond when they're derided or rejected by other kids.

➤ Ask them bluntly if there are kids they think are "funny" or "different," and explain why those kids, too, should be respected.

➤ Discuss differences freely (skin color, facial features, manners of speaking, and dress customs).

➤ Talk to them about well-known people (such as Tiger Woods) who can be role models because they have heritages and backgrounds similar to your grandkids'.

➤ Check with local colleges or universities to see if there are any programs scheduled that will deal with or celebrate racial and cultural diversity. Many colleges have an office of diversity or cultural affairs.

➤ Suggest ways they can avoid disagreeable confrontations, such as not getting involved physically or verbally with the attacker. Younger children should report any incidences to their parents, while older children might be able to handle confrontations on their own. A general response an older child could make is something such as, "What you said hurts me. I wish you could learn to respect that I'm different from you just as I've learned to respect that you're different from me."

➤ Teach them the toughest act of all: to be tolerant of, and polite to, other kids or adults who make fun of their background or appearance.

You are among millions of grandparents throughout the world who want things to be better for their grandkids. Helping them to honor and be proud of their own racial and cultural heritage, as well as to respect the heritages of others, will put action to your desires.

"I'm Pregnant!" "She's Pregnant!"

These are words that every parent or grandparent dreads hearing from an unmarried teen. Although there certainly is less stigma attached to unmarried pregnancy than there was in the past, it still is a major problem to deal with and overcome. If your grandson or granddaughter confides in you about a pregnancy, you can take comfort in the fact that his or her situation is not unique. Out of every 1,000 babies born in 1993, 310 of them were out of wedlock, compared to only 38 in 1,000 in 1940. This does not diminish the seriousness of the problem, however, and your grandchild is still likely to feel scared and alone.

As tempting as it might be to say something such as, "How could you have been so stupid (or careless, or dumb)," hold your tongue. What's been done is done. Your grandchild has probably asked himself or herself that question a thousand times and doesn't need to hear it again. Be as unemotional as possible, but reassure your grandchild that things will be okay. If you hear the news before the parents, you have a big job ahead of you.

If your grandchild (let's say granddaughter, in this case) is very upset, get her calmed down. Reassure her that you have her best interests at heart and want to help her in every

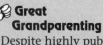

Great Grandparenting

Despite highly publicized campaigns to circulate information and contraceptives to young people, teenage pregnancies are steadily increasing. Two-thirds of them are out-of-wedlock pregnancies. Whatever you think about teenagers who engage in unprotected sex, they need our understanding, not our censure.

way possible. Let her know right away that she's going to have to tell her parents, and the sooner the better. Offer to be with her when she tells them. After that, you'll have to step back a little. As much as you love your granddaughter and want to help her, she and her parents should be the principal decision makers.

If your input is welcome, stay involved with the situation, as your advice is likely to be more objective and unemotional that of a parent. Be sure that your granddaughter sees a doctor as soon as possible to confirm the pregnancy.

Once her pregnancy has been confirmed and the initial reaction has passed, your granddaughter, her parents, and the father of the baby will need to discuss what alternatives are available. Again, if you are welcome to be involved in these discussions, you may be able to offer valuable advice. Let your granddaughter know that you will support her in whatever decision she makes. Take plenty of time to confirm the facts, discuss the options, and determine what your granddaughter's wishes are.

If you learn of the out-of-wedlock pregnancy after your granddaughter has told her parents, you have to decide what your role should be and how involved you should get. If the parents are compassionate and everyone involved has agreed to what seems to be a good course of action, you can simply show your love and affection. If your granddaughter is at odds with her parents over the situation, do what you can to smooth things over. Remind parents that the situation has occurred, and, while unfortunate, it does no good to cause more of a problem by alienating their daughter. Offer to help any way you can.

Hartt to Hartt

In Marilyn's extended family, some 40 years ago, a college student became pregnant and her father intended to ostracize her. He was a public figure, and could not bear the reproach he thought was sure to come. Marilyn was a teenager at the time, and felt sympathy for the student, but she could hardly believe it when her mother contacted this relative and volunteered to take the young woman into their home. Marilyn was amazed at her mother's generous spirit. Had not her mother warned Marilyn over and over about the dangers of premarital sex? Marilyn realized at that point that being a parent was different from being another relative. Now, as a grandparent, Marilyn fully understands this difference and further appreciates her mother's act of generosity.

Caring for Kids with Disabilities

If you have a grandchild who has physical disabilities or is mentally troubled, you can be of great help to the child, as well as to the parents. But you need to do some research so you can identify and understand the problems. Your resources include:

➤ *Your grandchild's pediatrician.* Since this is the person who probably diagnosed your grandchild's problem, he or she should be able to provide good information concerning it.

➤ *Associations.* Support groups have sprung up across the country for children and adults coping with almost every kind of mental or physical disability known. The best place to find what's available in your area is your phone book. Nearly all phone books list human service agencies, which include support groups and groups such as the March of Dimes and Easter Seals. These types of agencies will be happy to give you whatever information you require.

➤ *Government agencies.* These agencies, from which you can also obtain publications and sometimes direct aid, were formed to inform the public and help alleviate major diseases, such as muscular dystrophy, epilepsy, diabetes, and asthma. Again, look in your phone book for listings, or visit the reference section of your local library.

➤ *Public libraries.* Your library may contain books about specific diseases and impairments as well as other sources of information. Ask the reference librarian to assist you in your search.

➤ *Volunteer groups.* Most communities have volunteers who work with patients and family members to help those in need. These are excellent resources for you to know about because you can talk to people who are going through just the same kinds of anguish and anxiety as you are, and who can provide realistic advice. Many synagogues and churches sponsor support groups and advertise them in your local newspaper's religious pages. One church listed on the religion page of a mid-sized city newspaper offered support groups for people suffering or recovering from cancer, those caring for elderly parents, divorced and separated people, parents experiencing difficulties with their kids, elderly people, those grieving, and others. Your local United Way also may have information about such groups.

➤ *Your grandchild's school.* A counselor or nurse at your grandchild's school should have ample information on learning disabilities and other disabilities.

If you have a grandchild with disabilities, one of the most important ways you can help is to give the parents some relief from daily care. Offer as much time as you can. Caring for a child with disabilities can be physically and emotionally draining. You can offer to come to your grandchild's home and give the parents some time to themselves. You could help by arriving with a pre-cooked meal or offering to help with household chores. If you can take care of a grandchild with disabilities for a few hours by yourself, you could give the parents a chance to go out and enjoy themselves.

If you live far away or are otherwise unable to assist in person, consider helping financially so the parents can purchase some outside help. Think of providing your "special" grandchild with constant reminders of your love by choosing what is appropriate from the list of ideas in Chapter 21 where we talk about maintaining a long-distance relationship.

The Sexually Active Grandchild

You haven't seen Nancy, a granddaughter, who lives quite far away, for almost a year, and now you've just received a note saying she wants to come for a visit. You're thrilled! She's 20 now and in college, too busy to even call very often. As you read further down, however, your enthusiasm begins to lessen. By the time you finish reading the note, your stomach is in knots and you've got a bona fide dilemma on your hands.

It turns out that Nancy is in love—and living with—the most wonderful man ever. She wants so much to bring Tom along with her so you can get to know him and see for yourself how great he is. And, he's just got to meet you, she says. He's heard so much about you! You would love to see Nancy, and you'd really like to meet Tom, too. But, the idea of them staying together (okay, sleeping together) in your home makes you decidedly uncomfortable. What to do?

> **⚠ CAUTION Danger Zone**
> AIDS has added a new dimension of worry to the subject of teenage sex. A study by the Centers for Disease Control (CDC) found that 40 percent of American high school students regularly have sex without using protective devices. If you feel that your grandchild needs more information about AIDS and unprotected sex, contact a local agency that can provide it. Nearly every community has an AIDS information service.

Your best approach is to stand firm on your morals and ethics, whatever they may be. If you are uncomfortable with Nancy and Tom sleeping together in your home and you permit them to do so, you will resent it and not enjoy the visit. Meanwhile, they probably would be equally uncomfortable.

Call or write to Nancy and tell her you would love to see her and meet Mr. Right. You hope she understands that even though they live together, there will be separate bedrooms for them under your roof. Nancy most likely will be relieved to have the matter settled ahead of time, and everyone will know where they stand. You will have expressed no disapproval—only what the policy is in your home.

The Gay Grandchild

It used to be an almost overwhelming shock for a parent or grandparent to learn that a member of the family was gay or a lesbian. But today, gay people, although still the focus of much bias and prejudice, have been accepted at every level of society. Studies suggest that about one out of every 10 people you know is gay, whether acknowledged openly or not.

If you (and probably the rest of your family) know that a grandchild is gay or a lesbian, you need not treat him or her any differently than you would any other grandchild. Be understanding and loving, and participate in the same kinds of activities you think are appropriate for others their age.

The Least You Need to Know

➤ Talk to your grandchildren about prejudice and bigotry. Explain why they may be the targets of such behavior, and tell them they must never make anyone else a target.

➤ Be positive in dealing with grandchildren of mixed races.

➤ Treat teenage pregnancy with understanding and compassion.

➤ Do plenty of homework before trying to help grandchildren who have disabilities or are troubled.

➤ Use both good judgment and affection when dealing with a sexually active grandchild.

Aging—So What's New!

It used to be that by the time you were 35 or 40, your kids were pretty much taking care of themselves and you were looking ahead to having the house to yourself. Some folks were already grandparents, experiencing the joys of part-time parenting.

Nowadays, many people are just getting around to having babies at age 35 or 40, and probably won't be looking at grandparenting until they're well into their 60s or even 70s! Times do change!

Some people believe the trend toward older parents is a positive one. Parents in their 30s and 40s tend to be better educated and better off financially than those who start at very young ages. There are, however, some negative aspects to what physicians call "elderly prima gravida," that is, entering motherhood after age 35. Older parents may lack the energy to keep up with youngsters, lose the ability to relate to adolescents as they grow older, or be too involved with career and community commitments to have suitable time for parenting.

If older parents are going to be having these kinds of problems, whatever are older grandparents to do? A Pennsylvania grandfather was the source of much good-natured joking among his tennis buddies when he became a grandfather for the first time at age 66, and had six grandchildren, all ages seven or younger, by the time he was 73. Now, at age 77, this older grandfather is a source of much joy to all his grandchildren, but he does sometimes find it difficult keeping up with their antics.

Unless grandparents have managed to maintain the same stamina they had as the parents of teenagers, they'll have to be realistic, conserve strength, and expand ingenuity. The Pennsylvania grandfather can't get involved in his grandsons' basketball games, but he'll spend hours with them playing and tinkering with the model trains. You'll need to think of yourselves as aging tennis stars, holding your own against much younger competitors by using experience to anticipate where the ball is going next and using clever drop shots instead of sideline blasts to make points.

When you find you have to call it quits at the playground or when playing sports, try two strategies to help your grandkids understand what comes with growing older:

1. Tell them you need to stop playing for the time being, but you'll be happy to switch to another, less-demanding pastime, such as watching a video, going out for a snack, reading a story, or whatever else is suitable for their age and enables you to sit down.

2. Cheerfully admit that you have limited energy or physical endurance now that you're older. Yet, now you have more time to spend with them. Explain to your grandkids that the bonus of older age is leisure—more time to be with them and share the fun.

This concluding chapter looks at how to help your grandkids understand and accept your aging and all that goes with it so you can fully enjoy your time together.

Gauging Physical and Mental Agility

It's important that you have regular medical exams and are fully aware of your physical abilities for your own sake. If you intend to play a sport with your grandkids or to give lessons that are sometimes strenuous, consult with your physician. Are you within the limits for your age and condition, or are you pushing too far?

Physical therapists say that moderate exercise helps older people stay more physically limber and mentally alert, as long as they experience physical stimulation without stress. Focus on body conditioning as a vital part of any kind of athletic program. You can even

enjoy regular calisthenics and bodybuilding with your grandchildren. However, you need to read books to determine what exercises are and are not suitable for you. Some suggested reading is:

➤ *Medical and Health Guide for People Over 50*, by the Dartmouth Institute. Hanover, New Hampshire, 1995.

➤ *Fitness for Life*, by Ted Berland. Scott, Foresman & Company, Glenview, Illinois, 1986.

➤ *Jane Brody's Nutrition Book*, by Jane Brody. Times Books, New York, 1981.

➤ *Activity, Health and Fitness in Old Age*, by Jean Macheath. St. Martin's Press, New York, 1984.

➤ *Fit Over Forty: A Revolutionary Plan to Achieve Lifelong Physical and Spiritual Health and Well Being*, by James M. Rippe. Morrow, New York, 1996.

Don't forget about other sources, either. There are numerous health and fitness magazines on the market, and extensive information to be had from the Internet. Your doctor's office also can supply you with information about fitness and well-being.

Some sports that are especially suitable for grandparents include golf, walking, cycling, sailing, tennis (consider doubles), swimming, calisthenics, or fishing. Don't overlook everyday chores, such as gardening, mowing grass, or raking leaves as good sources of exercise, too.

In general, though, if you're not as active as you used to be, you may want to think less in terms of participating and more in terms of teaching. Can you give tennis lessons, supervise batting and pitching practice, teach skiing or skating, or show your grandchildren how to toss a football?

Smart Tips about Sitters

No matter how good your physical condition, you won't be able to engage in sports and recreational activities with some of your grandkids if you need to be at home to watch younger children. There will be times that you'll have to depend on a baby-sitter to give you time to enjoy activities with your older grandchildren.

Here are some pointers:

➤ Hire a sitter who knows and enjoys the sports in which you'll be engaged. That way, he or she can do a "mini" version of the same activity with the younger kids.

Great Grandparenting

Just as you, as a young parent, used sitters for your own children, you can use sitters now to watch younger children so you can spend more time with older ones. And if your grandchildren are staying for several days, consider engaging a sitter for when you'd like to have some quiet or private time. Be sure to let the parents know of your plan to hire a sitter.

➤ If possible, schedule sports programs so the sitter can accompany you with the younger grandkids and sit on the sidelines to watch the older grandkids play.

➤ Give the sitter a break from time to time and let him or her engage in the sport and perhaps give some pointers to the players, while you temporarily watch the younger kids.

➤ If the sitter has to remain at home and you'll be outdoors in a place where there's no phone, give him or her the name and number of another adult who will be readily available in case of an emergency.

Kids Make You Feel Young

There's no time for feeling old and tired when your grandkids are around (except maybe after having spent the entire day chasing after them!). There's too much to do, and too many new things to see to waste time sitting around. There are ponds to explore and books to read together. There are whole worlds waiting to be discovered.

Spending time with grandchildren gives you the marvelous opportunity to see things through their eyes—to discover anew all that you've been taking for granted. It also is a time for learning about how things have changed since you were a kid or your own kids were young. You might be surprised to find out things aren't so very different after all! There are many ways you can experience the joys of being young with your grandchildren. But you'll have to be the catalyst.

➤ Hone in on your grandchildren's areas of interest. When they come to visit you, encourage your grandchildren to bring books or materials on the subjects that seem most stimulating. These might be guidelines for bird watching, instructions for making and flying kites, a computer, information on rock collecting, or recipes.

➤ Set aside time (and a place, if appropriate) where you can discuss whatever subject you're going to pursue. Learn all about it, and look at it as a temporary hobby for as long as your grandchild is there.

➤ If you go to your grandkids' house for a visit, encourage them to show you their collections, hobbies, creative projects, and classroom assignments. Then focus on one or more that are unfamiliar to you or attract your interest, or on one you used to engage in years ago. With your grandchild as an enthusiastic teacher, you may learn something new and exciting, or be reintroduced to something you had long forgotten.

➤ Make a special effort to acquaint a grandchild with one of your own hobbies or pastimes that you think he or she would like. Watch the reactions, and get vicarious pleasure from the interest you've stimulated.

Whether it is working on a stamp collection, taking a nature walk, or shopping for a prom dress with your grandchildren, take time to experience and enjoy their worlds. Interesting people are interested people, and there is much out there to catch your interest.

Seize the opportunity to encourage fresh outlooks and opinions. One thing you can be sure of, your grandchildren will tell you what they think. (They hated the art exhibit, but they loved the concert in the park.) Enjoy the fun of getting candid opinions and unsolicited reactions from your grandchildren about places, events, people, and activities. What, for example, do they think about:

➤ The brand-new shopping mall that opened across town?

➤ The architecture of a famous building in town or a new house in your neighborhood?

➤ The people they meet at a neighborhood gathering of adults?

➤ New styles of cars at an auto dealer's?

➤ Animals on a farm?

➤ A pilot TV program?

It's also fun to set children loose with a cassette recorder and ask them to do a make-believe radio broadcast describing an event they attend in your town or sights they see on a nature walk.

You might not exactly feel young all over again, but you'll have some youthful comments and descriptions to think about and perhaps discuss that evening at the dinner table.

Hartt to Hartt

Our oldest grandsons, Max and Christopher, are anxious to talk about what they've learned at their pre-school. But we sometimes have to play referees, since they both want to talk simultaneously. We also need a chance to talk—both to them and to each other. Taking turns works very well around the dinner table, but it's important to shorten the turns we take, and not let either one of them take more than their fair share. A grandma we know uses a simple device for one garrulous grandson. When he gets started on a lengthy discourse, she sets out the egg timer and gives him a three-minute warning!

But Can I Keep Up with a 16-Year-Old?

Kids and teenagers have unlimited energy when they're doing something they enjoy. Now, cleaning rooms or doing homework might be another story, but give them a fun activity and watch them go! How do you ever keep up with a grandkid who is a mere fraction of your age?

A 61-year-old grandmother figured out an easy way to keep up with her 16-year-old granddaughter. "We come out about even because every time she outdistances me with one kind of game, I dream up a different one I can beat her at."

The key is to understand that when you're together, you'll choose your activities and times *in turn*. Thus, the situation never gets lopsided. For example:

➤ She suggests a game of Ping-Pong and beats you handily.

➤ You follow with a putting game on the carpet and make twice as many holes-in-one as she does.

➤ She turns to cards and clobbers you at gin rummy.

➤ You bring out a trivia game and edge her out in a thrilling finale.

➤ She puts on her roller blades and goes for a spin, while you, on your rusty old bike, are left far behind.

➤ You even the score for the afternoon by beating her at Croquet.

> **Great Grandparenting**
>
> If your teenage grand-child is going to visit and you haven't spent much time together during the past few years, don't panic. Give a call to a counselor at your local school, and ask for a quick briefing on the interests and activities of those your grandson's age. Or, observe or talk to kids around your neighborhood, grandchildren of your friends, or even other grandparents to find out special concerns, interests, and problems of teenagers.

You don't, of course, have to engage each other in contests of skill and endurance. You can both hold your own in discussions of current affairs, reading, evaluating the broadcast news, painting water colors, or collecting shells. And you can both end the day equally exhausted because you both were fired up with enthusiasm and the desire to enjoy every minute together.

When One Grandparent Is Spry and the Other Is Not

What do you do in this situation: The grandkids come to visit, and grandma is perfectly happy to be outside for eight hours a day, trudging up and down the hills of her property as she pulls out weeds, plants flowers, and cleans up dead wood. Grandpa, on the other hand, has trouble getting out of his chair to make a cup of coffee.

Or, what happens if Grandpa still goes into the office a couple of days a week to train younger workers and keep an eye on the business, but everyone agrees that Grandma has gotten a little scatterbrained and often can't remember what she started to say or where she had been earlier in the day.

If the physical and/or mental capacities of the grandparents vary dramatically, chances are you'll have to split up for different activities with the grandkids. But, with some preplanning and thought, everyone can have time to enjoy each other's company. The most important faculty you each need is *adaptability*.

Grandchildren aside for a moment, if either grandparent is becoming physically or mentally challenged, you need to sit down together and talk about what you'll do. Time is of the essence because you may have to start making changes that require study, the relearning of old skills, or the acquisition of new ones. If, for example, Grandpa has been handling banking, investing, and all financial matters, but he's failing mentally, Grandma had better acquire as much know-how as she can about such matters. And if Grandma is confined to her bed with a long illness, Grandpa would do well to brush up on cooking, laundry, and whatever other chores Grandma traditionally handled.

Enjoying Unequal Grandparents Equally

Illness and infirmity are unfortunate, but they're persistent aspects of life. They're not pleasant to be around. They fly in the face of our society's great quest for youth and health and good times. When a grandparent becomes ill, infirm, or mentally impaired, it's difficult for grandchildren to accept that Grandma isn't the same as she used to be. They may resent that she's unable to make their birthday cakes as she always did, or take them shopping for school shoes. They might be uncomfortable with the sight of a hospital bed, bedpan, or oxygen machine, or unable to understand why Grandma can't remember the rules when they all play Parcheesi together.

As a result, grandkids might start to avoid visiting or try to stay away from Grandma when they do visit. This can result in hurt feelings and guilt. With some planning and thought, you can lessen your grandchildren's anxiety and make visits more enjoyable:

➤ Schedule shorter visits, and make them for times when the ailing grandparent is likely to be on an upswing, rather than down.

➤ Select games and other pursuits that are challenging enough to be fun, but not over-demanding for the grandparent with reduced capabilities.

➤ Explain to grandkids, or have their parents explain, the condition in which they can expect to find Grandma when they go to visit. Tell them in simple terms what is wrong with Grandma, and what her limitations will be. If there is special medical equipment in use, explain what they will see and what it is for. Explain that

Great Grandparenting
The American Association of Retired Persons and many local senior groups conduct seminars for members who need to learn new skills. Some common subjects are bookkeeping, banking, investing, cooking, auto maintenance, plumbing, and home care. Check your phone book for the local AARP listing, or call their national number at 800-541-3717. You can also get such information from hospitals, retirement centers, churches or synagogues, and your local United Way chapter. Check your phone book under "Senior Citizens," "Aging," or "Retirement."

Grandma is looking forward to seeing them, and they will not hurt her by hugging or kissing her (unless, for some reason that is not true). Stress what she still can do (play games or tell stories) instead of what she is unable to do.

➤ Adjust the proportions of visits so you go less frequently to your grandchildren's homes, and they come instead to yours, where you can be more rested and better in control of the situation.

➤ If Granddad is totally unable to participate actively in games and diversions, plan for certain times when he can simply sit in the same room with the grandkids without having to be too responsive—watching TV, watching young ones perform, listening to someone read a book, or eating a snack.

Tackling Tough Topics

Our society, as a whole, doesn't like to talk about aging. We might joke about it, or complain about it, but it's not something that many of us are comfortable sitting around discussing. Your grandkids, however, might be curious about the changes occurring in you as you age. Some of them might be very frank, with questions such as, "Grandmom, why is your skin getting so wrinkly?" Some might not say much, but appear troubled as they see you starting to have trouble getting around or notice that you're not hearing well. When it's time to talk to your grandkids about issues such as aging and death, be frank and honest. Try to be as unemotional as possible, and consider the ages of the children you're talking to.

Help Them to Understand and Accept Aging

If your aging seems to be troubling a grandchild, try to make some time for a one-on-one conversation. Explain that you're not all that crazy about what's happening to you either, but you're making the best of it. Reassure him that you're happy and still have many good things in your life—him included. Be sure you don't sound sorry for yourself; this will only confirm his suspicion that something is wrong. You could compare your body to a machine, which doesn't operate as efficiently or well as it did when it was new. If the child is older, you might use a medical book (the *American Medical Association's Family Medical Guide* is good) to help him understand what happens to the human body as it ages. Try to make him understand that aging is a normal part of life.

If you foresee a time that your family will have to be caring for you, or making decisions about your care, you might want to get a copy of *Taking Care of Aging Family Members: A Practical Guide,* by Nancy R. Hooyman and Wendy Lustbader (published by the Free Press division of Simon and Schuster, New York).

It is difficult to keep young people from being impatient with your aging. It's a built-in part of their natures. Explain to them why you can't do everything you used to be able to. Relate your limitations to those they may have experienced: "Remember when you hurt your leg and couldn't play football for a while? Well, my knee hurts pretty bad today because of this darned arthritis, so I won't be able to go hiking with you." Make sure they understand that you do not choose to give up your activities with them, but that the situation is beyond your control. Speak with humor, not bitterness, when explaining your ailments. When you do plan to do something with your grandkids, allow a little extra time.

Present aging in a positive light. Tell your grandkids about the great guy you met at the library, or the bus trip you're looking forward to taking with the senior's group. Call your grandchildren when you've heard something that you know will interest them. Stay involved with their lives, even if it is in a less physical way. If they would be interested, take your grandkids along to any events or activities you may participate in. As much as possible, keep your sense of humor and try not to complain about your ailments.

Discuss Death and Dying with Your Grandkids

Losing a grandparent is often a child's first experience with death. As much as we might like to try, death cannot be ignored, and children can't be protected from it. You might want to introduce the idea of death by pointing out a dead bird or animal by the road-side, and explaining that, although we can still see the body, the animal is no longer alive. Children should be allowed to gradually get used to the idea that death is a normal part of the life cycle. If you have made peace with your own mortality, you'll more than likely be able to convey that to grandchildren.

If you are terminally ill or have a condition that makes it likely you'll die soon, you or the child's parent should try to prepare your grandchildren by saying something such as, "Grandpa is very sick and won't be able to be with us always." If your spouse dies first, allow your grandchildren to participate in grieving with the rest of the family.

In her book, *Teaching Your Child to Cope with Crisis*, author Suzanne Ramos recommends that children over the ages of eight should attend funerals or other mourning rituals. Children ages four to eight might attend part of a service, unless it's likely to be extremely emotional or hysterical. You will find more ideas on how to talk to your grandkids about death and dying in *Helping Your Child to Understand Death*, by Anna Wolf.

When considering these tough topics, keep in mind how lucky you've been to have had the opportunity to get to know your grandkids and be part of their lives. Nobody's life comes with a guaranteed number of years, so try to be glad for all that you've had and enjoy however many years you have left.

Not All Downhill: Growing Old with Grace

In a book published a generation ago titled *Then God Created Grandparents and It Was Very Good*, author Charlie W. Shedd asks a provocative question: "So what's a grandparent for?"

Answering his own question, Dr. Shedd, a minister with five children and three grandkids of his own, explains in lively detail that:

➤ Grandparents are for wondering with you.

➤ Grandparents are for listening.

➤ Grandparents are for saying "no" sometimes.

➤ Grandparents are for having fun with you.

➤ Grandparents are for telling you what it used to be like, but not too much.

➤ Grandparents are for saying, "I think you're okay."

In lyrical text and captivating photography, he tells and shows how grandparents are the epitome of graciousness, compassion, and empathy, yet they have fortitude and strength that inspire and hearten the young.

> ### Hartt to Hartt
>
> Of all the things that grandparents are for, the one we try to keep most in mind when we are with our grandchildren is "Grandparents are for saying 'I think you're okay.'" We know that the parents of our grandkids have to prepare them to live in the real world by telling them of the many things they should do and not do. But, we like to let them know they are loved just the way they are—straight hair or curly, fat or thin, brown eyes or blue, shy or assertive, scholar or athlete. *That's the way it is.*

The Least You Need to Know

➤ Evaluate your physical condition and capacity thoroughly before engaging in sports and exercise with the young.

➤ Loosen your inhibitions and reawaken the joys of yesteryear with the grandkids.

➤ Employ ingenuity and strategy to show how well you can keep pace with the young, without risking life and limb.

➤ When one grandparent is in better physical and/or mental health than the other, the responsibilities and duties must be shifted accordingly.

➤ Discuss aging and death with grandkids.

➤ Relish the fact that, though advancing age can be worrisome, there are many blessings that come with being a grandparent.

Recommended Reading

Your local library will contain many books relating to health, pregnancy, birth, and other grandparenting-related issues. A few suggestions follow.

Caplan, Theresa. *The First Twelve Months of Life.* New York: Grosset & Dunlap, 1973.

Editors of *Prevention* magazine. "Symptoms, Their Causes and Cures." Emmaus, PA: Rodale Press, 1994.

Editors of *Prevention* magazine. "Your Perfect Weight." Emmaus, PA: Rodale Press, 1995.

Eisenberg, Arlene, et al. *What to Eat When You're Expecting.* New York: Workman Publishing, 1996.

Eisenberg, Arlene, Heidi E. Murkoff, and Sandee E. Hathaway, B.S.N. *What to Expect When You're Expecting.* New York: Workman Publishing, 1994.

Ferber, Richard A., M.D. *Solve Your Child's Sleep Problems.* Cambridge, MA: Harvard Medical School, 1986.

Jones, Sandy, with Werner Freitag. *Guide to Baby Products.* 4th ed. Mount Vernon, NY: *Consumer Reports,* 1991.

Leach, Penelope. *Your Baby & Child (from Birth to Age Five).* New York: Alfred A. Knopf, 1989.

Pryor, Karen and Gale Pryor. *Nursing Your Baby.* New York: Pocket Books, 1991.

Roberts, Bonnie Worthington and Sue Rodwell Williams. *Nutrition in Pregnancy and Lactation.* 5th ed. St. Louis: Times Mirror/Mosby College Publications, 1993.

Simkin, Whalley, Keppler. *Pregnancy, Childbirth and the Newborn.* New York: Simon & Schuster, 1991.

Sears, William, M.D. and Martha Sears, R.N. *The Baby Book.* Boston: Little, Brown & Co., 1993.

Sears, William, M.D. and Martha Sears, R.N. *The Birth Book: Everything You Need to Know.* Boston: Little, Brown & Co., 1994.

Tamborlane, William V., M.D., ed. *The Yale Guide to Children's Nutrition.* New Haven, Conn.: Yale University Press, 1997.

Tunler, Julie, R.N. *Maternal Fitness.* New York: Fireside Books, 1996.

Resource Directory

The following organizations are reliable sources of information, publications, and counsel.

General Organizations with Grandparenting Interests

AARP Grandparenting Information
Center
601 E Street, NW
Washington, DC 20049
(202) 434-2296
Fax: (202) 434-6466
(Publisher of many helpful publications,
including *Tips for Grandparents*)

Active Parenting Publishers
810 Franklin Court
Marietta, GA 30067
(800) 825-0060

Foster Grandparenting Program
2500 Martin Luther King Jr. Avenue, SE
Washington, DC 20020
(202) 678-4215

Foundation for Grandparenting
5 Casa del Oro Lane
Santa Fe, NM 87505-9108
Phone and Fax: (505) 466-1336

Grandparents Anonymous
1924 Beverly Street
Sylvan Lake, MI 48320
(810) 682-8384

Grandparents Raising Grandchildren
P.O. Box 104
Colleyville, TX 76034
(817) 577-0435

Grandparents Rights Organization
555 South Woodward Avenue
Birmingham, MI 48009
(810) 646-7191
Fax: (810) 646-9722

National Association of Foster
Grandparent Program Directors
Laurelton Center, Box 300
Laurelton, PA 17835
(717) 922-4799
Fax: (717) 922-4799

National Council on Aging
West Wing 100
600 Maryland Avenue, SW
Washington, DC 20024
(202) 479-1200

National Federation of Grandmother
Clubs of America
P.O. Box 786
Wauconda, IL 60084-0786
(847) 526-4811

National Organization of Mothers of
Twins Clubs
P.O. Box 23188
Albuquerque, NM 87192
(505) 275-0955

Relatives as Parents Program (RAPP)
The Brookdale Foundation Group
126 East 56th Street
New York, NY 10022-3668
(Mail contacts only)

Legal Issues

Commission on Legal Problems of
the Elderly
American Bar Association
1800 M Street, NW
Washington, DC 20036
(202) 331-2297 or (800) 621-6159

Legal Services for the Elderly
132 West 43rd Street
New York, NY 10036
(212) 391-0120

National Senior Citizens Law Center
1052 West 6th Street
Los Angeles, CA 90017
(213) 482-3550

Medical and Health Organizations

American Academy of Pediatrics
172 W. State Street, Suite 303
Trenton, NJ 08608
(609) 393-3350
(General information on pediatric
issues and care)

American Medical Association
535 North Dearborn Street
Chicago, IL 60610
(312) 464-5000
Fax: (312) 464-4184

Asthma and Allergy Foundation of
America
1717 Massachusetts Avenue, NW
Washington, DC 20036
(202) 265-0265

Caesarian Support, Education,
and Concern
22 Forest Road
Framingham, MA 01701
(508) 877-8266

Confinement Line
P.O. Box 1609
Springfield, VA 22151
(703) 941-7183
(Telephone support counseling, referrals
for high-risk pregnancy)

Council on Family Health
420 Lexington Avenue
New York, NY 10017
(212) 210-8836

La Leche League International
(908) 233-0857
(Worldwide breast feeding advocacy
and information)

National Health/Education Consortium
1001 Connecticut Avenue, NW
Washington, DC 20036
(202) 822-8405

New Jersey Coalition for Downs Syndrome
(908) 264-0824 or (908) 290-9248

Sidelines
P.O. Box 1808
Laguna Beach, CA 92652
(714) 497-5722
(High-risk pregnancy support)

SIDS Alliance
10500 Little Patent Parkway, Suite 420
Columbia, MD 21044
(800) 221-SIDS
(Prevention of Sudden Infant Death
Syndrome and bereavement support)

Society for Nutrition Education
1736 Franklin Street
Oakland, CA 94612
(415) 444-7133

Monetary and Economic Problems

AARP Tax Aide Program
601 E Street, NW
Washington, DC 20049
(202) 434-6000

American Financial Services Association
919 18th Street, NW
Washington, DC 20006
(202) 296-5544
Fax: (202) 223-0321

Earned Income Tax Credit (EIC) Program
(Information provided by the Internal
Revenue Service)
(800) 829-1040

Substance Abuse

Al-Anon/Alateen Family Group
Headquarters
P.O. Box 862
Midtown Station
New York, NY 10018-0862
(800) 344-2666

Drug Abuse Resistance Education (DARE)
P.O. Box 2090
Los Angeles, CA 90051
(800) 223-DARE

"Just Say No" International
1777 North California Boulevard
Walnut Creek, CA 94596
(510) 939-6666

Mothers Against Drunk Driving (MADD)
511 East John Carpenter Freeway, #700
Irving, TX 75062
(212) 744-6233 or (800) GET-MADD

National Clearinghouse for Alcohol and
Drug Information
P.O. Box 2345
Rockville, MD 20852
(800) 622-HELP or (800) 729-6686

Tools of the Trade Checklist

Here is a selected list of equipment every new grandparent should have when the grandbabies or young grandchildren come to visit. The parents will be able to supply many of these items; some you may wish to stock up on your own. Be sure to check with the parents before you buy any of the materials listed here to see what they already have to lend you, and also to see if there are particular brands or types they prefer you to buy.

Kids In the Kitchen

Baby bottles

Bibs

Dinnerware (unbreakable)

Face and hand wipes

Floor mats

Highchair or booster seat

Sipper cups

Bedtime Basics

Bed or crib

Intercom

Night light

Child's own security blanket

Stuffed animals

Bathroom Basics

Baby oil or ointment

Baby wipes (non-alcohol)

Bath toys

Bathtub rubber mat or bath ring

Diapers

Soap, shampoo, and lotion (for babies)

Washcloth (small and soft)

Fun Stuff

Baby swing

Books (soft books or picture books for the very young)

Building blocks

Card games (such as Old Maid, Go Fish, Crazy Eights)

Cars and trucks

Audio cassettes or CDs of children's songs and/or recorded children's books

Chalkboard and colored chalks (chalks are also good for drawing on sidewalks and driveways)

Child-oriented musical instruments

Colored clay or processed dough

Construction sets

Craft supplies (child-safe scissors, glue stick, tape, ribbons, felt, etc.)

Crayons and washable felt-tip markers

Dolls, with dolls' clothes

Finger paints (non-toxic) and paper

Games of skill and imagination, such as Monopoly, checkers, chess, and Scrabble

Indoor golf putting sets

Kites, planes, and other things that fly

Musical instruments

Paint sets

Playpen (with hanging chimes, an unbreakable mirror, an overhead mobile)

Boardgames (to fill those rainy days)

Skateboards or in-line skates with protective helmets, knee pads, and wrist pads

Small bike (with training wheels, if needed)

Sports equipment (balls, bats, etc.)

Stuffed animals

Toys that roll or have sound effects

Tricycle

Videocassettes of cartoons, films, and home-recorded children's TV shows

On the Move

Car seat

Stroller

Just in Case

Acetaminophen, in liquid or chewable form

Band-Aids of various sizes

Ace bandage (to reduce swelling in ankles and wrists)

Adhesive tape

Antibacterial first aid cream

Calamine lotion or other soothing lotion

Calibrated medicine dropper, spoon, or syringe

Cotton balls

Eyewash bowl

Family medical/first aid guide

Heat pack (after using an ice pack, to increase circulation for faster healing)

Ice pack (immediately after an injury, to reduce aching and swelling)

Pain reliever for teething (herbal or medicinal)

Spray for relieving the pain of bee stings and insect bites

Syrup of ipecac (to induce vomiting in case of poisoning)

Tweezers and sterile needles (for removing splinters)

Other Things Perhaps to Have on Hand

Baby bottle carrier (insulated to keep milk cold)

Baby rattles

Pacifier

Teething ring

Grandchild's Favorite Things

Sometimes it's difficult to keep up with your grandchildren's likes and dislikes as they grow. This worksheet will help you stay current on your grandchild's favorite hobbies and passions. Have the parents fill out the list (you may ask them to update it year to year) so you'll know what's going on in your grandchildren's life. The list can also be a great source of inspiration for special activities to share during visits. And you'll always be full of ideas for the perfect holiday or birthday gifts for your grandchildren!

Grandchild's name: _____

Grandchild's age: _____

Clothing

A growing grandchild can change clothing sizes and clothing tastes almost weekly—not to mention that clothing trends seem to change daily. This is an important thing to keep track of because you don't want to give your grandchild a shirt with a floral print when it's pinstripes that are in! Knowing these things will make shopping for a long distance grandchild easier, and possibly even allow a pleasant trip to mall with your grandchild.

Shirt size: _____

Pants size: _____

Dress size: _____

Shoe size: _____

Favorite colors: _____

Favorite styles: _____

_____

Facing the Future

Your younger grandchildren may not want to be anything else except a firefighter or a policeman, but your older grandchildren may have more specific goals in mind. Both of the items below can change frequently, so try to keep up as best you can. You never know when your grandchild will be interested in following in your footsteps.

Dream job(s): _____

Favorite place to live: _____

Foods

There's nothing wrong with spoiling your grandchildren a little bit! Having their favorite snacks around when they come to visit, or making their favorite meal is a great way to show them that you remember those important little things.

Favorite foods: _____

Least favorite foods: _____

Favorite breakfast: _____

Favorite lunch: _____

Favorite dinner: _____

Favorite dessert: _____

Favorite snacks: _____

Favorite drinks: _____

Favorite cuisine (Mexican, Italian, etc.): _____

Least favorite cuisine: _____

Hobbies

Which hobbies does your grandchild enjoy most? Find out as many of these as possible so you'll be able to plan activities that your grandchild will really enjoy doing with you. Don't worry if you don't have answers for all of them, it will just give you a chance to maybe try some activities that your grandchild has never done before.

Art (favorite arts and crafts): _____

_____

Athletics (favorite sports to play): _____

_____

Books (favorite series, characters, and authors): _____

_____

Collections (favorite collectibles): _____

_____

Computers (favorite computer games or Web sites): _____

_____

Fitness (favorite athletic hobbies): _____

_____

Games (favorite card games, board games): _____

_____

Movies (favorite movies and stars): _____

_____

Music (instruments played): _____

_____

Music (favorite musicians or bands): _____

_____

Music (favorite tapes and CDs): _____

_____

Pets (pets or desired pets): _____

_____

Sports (favorite sports teams): _____

_____

Sports (favorite athletes): _____

_____

Television (favorite shows and characters): _____

_____

Videos (favorite videos to rent): _____

_____

School Days

There is always a lot going on when the grandchildren are school age: plays to attend, teams to cheer for, homework to help with, to name just a few. Keep the below items up-to-date so you can be at the top of your academic game!

Grade in school: _____

Name of school: _____

Favorite academic subjects: _____

Least favorite academic subjects: _____

Favorite non-academic subjects: _____

Least favorite non-academic subjects: _____

Recent academic achievement: _____

After-school activities: _____

Activities Idea List

Stumped for ideas when you get together with the grandkids? The following lists should help inspire you to find something fun to do.

Special Sports

The following energetic activities will get you and your grandchildren up and moving:

Bicycling and tricycling

Calisthenics (indoors or out)

Dancing

Fishing

Hide-and-Seek, Tag, and other active games

Hiking

Jogging or walking

Jumping rope (indoors or out)

Playing informal sports (football, basketball, softball, badminton) with neighborhood kids

Roller skating and in-line skating

Swimming

Tossing a ball or Frisbee

Visiting a playground

Risky Business

Here are some wild outdoor ideas for the adventurous grandchild and grandparent:

Ballooning in a hot-air balloon

Camping by packhorse

Canoeing

Cruising in an old-fashioned schooner

Going aloft in a motorized hang-glider or ultralight plane

Helicopter-hopping

Kayaking

Motor boating

River rafting

Scuba diving or snorkeling

Sledding or skiing (cross country and downhill)

Spelunking—exploring caves and caverns

Waterskiing

Whale-watching

Imagination Sparkers

The following activities will spark your grandchildren's creativity and imagination (and yours, too):

Body painting

Charades

Drawing and coloring

Dressing up

Hunting treasure

Lip-synch performances

Making crafts of all kinds

Making your own music; singing your own song

Putting on a play

Reading or telling stories aloud

Reciting your own poetry

Special Ed

Here are some special subjects you and your grandchildren can have fun learning together:

Archeology (go on a dig)

Art (visit a museum)

Card tricks or magic tricks

Ceramics (make your own things from clay or decorate pre-made, unglazed cups, vases, animals, etc. before they're fired)

Computers (try out software at the library or computer store)

Foreign languages (listen to an instructional cassette together)

Geography (examine a globe or map together)

Music (go to a concert)

Nature (visit an arboretum or public garden; take a nature walk and identify flowers and trees, animals and birds, clouds, etc.)

Science (visit exhibits at the local museums)

Sign language

Theater (go to a play)

Family History

Here are ways to spark your grandchildren's interest in family history and lore:

Create a family tree together

Explore treasures in the attic

Leaf through old photograph albums

Relate family experiences from the past

Visit your old house, town, school, etc.

Watch family movies and videos together

Cooking Basics

It's fun for both you and your grandchildren to have them help out in the kitchen. Here's what they can do:

Breadmaking (especially kneading the dough)

Cooking a favorite dish (see children's cookbooks or choose a simple recipe)

Cutting vegetables (for older grandchildren)

Decorating a cake or cupcakes

Food shopping

Growing herbs or vegetables in the garden

Making cookies (the refrigerated cut-and-bake kind are especially good for little children)

Menu planning

Mixing batter

Playing waiter or waitress

Sprinkling in herbs or garnishes

Stirring soup

Reading recipes

Another good thing to do is cut out any fun recipes; such as holiday recipes, or something your grandkids can share with friends or classmates when they go back home; or activities, like making Play-doh™ and fingerpaints, from magazines. You can save these for when your grandchildren are visiting and let them pick what they would like to do.

Stepping Out

Don't feel like staying in? Chances are your neighborhood has a wealth of special places your grandchildren will love to explore:

Airports

Amusement parks

Animal sanctuaries

Aquariums

Archaeological digs and restorations

Art exhibits and showings

Aviaries

Bike trails

Car shows

Concerts

Craft exhibits

Dog shows

Festivals or fairs

Historic sites

Horse shows

Movies

Museums

Nature preserves and walks

Plays and musicals

Restaurants

Stores (especially those that display computer software, pets, science and nature products, toys)

Wildlife refuges

Zoos

Emergency Information Sheet

If your grandchildren visit regularly and stay overnight, it's a good idea to keep emergency information on each of them, or on each family of grandchildren, handy. You never know when you'll need quick information or when someone else who's minding them at your home will. You can make up your own emergency sheets, or you can make copies of this form to fill in.

Grandchildren's complete names, their parents' names, home addresses, and phone numbers (parents' home and work phones):

_____

_____

_____

_____

_____

Your grandchildren's ages and weights:

_____

_____

_____

_____

_____

Any special medical conditions or allergies your grandchildren might have:

_____
_____
_____
_____
_____

Your own work addresses and phone numbers:

_____
_____
_____
_____

Your doctor's name, address, and phone number:

_____
_____
_____

Your grandchildren's doctors' names, addresses, and phone numbers:

_____
_____
_____
_____

The name, address, and phone number of the nearest hospital to you:

_____
_____
_____
_____
_____

Names, address, and phone number of nearby friends or relatives:

_____

_____

_____

_____

_____

Police phone number:_____

Fire department phone number: _____

Ambulance phone number: _____

Local or national poison control center phone number: ____

_____

Index

Symbols

911, dialing, 64

A

AARP Grandparenting
  Information Center, 277
AARP Tax Aide Program, 279
abrupitio placenta, 17
abuse
  drug and alcohol
    among parents, 246-247
    recognizing, 207-208
  physical, 247-248
acceptability of attire, 205-206
accessibility
  doors, 53
  Internet, 118
  television, 116-117
  windows, 53
accidents, 63-64
  preparing for, 94
  water safety, 69-70
accommodations, limited space,
  235
accumulating possessions,
  affluenza, 220
Active Parenting
  Publishers, 277
activities
  birdwatching, 159-160
  birthday parties, planning,
    175-176
  camping, 162
  chaperoning, 137
  competing with
    grandchildren, 269-270
  cooking, 292
  educational, 149-150, 291
  expeditions, 140-141
  exploring, 292-293
    woodlands, 160-162
  for infirmed grandparents,
    271-272
  games
    capture the flag, 140
    cat's cradle, 139
    kick the can, 139
    pick up sticks, 139
    ringalevio, 140

sportsmanship, 141
    TV tag, 139
  gardening, 165-166
  geneaology, 291-292
  hobbies, 136-137
  indoor, preparing, 112-113
  inexpensive, 227-228
  movies, 146-147
  outdoors, 290
  planning, 110-112
  shopping, 152-153
  splitting between
    grandparents, 270-272
  sports, 132-133, 289-290
    equipment, 135-137
    losing, 133
    permission, 136
  trips
    amusement parks, 150-152
    expenditures, 152
    movie theaters, 146-147
    zoos, 147-149
adaptability, 270-272
addressing religious issues,
  216-217
adolescents, teenagers
  bonding, 201-202
  rules for visits, 118-119
  visiting, 200
adopted children, 251
adventures, 140-141
affirming grandchildren, 274
affluenza, 220
agility, gauging, 266-267
aging
  discussing, 266, 272-273
  elderly prima gravida, 265
  infirmities, 270-272
  lessening anxiety, 271-272
  stamina, 266-267
air bags, 42-43
Al-Anon/Alateen Family Group
  Headquarters, 279
alcoholism, recognizing,
  207-208
allergies, 71-72
  from pets, 61, 72
  insect stings, 95
American Academy of
  Pediatrics, 278

American Financial Services
  Association, 279
American Medical
  Association, 278
ammunition, storing, 55
amniocentesis, 12, 16
anaphylactic shock, 96
ancestors, family trees, 183
anecdotes, telling, 185-186
animals
  allergies, 61
  birds, 63
  birdwatching, 159-160
  bites, first aid, 96
  pets, 61-63
  wildlife, 163-164
    bats, 163
    daddy longlegs, 164
    praying mantises, 163
    spiders, 163
    toads, 163
    walking sticks, 163
  zoos, 147-149
anxiety, nightmares, 104-105
appliances, childproofing, 54-55
  cooking appliances, 55-56
applying sunscreen, 68
appreciating
  nature, 161
  non-material possessions, 220
aquariums, 63
arguments
  fights between grandchildren,
    stopping, 85-86
  religious beliefs, resolving,
    214-215
  resolving, 82-84
asthma, first aid, 98-99
Asthma and Allergy Foundation of
  America, 278
athletics, 132-133
  see also sports
attacks
  allergies, 71-72
  animals, first aid, 96
  asthma, first aid, 98-99
  prejudicial, comforting
    grandchildren, 258
attending church with grandchildren, 213

When You're Smart Enough to Know That You Don't Know It All

For all the ups and downs you're sure to encounter in life, The Complete Idiot's Guides give you down-to-earth answers and practical solutions.

The Complete Idiot's Guide to Learning French on Your Own
ISBN: 0-02-861043-1 ▪ $16.95

The Complete Idiot's Guide to Dating
ISBN: 0-02-861052-0 ▪ $14.95

The Complete Idiot's Guide to Hiking and Camping
ISBN: 0-02-861100-4 ▪ $16.95

The Complete Idiot's Guide to Cooking Basics, 2E
ISBN: 0-02-861974-9 ▪ $16.95
Available November 1997!

The Complete Idiot's Guide to Learning Spanish on Your Own
ISBN: 0-02-861040-7 ▪ $16.95

The Complete Idiot's Guide to Gambling Like a Pro
ISBN: 0-02-861102-0 ▪ $16.95

The Complete Idiot's Guide to Choosing, Training, and Raising a Dog
ISBN: 0-02-861098-9 ▪ $16.95

**The Complete Idiot's Guide
to Trouble-Free Car Care**
ISBN: 0-02-861041-5 ▪ $16.95

**The Complete Idiot's Guide
to the Perfect Wedding, 2E**
ISBN: 0-02-861963-3 ▪ $17.99

**The Complete Idiot's Guide
to Trouble-Free Home
Repair**
ISBN: 0-02-861042-3 ▪ $16.95

**The Complete Idiot's Guide
to Getting into College**
ISBN: 1-56761-508-2 ▪ $14.95

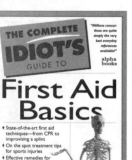

**The Complete Idiot's Guide
to the Perfect Vacation**
ISBN: 1-56761-531-7 ▪ $14.99

**The Complete Idiot's Guide
to First Aid Basics**
ISBN: 0-02-861099-7 ▪ $16.95

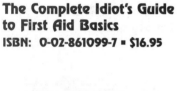

You can handle it!